D1596421

REGIS COLLEGE LIBRARY
100 Wellesley Street West
Toronto, Ontario
Canada M5S 2Z5

WITHDRAWN

Christian Dying

REGIS COLLEGE LIBRARY
100 Wellesley Street West
Toronto, Ontario
Canada M5S 2Z5

Christian Dying

WITNESSES FROM THE TRADITION

edited by

George Kalantzis
and Matthew Levering

foreword by J. Todd Billings

REGIS COLLEGE LIBRARY
100 Wellesley Street West
Toronto, Ontario
Canada M5S 2Z5

BT
825
C 47
2018

 CASCADE *Books* · Eugene, Oregon

CHRISTIAN DYING
Witnesses from the Tradition

Copyright © 2018 Wipf and Stock. All rights reserved. Except for brief quotations in critical publications or reviews, no part of this book may be reproduced in any manner without prior written permission from the publisher. Write: Permissions, Wipf and Stock Publishers, 199 W. 8th Ave., Suite 3, Eugene, OR 97401.

Cascade Books
An Imprint of Wipf and Stock Publishers
199 W. 8th Ave., Suite 3
Eugene, OR 97401

www.wipfandstock.com

PAPERBACK ISBN: 978-1-5326-3096-5
HARDCOVER ISBN: 978-1-5326-3098-9
EBOOK ISBN: 978-1-5326-3097-2

Cataloguing-in-Publication data:

Names: Kalantzis, George, editor. | Levering, Matthew, editor.

Title: Christian dying : witnesses from the tradition / George Kalantzis and Matthew Levering, editors.

Description: Eugene, OR: Cascade Books, 2018 | Includes bibliographical references and index.

Identifiers: ISBN 978-1-5326-3096-5 (paperback) | ISBN 978-1-5326-3098-9 (hardcover) | ISBN 978-1-5326-3097-2 (ebook)

Subjects: LCSH: Death—Religious aspects—Christianity.

Classification: BV4905.3 C486 2018 (print) | BV4905 (ebook)

Manufactured in the U.S.A.   JULY 13, 2018

REGIS COLLEGE LIBRARY
100 Wellesley Street West
Toronto, Ontario
Canada M5S 2Z5

Table of Contents

Foreword

J. Todd Billings

It is a stubborn, indisputable fact: everyone reading these words is dying. We live and breathe, yes. But we do so as mortal creatures—creatures that not only have a terminus, but whose bodies slowly deteriorate and decay. We fall ill, and sometimes we recover. We break a bone, and sometimes it heals. But all of this recovery and healing is temporary. The process of dying appears to have the final word: "You are dust, and to dust you shall return" (Gen 3:19). These words hold just as true for a Christian who has received the imposition of ashes on their forehead on Ash Wednesday as for a medical doctor who has never entered a church. Nothing seems more universally certain: we are dying creatures who shall return to dust.

What can we do in the face of this stark reality? In the late modern West, we often push death to the edges of our lives. Concealing the signs of physical aging has become big business. We have moved those in their final days from our homes and our faith communities to hospitals and hospice centers. Except for the spectacle of death in the news and in entertainment, the dying are hidden from sight. But even when seen, death usually comes to us as an anomaly— a mystery to be solved, an injustice to be protested—not as the inevitable earthly end of us all, an indelible feature of my identity and yours.

Creaturely life has a way of disrupting our attempts to distract ourselves from the reality of death. When I was diagnosed with a terminal illness at the age of 39, many in my community opined that it was not fair. I deserved to see my one- and three-year-old children grow to adulthood. I deserved to live into retirement with my wife Rachel, the love of my life. We lamented together. Yet, I knew that I had already been given more years than many of the Ugandans among whom I had worked in college, than many of the African Americans living in tough neighborhoods in Chicago, and than many of my fellow Homo sapiens throughout human history. I had temporalized death—assumed that I would "deal with it" three or four decades in the future. Until then, I could almost live as if there were no death. But that is an illusion. As a patient with incurable cancer, dying has become a part of my daily life. I sit by my son and daughter at meals, swallowing a poison (chemotherapy) pill as we share our food. Each day, I manage the pain caused by the toxins that my body has already received. Planning for future years takes place under a cloud of uncertainty. Although my body has always been dying, my recognition of this reality is new.

And yet, this recognition need not lead to despair. The hard ground of mortality might seem like infertile soil for hope. But for Christians, whether Roman Catholic, Eastern Orthodox, or Protestant, this hard ground is the context for our deepest hope. For Jesus Christ broke through the hard ground of mortality, taking death upon himself, so that death and sin and the devil do not have the final word. Yes, they still have a word. But not the *final* word. The word of death stings. It still stings for parents who have lost a young child to cancer. It stings for the mother who has lost her son to gang violence. It stings for the refugee family who loses their father while fleeing to safety. But as the apostle Paul testifies, in light of the astonishing resurrection of Jesus Christ, there will be a day when the sting of death will be no more. Through Jesus Christ, on that day "this perishable body" will "put on imperishability" and "this mortal body" will "put on immortality" (1 Cor 15:53).

But what does all of this mean for Christians today? In order to answer that, we need to stop thinking of "death" as simply the end of our earthly life, and start recognizing mortality as an indelible feature of our identity. We are dust. And yet, we have immense hope in Jesus Christ. Dust. Hope. Together. Because of this paradoxical pairing, this book on Christian dying is a powerful resource for the whole Christian life, not just the end of life.

Precisely because the late modern West medicalizes dying and pushes the concerns of our mortality to the edges of our lives, this book is an urgent and extraordinary gift to today's church and academy. Leading Roman Catholic, Eastern Orthodox, and Protestant scholars probe the significance of death in earlier eras, exposing our self-deceiving illusions and pointing to manifold ways of living as mortals who hope in the crucified and risen Lord. While attending the conference that included earlier drafts of these essays, I felt a thrill of excitement. As a cancer patient, I often feel that I've traveled to a far off land that only other patients with serious illnesses can understand. But here, in Augustine and Irenaeus, in Gregory of Nyssa and Luther, in Bulgakov and Barth, I found companions. They often disagreed with each other. But they inhabit the same hard ground and walk in the same dark space illumined by the candle of resurrection hope. Even the disagreements help us move from the shadows to further light. Is mortality essential to what it means to be human, or is death always the enemy for Christians? How does death relate to the fall of humans into sin? What might it mean to be liberated from the fear of death? In what sense can Christians speak of a "good death," and how should individual Christians and their faith communities prepare themselves for death? These essays present divergent yet mutually enlightening responses to questions such as these. Readers who tire of the death-denying ways of the modern West are in for some good news: the Christian tradition is deep and wide in its reflections upon human mortality in light of the risen Lord. For mortals like ourselves, that is good news indeed.

Acknowledgements

THE EDITORS WISH FIRST to thank the extraordinary contributors to this volume, each of whom participated in the March 2016 Colloquium from which this volume comes. The Colloquium took place at Wheaton College's Harbor House. Its co-sponsors were the The Wheaton Center for Early Christian Studies and the Center for Scriptural Exegesis, Philosophy, and Doctrine at Mundelein Seminary. Wheaton College and Mundelein Seminary deserve thanks for making this initiative possible and for being such congenial places for Christian teaching and research.

We owe a special thanks to David Augustine, a superb doctoral candidate in systematic theology at the Catholic University of America. After we had collected the essays and written the introduction, David used the Cascade author's guide to prepare the manuscript for publication, a very extensive task. He also graciously compiled the indices. We also owe great thanks to Rodney Clapp of Wipf and Stock. Rodney is a longtime friend, and he enthusiastically greeted our proposal to publish this volume with Cascade. Thanks also to Brian Palmer of Wipf and Stock, who helped us significantly in the contracting process and in the process by which the manuscript became a book. Thanks also to Jack Bates and Ryan Clevenger, doctoral candidates at Wheaton who, as students of George, gave much help during the conference itself. During the time period of this conference, we also teamed with David Luy of Trinity Evangelical Divinity School to form the Chicago Theological Initiative, a project that we hope will grow in the future and that has already born good fruit.

Above all, we thank God for the collaboration that has led to this book. And we thank our wonderful wives, Irene Kalantzis and Joy Levering, for their faithfulness to Christ, their encouragement, and their support.

Introduction

THE PREMISE OF THIS book is that contemporary Christians not only can learn about dying from our predecessors, but must do so. The "cloud of witnesses" (Heb 12:1) must be questioned for what they have to say about dying. We focus here on the task of dying in one's bed, which will likely be the fate of most of us, though martyrdom, violence, and sudden death still afflict many Christians today. For people today, facing imminent death can feel like a terrifying blind leap into nothingness or into the judgment of a God who sees and knows all our sins. Essentially everything that we work for in this life cannot be carried past the gate of death; we must leave it behind, and the world will go on without us, generally as if we had never existed.

Christians, however, are identified by the fact that we follow Jesus Christ who died and rose again. Our task is to die in Christ and with his love, through the grace of the Holy Spirit. But we cannot claim to be taking our dying seriously if we refuse to take the time to inquire of Christians who have gone before us: how should we die? And thus also: how should we live?

After his Resurrection, Jesus Christ sent forth his apostles into the world to proclaim the gospel, and for twenty centuries he has continued to send disciples, filled with the Spirit, into the world to bring his transformative gospel to the world. Insofar as these disciples were *performative* interpreters of the Word, we need to listen to what they have said about dying and to be instructed by their own dying.

There are other books that have done something similar to what we are trying to do here. Kerry Walters's *The Art of Dying and Living* tells the stories of seven twentieth-century Christians—Joseph Bernardin, Thea Bowman, Etty Hillesum, Jonathan Daniels, Dietrich Bonhoeffer, John Paul II, and Caryll Houselander—in order to teach us about dying (and living). David Albert Jones's *Approaching the End* examines the

1

contrasting theologies of death found in Ambrose, Augustine, Thomas Aquinas, and Karl Rahner. Vigen Guroian and John Behr have written about dying from an Orthodox perspective, and Todd Billings has done the same from the perspective of the Psalms and Reformed theology. Allen Verhey has reflected upon the hospice movement and modern medicine in light of the late medieval *Ars Moriendi* (art of dying) tradition. Christopher Vogt has delved into the *Ars Moriendi* tradition and other resources from a Catholic perspective.[1]

Inspired by such work, the present book retrieves the "cloud of witnesses" more systematically. The chapters of our book offer detailed engagements with the Book of Job, Irenaeus, Gregory of Nyssa, Augustine, John of Damascus, Maximus the Confessor, Thomas Aquinas, Martin Luther, Sergius Bulgakov, Hans Urs von Balthasar, Edith Stein, Erich Przywara, and Karl Barth. Moreover, while the essays in this volume are scholarly, they are also efforts to wrestle personally—as Christians who face death—with the meaning of our dying.

In her recent book, *The Violet Hour*, popular author Katie Roiphe examines the deaths of six "writers and artists who are especially sensitive or attuned to death, who have worked through the problem of death in their art, in their letters, in their love affairs, in their dreams."[2] Roiphe finds that these writers and artists discover no real meaning in death, which they conceive of as annihilation (the exception in her book is John Updike, who died a Christian). Characteristically, Roiphe thanks one of her sources "for several conversations in which he helped and dazzled me enormously with his erudition and insight while adroitly answering exactly none of my questions."[3] In fact, he had no answers. Her concluding line is: "We make our own comfort."[4] Thus, when Roiphe studies the most prominent intellectuals—literary figures and artists—of our time, she comes up with cold comfort.

For us, her book is both a warning and an invitation. It is a warning not to rely upon our culture for answers to our most pressing questions. It is an invitation to seek deeper and to ask whether those who have long preceded us in death, including the inspired author of the Book of Job,

1. Walters, *Art of Dying*; Jones, *Approaching the End*; Guroian, *Life's Living*; Behr, "Life and Death," 79–95; Billings, *Rejoicing in Lament*; Verhey, *Christian Art of Dying*; Vogt, *Patience, Compassion, Hope*.

2. Roiphe, *The Violet Hour*, 8.

3. Ibid., 291.

4. Ibid., 287.

Irenaeus, Gregory of Nyssa, Augustine, John of Damascus, Aquinas, and Luther, as well as giants of the twentieth century such as Bulgakov, von Balthasar, and Barth, can tell us more. That in fact they *can* do so is due to their receptivity to divine revelation and to the depth of their questions. Their probings need to be known today by dying Christians. The twelve chapters of this book are a step in that direction.

Survey of the Chapters

Let us briefly survey the arguments of each chapter. Chapter 1 takes up the Book of Job, the greatest exemplar of mortal suffering other than Jesus Christ. Matthew Levering argues that the Book of Job is neither about why an omnipotent God permits such terrible suffering (as many scholars hold), nor about whether Job will be rescued by God from the tragedy of dying without descendents (as Jon Levenson suggests). Rather, Levering argues that the Book of Job is about how cruel and unjust it would be for a God who has created humans and blessed them with communion with himself to allow them to be annihilated by death. Job cries out repeatedly against annihilation; he does not want death to be the end, since he insists that he has been created for communion and that if death deprives us forever of communion, then death is an utterly unbearable prospect. Levering argues that in this sense, God's goodness is at stake throughout the Book of Job.

The second chapter engages the Church Fathers from the deeply personal perspective of a scholar aware of the looming presence of death over every person's life, and who recounts the pastoral experience of having to console a young husband over the sudden death of his 24-year-old wife. Michel René Barnes notes that by contrast to pagans, Christians believe that human death has a particular origin (the fall, as well as human sexual reproduction) and an endpoint—resurrection. He raises the question of whether, given the sure hope of resurrection, Christians should actually grieve death. He first attends to how Cicero sought to manage his own grief after the death of his adult daughter Tullia. After weighing the philosophical remedies, Cicero finally decided to console himself by having Tullia publicly proclaimed as now a goddess with her own temple! In this striking light, Barnes turns to Gregory of Nyssa's warning that marriage and family (and Gregory was married) means exposing oneself to the death of one's wife and to the deaths of one's children. In light of such mortal turmoil, consecrated virgins such as Gregory's sister Macrina have an advantage with respect to peace and serenity in dying. Turning to Augustine, Barnes notes that Augustine shows that the key is to order our loves rightly. For Augustine, our true happiness is to be found only in the life to come, revealed to us by the divine physician who himself, as a self-humbling lover, underwent death for us.

In the third chapter, Brian E. Daley addresses the biblical scholar Oscar Cullmann's famous concern that Christian faith in bodily resurrection is incompatible with Platonic belief in the immortality of the soul. Daley notes that the immortality of the soul, in the way Plato typically conceives of it, did not become a central part of Christian anthropology and eschatology until the mid-fourth century. On this basis, Daley turns to Gregory of Nyssa's perspective. For Gregory, the life of the soul in the body is always something of an exile, since the body, unlike the soul, is subject to death, and also since life in the flesh generally involves much suffering. At the same time, Gregory insists upon the goodness of the resurrection of the body, and he looks forward to possessing a transformed body—whose character and possibility he explores in detail. He argues that our body and soul are united in such a way that, when their union is broken, the soul and bodily elements remain teleologically ordered to reunion. After canvassing the full spectrum of Gregory's writings on death and the life to come, Daley concludes that contrary to Cullmann's concern, Gregory is right to take up the philosophical and cultural assumptions of his time and to integrate them into his radically biblical defense of the goodness of bodily resurrection. Gregory places Scripture's witness to resurrection and salvation (involving purification and transformation) at the center of his approach, and Gregory rightly defends the role of the soul in assuring continuity between the person who dies and the person who is resurrected.

In chapter four, John C. Cavadini directs attention to Irenaeus and Augustine on suffering and death. These two great Fathers explain suffering and death quite differently. Irenaeus suggests that the fall had roots in the fact that Adam and Eve were not yet fully developed. On this view, humans require a process of maturation and development, and so our abuse of freedom, while unfortunate, is not the utter disaster that it would be if we were not created to grow through experience, struggle, and training. Indeed, for Irenaeus we are created for the Incarnation, in which the purpose of longsuffering patience becomes clear. Through Christ's death, we can see the mature human being who loves us despite our sin, and we can see that immortal life per se would not satisfy us, since we were made for life in God and for love. By contrast with Irenaeus's view of death as remedial, Augustine holds that death constitutes a devastating punishment. Augustine thinks that Adam and Eve knew precisely what they were doing, and absurdly and wickedly sinned nonetheless. Death rips apart the body-soul unity that is the human person, and in response to such a devastation, God rescues us through the Incarnation. For Irenaeus, therefore, suffering is pedagogical and gradually helps us to attain maturity in Christ, whereas for Augustine suffering is dreadful and can be overcome only by Christ. Cavadini argues that in a real way, both are right. We should affirm Irenaeus's point about mortal suffering helping us to grow toward God, but with Augustine we should also insist that mortal suffering in itself (outside of union with Christ), along with those who by their wicked actions make others suffer, must not be sentimentalized as somehow good. Cavadini concludes that only a combination of the Irenaean and Augustinian streams characterizes a fully healthy Christian spirituality of suffering and death, such as he finds in Pope John Paul II's *Salvifici Doloris*.

Chapter 5, by Marcus Plested, examines the liturgical materials of Orthodox Christianity with respect to death and dying. Plested begins with a set of quotations from John of Damascus that are included in the Orthodox funeral service for a layperson. As Plested shows, John bemoans death as a bitter, fearful, and grievous separation of body and soul. Death offers reason for deep lamentation at the transitory character of earthly life and earthly beauty. The once-beautiful human body, now a corpse, becomes food for worms. Separated from the body, the soul is separated from all earthly privileges and pleasures, and stands naked before the divine judge, in need of our prayers and dependent upon Christ's mercy. Plested emphasizes the reverence that Orthodox liturgy and burial practice shows for the body of the deceased person, despite the soul's departure. He mentions, too, the anointing of the sick and the memorial services commemorating a person's death, as well as the admonitory prayers of the Lenten services and the conversations between saints and dead persons recorded in the *Sayings of the Desert Fathers*. In undermining stereotypes of Greek patristic "flight from this world" and rejection of the body, Plested makes clear that the center of the Orthodox perspective on death and dying is a realistic confrontation with the bitterness of death in combination with an equally realistic joy in Christ's Resurrection.

Mark A. McIntosh, in chapter 6, views death through the lens of the divine ideas tradition. The divine ideas tradition perceives both the sheer gratuity of creatures and the fact that God eternally knows and loves them into existence. Since God's mind is the ground of creatures, their falling into ruin need not be their end, since God knows what they are meant to be. Drawing especially upon Augustine, Maximus the Confessor, Anselm, and Thomas Aquinas, McIntosh makes clear that death's hold seems much less firm upon us when we realize the vibrant way in which the Trinity knows and loves us into existence. Although we are sinners, this fallen identity is not our deepest identity, which God knows and can bring to be. We can thus offer our mortal, transient, and distorted selves to God with assurance that, in the Word, God can make us who we should be. The Father knows us in his Word, and the incarnate Word, bearer of the deepest truth of each person, dies for our sins and renews the wellsprings of our true life, transforming us through the Spirit into the Father's idea of us. The mortal truth of the world is transformed by the death of the Word in whom the eternal truth of the world becomes known—a truth that is Trinitarian, and that is made present in time by the Resurrection of Christ, his conquest of the mortal hash that sin has made of the world and his manifestation of the Spirit's joy in the Truth known from all eternity by the Father.

In chapter 7, David Luy explores Martin Luther's teachings about dying. As Luy shows, Luther offers spiritual strategies for preparing to die, and indeed Luther argues that the whole life of the Christian should be regarded as a preparation for death. For Luther, Christian life is an ascetic or purgative training, which we need because we are tempted by concupiscence to cling to this world rather than to God. Especially when we are dying, we are deeply tempted to fight against being separated from our worldly life, and it is precisely during this existential trial that we need to be able to draw upon the purgative training of our Christian life in order to stay the Godward course. What is needed is faith and complete dependence upon God. Only this can restore us, and no works performed outside of this posture have any spiritual value. Because of concupiscence, however, fallen human nature continually asserts itself over against God. The Christian life, therefore, consists in the struggle of the spirit against the flesh, a purgative struggle flowing from baptism and requiring radical repentance in the sense of turning away completely from all things other than God and turning to God (repentantly and obediently) with our whole heart. Trials often expose how we cling to worldly things, including experiential consolations upon which we wrongly depend. God permits these trials so as to purify us from our wayward inclinations and to call us once more to put our faith solely in Christ and his promise of mercy. God also seeks to awaken us to the fact that death is a divine punishment, rooted in the wrath of God, and that to escape this wrath we need faith in Christ and his grace. Trained by mortifications to depend solely upon God in Christ, rather than depending upon our sense experience, the Christian will be prepared to die in the peace, pardon, and strength given by Christ to all who have true faith and trust in his Cross and Resurrection.

In chapter 8, Paul L. Gavrilyuk probes some previously untranslated and little known writings of Sergius Bulgakov on death and dying. He argues that Bulgakov's "sophiological" teaching about Godmanhood— the existence of all things "in God" or "divine-human unity"—may have existential roots in Bulgakov's encounters with death, beginning as a young child, when his father earned his livelihood as a Russian priest by presiding over funerals. Bulgakov's own son Ivan died in 1909, and Gavrilyuk shows how Ivan's death marked a profound transformation for Bulgakov, who experienced himself loving his dead son with the love of Christ, communicating mystically with God and his son, and believing with a sudden certainty in the general resurrection of the dead. Bulgakov thereby discovered death as the place of (transfigured) life, an eschatological thrust that marks all his later theology. Gavrilyuk mines his *Spiritual Diary* (1924–26) for evidence of his traditional piety and sense of life as a continual dying for Christ, on the path to the joy of eternal life where we will be fully united with those whom we love. In 1926, Bulgakov suffered from a dangerous fever and experienced a separation and intensification of his "I," along with the enactment of divine judgment and mercy, capped by intense joy and freedom from fear of death. But Bulgakov encountered death in a different way while undergoing surgery for throat cancer in 1939. He underwent an experience of painful co-crucifixion with Christ, of being enveloped by the profound darkness of abandonment to mortal threat. Gavrilyuk concludes by examining Bulgakov's theology of death in *The Bride of the Lamb* and "The Sophiology of Death," showing that the sophiological theme of *kenosis* and co-dying (Christ's *kenotic* co-dying with us and ours with him) becomes explicit only after his experience of 1939, without undermining the power of his earlier experiences.

Cyril O'Regan, in chapter 9, directs our attention to Christ's ordering of existence toward death in contrast with Heidegger's ordering of existence toward death. Heidegger promotes a dramatic view of human finitude and living-toward-death, but Heidegger also proscribes thinking about God or life after death, insisting that the boundary of finitude is not God but "nothing." Heidegger insists that we must stand before death as before an absolute, utter finality; only thus can we authentically accept our non-teleological finitude and live toward death as our own apocalyptic annihilation. For Heidegger, as O'Regan notes, Christianity is a costly forgetting of death, a self-blinding and self-destroying attempt to get around the tragic character of human finitude. Heidegger urges in this regard that Augustine (as a Platonist) deeply distorted the best impulse of Christianity, namely Christianity's existential openness to the radical inbreaking of a transformative event (which Heidegger describes as the phenomenon of coming, heroically or humbly apocalyptic but decidedly non-redemptive). O'Regan carefully reviews major Catholic respondents to Heidegger's position: Hans Urs von Balthasar (who notes the connections to Friedrich Nietzsche and Ranier Maria Rilke), Erich Przywara, Karl Rahner, and Edith Stein. All contest Heidegger's finitism and *a priori* rejection of God, and Stein in particular shows how we can advance along the lines of the "dark night" (or "mystic death") of the humble Christ as the answer to, and proper appropriation of, Heidegger's claims. O'Regan concludes by reflecting upon the disastrous consequences for Christian eschatology of Heidegger's "eschatological contraction," as well as upon the ongoing fruitfulness of the (post-Heidegger) Augustinian alternative advanced by Przywara and von Balthasar.

Chapter 10, by Marc Cortez, focuses on Karl Barth's theology of death and dying as unfolded by Barth in a series of volumes of his *Church Dogmatics*. As Cortez shows, Barth distinguishes between death in itself and death as we now experience it. The latter is the result of original sin, and it is death in this sense that the Bible describes as unnatural and negative, rooted in divine judgment. In itself, death need not have been negative, but after sin it is experienced as judgment. By dying on the Cross, Jesus has borne death-as-judgment for us. Barth adds that because Christ died, we know that mortality (death-as-transition) and finitude belong to sinless human nature. Barth holds that such limits are to our benefit, since in his view our identity arises in the acts that we perform, and so a temporal end is required to bring completion and closure to our "identity." Endless temporal life would endlessly put our salvation in jeopardy, not least since Jesus' act of atonement is not undertaken for an endless temporal series of sins. Barth critiques the notion of the immortality of the soul and holds that our existence after death can only be guaranteed by God's free grace; we have nothing of "our own" after death. For Cortez, granting that human existence always depends upon the Creator, Barth's rejection of the soul raises the question of what grounds the continuity of our earthly existence with our resurrected existence. Cortez also notes that Barth's position suggests that the Incarnation would have ended at the moment of Christ's death, only to resume again at Christ's Resurrection. Thus, while Cortez strongly approves Barth's christological starting-point for reflecting on death, he argues that Barth runs into problems with the nature of creaturely existence after death.

In chapter 11, Brent Waters investigates the question of what constitutes a "good" Christian death. Certainly such a death must be a faithful one, in which we consent to God's will and die with love of God and of neighbor. Over all our loves, love of God must be primary, and we should understand our lives to be a divine "gift" and "loan" which we must ultimately surrender to God. Waters describes us as custodians or caretakers of the gift of our lives; we do not possess them in an autonomous fashion, and we must treasure our time (and the finitude of our time) as part of what makes us the creature that we are. Indebted to Barth, Waters identifies the church as the place where we learn how to live as people who have died with Christ and who seek to imitate his self-surrender. In this way, it is important to prepare daily for death. Waters also reflects upon the status and claims of modern medicine, especially its oft-present sense that humans can be what we will ourselves to be, which in the face of death prompts calls for euthanasia. While recognizing that euthanasia will be a real temptation even for Christians, Waters insists that fidelity to God requires bearing witness to the fact that we are not in control of the gift of our life, and he points out that when "curing" is no longer possible, "caring" and palliative care—along with accompaniment by friends and relatives—are still possible. He concludes by warning against the contemporary exaggerations of the goal of mastering nature, as exhibited by transhumanism, and by noting that the truth of life is found not in mastery but in love.

The final chapter is authored by Gilbert Meilaender, who, like Waters, is a well known Christian ethicist. Indebted to Barth, he examines death from the threefold perspective of creation, reconciliation, and redemption. Since earthly life cannot satisfy our yearnings, the gradual bodily decline that we endure in aging is a good thing. We are temporal creatures, and despite our desire for more temporal life, we should be able to appreciate that our finitude makes endless earthly life unappealing For Meilaender, the key aspect of human life is our thirst for a deeper union with God and a greater freedom, as befits creatures endowed with a spiritual soul. Having said this from the perspective of creation, Meilaender adds that from the perspective of reconciliation we can recognize that death, when it comes, comes as a judgment; we are called to appear before God, and all our illusions of autonomy fall away. Here we should know in faith that Christ has borne our judgment for us. Finally, in terms of redemption, even now we can participate in the self-surrender that characterizes the holy Trinity. In Christ, we already live this self-surrendered life, and our sinful self-centered life has been put to death. Although Meilaender affirms that death does not reduce us to nothing, he suggests that rather than trying to conceive of a truly human life that somehow could be bodiless, it is better to think of the period between death and the general resurrection as a "sleep" during which we are sustained by God and are at home with the risen and living Christ.

BIBLIOGRAPHY

Behr, John. "Life and Death in an Age of Martyrdom." In *The Role of Death in Life: A Multidisciplinary Examination of the Relationship between Life and Death*, edited by John Behr and Conor Cunningham, 79–95. Eugene, OR: Cascade, 2015.

Billings, J. Todd. *Rejoicing in Lament: Wrestling with Incurable Cancer and Life in Christ*. Grand Rapids: Brazos, 2015.

Guroian, Vigen. *Life's Living toward Dying: A Theological and Medical-Ethical Study*. Grand Rapids: Eerdmans, 1996.

Jones, David Albert. *Approaching the End: A Theological Exploration of Death and Dying*. Oxford: Oxford University Press, 2007.

Roiphe, Katie. *The Violet Hour: Great Writers at the End*. New York: Random House, 2016.

Verhey, Allen. *The Christian Art of Dying: Learning from Jesus*. Grand Rapids: Eerdmans, 2011.

Vogt, Christopher P. *Patience, Compassion, Hope, and the Christian Art of Dying Well*. Lanham, MD: Rowman & Littlefield, 2004.

Walters, Kerry. *The Art of Dying and Living: Lessons from Saints of Our Time*. Maryknoll, NY: Orbis, 2011.

Chapter 1

The Unbearability of Annihilation

Job's Challenge to His Creator

Matthew Levering

Jon D. Levenson argues that the central question of the book of Job is whether Job can "legitimately rely on God's much-acclaimed faithfulness to rescue from Sheol—not at the end of days, to be sure, but in his own time of lethal torment."[1] According to Levenson, the book of Job is about whether God will rescue Job from mortal suffering, rather than being about the problem of everlasting death. Citing Bildad the Shuhite's response to Job, Levenson notes that Bildad thinks that Sheol is only "the place of him who knows not God" (Job 18:21). Levenson makes clear that he is not claiming that Bildad recognizes "an eschatological resurrection of the dead along the same lines of the Second Temple and rabbinic doctrine that emerged centuries later," nor indeed that Bildad recognizes any kind of resurrection of the dead.[2] Rather, Levenson is simply claiming that for Bildad and also most importantly for the author(s) of the book of Job, Job's vision of "hopelessness and gloom" is not the "universal human

---

1. Levenson, *Resurrection*, 68. A version of this chapter has previously appeared as chapter 1 of Matthew Levering, Dying and the Virtues (Grand Rapids: Eerdmans, 2018).

2. Ibid., 70.

destiny," because "Sheol" means only a terrible earthly fate, namely an early and miserable death.[3]

Levenson fully accepts the later Second Temple and rabbinic doctrine of the resurrection of the dead, and his book offers a subtle and valuable defense of that doctrine. But according to Levenson, "in the Hebrew Bible, death is malign only to the extent that it expresses punishment or otherwise communicates a negative judgment on the life that is ending."[4] On this view, to die at the end of a long and praiseworthy life is not a problem for the Hebrew Bible, and neither is it a problem for the book of Job, which concludes happily with Job recovering from his mortal illness and living 140 more years. The final verse of the book of Job, meant to be a happy ending, is that "Job died, an old man, and full of days" (Job 42:17). Levenson emphasizes that Sheol is a punishment, whereas "the texts about the demise of Abraham, Moses, and Job . . . give no hint that at that moment they fear Sheol, for their impending death does not negate God's evident and abundant favor. They die with lives fulfilled and certainly seem to face no future terrors or miseries whatsoever."[5]

It would seem, however, that in the face of impending death, Abraham, Moses, and Job actually face nothing whatsoever, let alone "future terrors and miseries." If there were nothing after death, as Levenson assumes the ancient Israelites believed, then surely death would annihilate Abraham, Moses, and Job once and for all. In Levenson's view, however, to think along those lines is to miss the way in which personal identity was constructed in this period of ancient Israel's life. Since personal identity was linked tightly with one's extended family, the survival of the family sufficed to enable the person to face everlasting death with equanimity. In Job's case, he gained an entirely new family that overcame the deaths of his seven sons and three daughters. Levenson explains the difference between our perspective on death and that of the book of Job (and of ancient Israel generally): "To us, the shadow of death always overcasts to an appreciable degree the felicity that the books of Ruth and Job predicate of Naomi and Job at the end of their travail. We look in vain for some acknowledgment that the newfound or recovered felicity is not absolute, since death is. The authors of these books thought otherwise."[6] Death

3. Ibid.
4. Ibid., 72.
5. Ibid., 73.
6. Ibid., 119.

remains a threat for the book of Job, but it is a threat only insofar as it raises the possibility that the family (not the person) will come to an end.

Levenson admits that the evidence of the Psalms shows that individual Israelites did indeed experience existential terror in the face of death. But he contends that in Genesis and throughout the Hebrew Bible, "the great enemy" is "death in the twin forms of barrenness and loss of children," not the death of the individual person.[7]

I accept that for biblical Israel, the most central fear was dying without children; and I recognize that the book of Job ends on a happy note by having Job die in old age with a prosperous family surrounding him. Nonetheless, I think that the book of Job confronts head-on, with real terror and agony, the problem of personal death understood as annihilation. My contention is that Job challenges God precisely on the grounds that it would be cruel and unjust for God to annihilate (or to permit to be annihilated) a human being such as Job, who obeys God and who yearns for an ongoing relationship with God.

I do not think that Job's major concern is his lack of children. In fact, he hardly speaks about his relations except to complain that they do not honor him now that he is incapacitated and worn down by his mortal suffering. Instead of worrying about family, Job's central concern throughout the book is that his impending death is unjust and unbearable.

Before I turn to the book of Job, however, I will devote a good bit of attention to the view of God and death found in Katherine Sonderegger's recent work. Sonderegger describes God in terms of fiery and life-giving power, and she recognizes God to be untamable and overwhelming. She argues that in dealing with such a God, the question for everyone who suffers deeply is whether God is in fact good. Given what some friends of God endure in their encounter with God, Sonderegger argues that we can affirm that God is good but we cannot *explain* God's goodness in the face of the suffering of his friends. She thinks we can defend God's goodness, but not in a truly explanatory way; and in the end, we must simply be silent.

I agree that silence in the face of suffering can be appropriate. Why God's plan for creation involves so much suffering is ultimately, in my view, an impossible question to answer. For instance, I assume that God could have simply created all creatures, with Christ at the center, in a glorified state and that this universe, while excluding some kinds

7. Ibid., 120.

of perfection, would nonetheless have had its own perfection. Unlike Sonderegger, however, I think that God's goodness in the midst of the suffering of his friends must be intelligible. We must be able to explain—not solely defend, let alone lapse into silence about—why we believe that God is never abusive toward those who love him. In the case of the Book of Job, God's handing Job over to the Satan for testing (see Job 1:12) is sometimes seen as evidence for a God who inflicts pain on the innocent, but the framing device of Job's first two chapters should not be taken literally. We need to be able to show that God is not Job's abuser, since this is the charge that Job repeatedly makes against God and since an abusive God would not be worthy of worship. Job's existential challenge is how a good God could permit the everlasting destruction or annihilation of those whom God has made and loved, and who (for their part) love God.

In what follows, therefore, I first survey Sonderegger's position on God and human death. I then argue that Job's profound and unblinking encounter with the terrible absurdity of death (abstracted from the context of sin and its punishment) is the fundamental root of Job's suffering, which is more spiritual than it is physical, though it is certainly both. Certainly, God permits Job to face with terrifying immediacy his vulnerability to annihilation. But far from abusing Job, God speaks at the end of the dialogue to reassure Job that God is the wise Giver of life, possessed of the power to restore Job's standing and to overcome human death.

I. Katherine Sonderegger: God and the Suffering and Death of His Beloved People

The first volume of Sonderegger's *Systematic Theology* treats the doctrine of God. I focus here upon something of a side issue, but one that she handles at length: namely, the problem of suffering and death in relation to God. As she writes, "we cannot deny that human history, borne and sustained by the Lowly One, is also frightful in its cruelty and indifference. No one who scans human history with an open eye can fail to recoil at the violence, the random and ceaseless bloodletting, the pathetic grandeur of rulers and their empires, tyrants all for a brief day."[8] In the "cruelty and indifference" of history, death obviously plays a major role; the violence and bloodletting produce not only suffering but the death of

---

8. Sonderegger, *Systematic Theology*, vol. 1, 151.

numberless innocent victims, so many of whom are completely crushed and forgotten, their desires and dreams for life utterly thwarted.

Sonderegger quotes a marvelous passage from John Henry Newman in which he remarks upon "the greatness and littleness of man, his far-reaching aims, his short duration, the curtain hung over his futurity, the disappointments of life, the defeat of good, the success of evil, physical pain, mental anguish, the prevalence and intensity of sin, the pervading idolatries, the corruptions, the dreary hopeless irreligion, that condition of the whole race."[9] Death cuts deeply in this mournful passage, since our hopes and dreams for this life, as Newman says, are cut short by death, beyond which we cannot see by our own powers. Sin makes death even more bitter, because what life we do have is so often marred by "the success of evil" and by "the pervading idolatries" and "corruptions."

In response to the "cruelty and indifference" of human history, Sonderegger first emphasizes that God is not absent. She describes God's presence using the biblical image of fire, in addition to undertaking metaphysical reflection upon the presence of God. Since "Dynamic Life exists," she holds that "life after death, and even more, life in the face of death, is not a concept or a doctrine or a pious hope—not first or principally!—but rather the simple and profound acknowledgement of the creature standing before, and so bathed in, this Omnipotence, this fiery Life."[10] When confronting death, believers can endure and rejoice because believers are bathed in the fiery Life of God. For believers, God's presence shines so brightly through the beings that exist that we can endure the cruelty and indifference of death, the way it cuts short our lives and those of our loved ones. God makes the cruel and indifferent sickle of death bearable. We are bathed in Life, not bathed in death, despite the incontestable grimness of human history.

Sonderegger emphasizes that she is not grounding herself in natural theology or in philosophical or epistemological warrants for belief. Rather, she is simply expressing what believers know from God's descent upon them, not from their ascent by any powers of their own. Speaking for believers, she states, "In prayer, in times of testing and trial, in the haunting melancholy and passion of this life, we simply know this Vitality; more, we *encounter* its mighty Power that crushes death and sin."[11]

9. Newman, *Apologia*, 242; cited in Sonderegger, *Systematic Theology*, vol. 1, 152.

10. Sonderegger, *Systematic Theology*, vol. 1, 187.

11. Ibid., 186.

Our encounter with "fiery Life" does not answer questions about why God permits the evils of history. When God descends upon us, he shows us that God is God; he does not answer the questions by which we would wish to ascend to God. God simply suffuses us and irradiates us with himself; he does not meet us here on the level of mere introspection, epistemological warrant, or doctrinal affirmation.

Sonderegger explains that this encounter with the descending God "is why believers who suffer, sometimes brutally, sometimes through a long, harrowing life, can nevertheless lift up their voices to God not only in lament but also and much more in praise."[12] For such believers, the "encounter with Reality itself" means that in the encounter, "the veil of this mortal life has been lifted, the door opened to the heavenly realm, and Life bursts forth."[13] Without denying the cruelty of death, then, the saints bear witness to what they have experienced, not as a matter of trying to give warrant to their faith, but as a matter of professing the God who has descended upon them so that they have been "enveloped, irradiated with Life, the blazing Lord of Light."[14]

The encounter with "the blazing Lord of Light" makes clear to believers that the power of death is nothing in comparison to God. Having been met by the Lord, believers know that all powers, including death, "will bow the knee before this Living Lord."[15] Sonderegger observes, "*That* is first and principally what the faithful mean when they scoff at death, and what Athanasius praises when he sees the Roman world freed from the feverish fear of death."[16] Now that Life has made himself known, those who have encountered this Life know that nothing can be held by the power of death, which pales in comparison to this Life. The "whole created order will rise again," because the merest touch from this fiery Life banishes death by its divinely radiating Power.[17] As Sonderegger says, testifying to this fiery Life constitutes the purpose of every page of Scripture. Pairing the Old Testament theophanies with those of the New, she ends by giving praise to "the blazing Light that sears and emblazons the face of Moses and the very garments of Christ" in the Transfiguration, and

12. Ibid.
13. Ibid.
14. Ibid., 187.
15. Ibid.
16. Ibid.
17. Ibid.

by giving praise to "the sheer fire of resurrection, the Light that streams forth from the grave, the great Hope, the exceeding weight of Glory, that is the Vitality of the Lord God, seizing His creature home."[18]

In this way, Sonderegger connects what God does in Christ—namely, conquering death—with who God is as infinite fiery Life. She also emphasizes that the God who is present in the graves of victims is the Christ, who shows himself to be "the One who is with us."[19] Christ has "tasted" our sin and borne it "vicariously," as "the Life, the Vitality, within the death of sin" and as "the Life laid down for sinners," so much so that "He becomes the lost" and enters into "the darkest pitch of grief."[20] His corpse, the corpse of the incarnate Son, is the corpse of Life.

God meets the dead as One who is dead, and therefore the dead are never simply dead: "in the midst of death, we are in Life," because Christ's "own Light flames out in this darkness, and the darkness does not overcome it."[21] The "Power of the Living" irradiates the realm of death even when Christ is dead.[22]

Despite her emphasis on the believer's experience of God's fiery Life in the face of suffering and death, Sonderegger does not want us to accept too easily that God is "good." She points to the prophet Jeremiah's wrenching experience of knowing the Lord, an encounter which even leaves him cursing the day he was born. Sonderegger observes that Jeremiah's anguish and suffering "can only remind us of that other Prophet [Christ] in Jerusalem, eaten up by zeal for the Lord's house, consumed by His terrible mission. Jeremiah's prophecy is a living apocalypse, a vivid torment that cannot let go of the encounter with the Lord God in His raw Subjectivity."[23] Ultimately, it is not the people that torment Jeremiah, but rather it is the Lord himself who compels Jeremiah to suffer for his people, and it is this same Lord who seems to fail Jeremiah. Sonderegger describes "the uncanny power and terror of Jeremiah's interior nakedness before and *within* the Lord."[24]

18. Ibid., 188.
19. Ibid., 217.
20. Ibid.
21. Ibid., 218–19.
22. Ibid., 219.
23. Ibid., 224.
24. Ibid., 225.

Why does God, if he is in fact good, sear Jeremiah so profoundly, just as God sears Job even to the point of "Job's self-loathing and longing for death"?[25] It seems as though God, in his fiery Presence, simply burns away or scorches the human ego of some of those whom he calls, to the point where God does not care about the pain and the desire for death of precisely those whom, more than other humans, God claims to love. How is it that God, in his very Presence to those whom he loves, can break his beloved ones and permit them to feel utterly desolate? At certain points in the book of Jeremiah, Jeremiah proclaims his joy in God's Presence, while at other points "the Lord's Presence can only wound and tear open the prophet's flesh in incurable misery."[26] It would seem that such a dangerous and disturbing God can hardly be good, if in response to Jeremiah's love for him, he tears Jeremiah apart interiorly as an "annihilating fire" rather than identifiably as "Blessing."[27]

Sonderegger makes clear that it is not simply that God *permits* suffering; it is also that God's particular closeness to some of those whom he loves *causes* them excruciating suffering, and God allows them to drink this suffering to the dregs. With regard to such challenges to the doctrine of God's goodness, she notes that theologians "have grown accustomed to putting away the urgency and starkness of such questions by relating the agony of Jeremiah, or of Job, or of the psalmist to a literary device of Israel's scribes, or more doctrinally, to an abrupt 'anthropomorphism' in the doctrine of God."[28] Sonderegger resolutely and rightly refuses to follow this path of evasion. Pertinently, she notes that "the incarnate Son . . . is broken on the cross with the Father's Name on his lips."[29] At issue, then, is not just the status of suffering and death, not just the question of how God could allow us to die like mere animals, with no physical basis for hope for any further life. God not only allows us to set forth into such a nightmarish and (from all outward appearances) endless chasm, but also, to some whom he specially chooses for his service, his Presence shakes them with literal agony. Viewed in this light, he cannot be called a "good" God without also being called a "terrible" and "dangerous" God.[30]

---

25. Ibid., 226.
26. Ibid., 227.
27. Ibid., 228.
28. Ibid.
29. Ibid., 229.
30. Ibid.

Sonderegger argues that theologians must "fall silent" in the face of the mystery of God's presence painfully consuming his servants.[31] In her view, we must not be like Job's friends, trying to justify the ways of God as though they could be explained by an easy application of human reasoning. She avers: "I say that we simply do not know what to say about the dereliction that is Job's or Jeremiah's, the trial and great testing that some must undergo in their encounter with the Lord God and His awe-ful Subjectivity."[32] She adds, however, that it is God's Love in its adaman-tine Presence that scorches and breaks his chosen people. She explains that "Love is the name of Divine Presence" and that "the Love of God" is "holy Fire" and "an unchecked Flame, red hot, incendiary."[33] God's Love is "Rock, adamantine Reality," says Sonderegger, and "[w]e are broken on God in just this way."[34]

Repeatedly, then, Sonderegger connects divine Love with pain on the part of his beloved people: we are scorched, burnt, ashen, not spared, broken by God's Love. But these descriptions, surely, are appropriate only in our condition of sin, or at least in the context of a world marred by sin. I do not see how these descriptions of pain and suffering would be appropriate absent the world's fallen condition. And if this is so, then theologians should do more than "fall silent" in the face of the pain that God allows his beloved ones to endure.[35] Theologians should make clear that this pain has to do with the process of overcoming the state of hu-man alienation resulting from sin.

Along these very lines, Sonderegger herself shows that the book of Numbers displays the painful way in which humans, both as a society and as individuals, emerge from the condition of sin. She states: "The Power of God, turned toward the creature, is *personal*: it concerns liberty, the birth of persons. No abstract Power this, but rather the breaking of slavery, the wrenching transformation and cost that is exacted when lib-erty is announced and seized."[36] In Numbers, the people, including Moses

31. Ibid.

32. Ibid.

33. Ibid., 489–90.

34. Ibid., 489. In the same vein, she states that God's Love is "an unquenchable Fire that simply Lives, Abides, Burns, in the midst of Israel, scorched and purified and ashen before it. The Dynamism, the Energy, that is God radiates Love and Light: nothing is spared from its burning Heat" (ibid.).

35. Ibid., 108.

36. Ibid., 287.

(whose own sin against the Lord eventually bars him from the promised land), constantly endure dire threats and real pain from the Lord. Sonderegger remarks that the encounter between the holy Lord and his sinful people inevitably causes the people pain: "The hard Objectivity of the Lord bruises the people . . . The Lord appears to rage like a blind Force: the camp is scorched wherever the Lord touches down, an uncontrollable Fury."[37] Here, Sonderegger rightly explains the biblical text in terms of the people's sin and the painful difficulty of gaining freedom from sin, so that the Fire of God is in fact his purifying Love.

Yet, in her analysis of Jeremiah's suffering (and Job's), Sonderegger insists that we cannot offer explanations of this kind.[38] Instead, we must accept God's Subjectivity and Freedom, and not try to account for God's scorching and wounding of some of his most beloved, innocent people. We cannot claim that in the subjective experience of Jeremiah, the torment he endured from God was balanced by something positive. Against explanations like this one, Sonderegger states: "The breaking and crushing of Jeremiah, the fire that burns him within, is not *balanced* by or equaled to the Word that is sweet, the intimacy that is Life Itself."[39] Nor is Christ's suffering balanced by an interior apprehension of God.

Sonderegger allows herself one explanation, although she proceeds to deny that it can explain. The explanation is that after God's terrifying rending apart of his beloved—after the internal and external *exile* that encounter with God means for Jeremiah and Jesus—there follows a *return*. In Jeremiah and in Christ, God reveals the exile-return pattern that is the truth about history: "Human life, each of them, and all of them, live under the expansive arch of this pattern, this on-rush of life: from the terror of exile to the exceeding weight of glory, the mansion of many rooms, the return prepared for us by the One who tasted death for us all."[40] But although this is the inner "secret" and indeed the "plain fact" of all history, nonetheless Sonderegger denies that it can really function as an explanation.[41] Silence remains the only possible stance in the face of God's inflicting pain upon his beloved ones: "The movement from exile to return is not an *explanation*, still less a *justification*, of the broken spirit

37. Ibid., 280.
38. Ibid., 230.
39. Ibid., 233.
40. Ibid., 234.
41. Ibid., 235.

that descends on some of the faithful, wounded by God."[42] She notes that Jeremiah, during his life, experienced the wounding and the tragic exile, but never experienced a return. He died in torment and/or in exile. Admittedly, he prophesied the return and the restoration, but he did not live to experience it. We cannot allow the Resurrection to shield our eyes from the agony of the Crucifixion. Instead, the distance between exile and return, between Good Friday and Easter Sunday, for Jeremiah and for Jesus as for us, must be crossed in silence: our words cannot explain away the horror of God wounding his beloved. She insists once more, "We cannot break or explain away the silence of suffering divine things; there is no proclamation that renders such brokenness intelligible or comprehended. No, the dark mystery remains."[43]

Naturally, Sonderegger has to face the question of whether the God she has portrayed is an abusive God. Why is it that those who are lifted up as the greatest exemplars of service to God are the ones who are "crushed by divine service"?[44] Sonderegger knows that this pattern fits with what psychologists have identified as the cycle of abuse, in which the abused person constantly seeks the approval of the abuser and does so by submitting to further abuse. In answer to this concern, Sonderegger denies that it is divine abuse, but she also argues that no explanation of her denial can be given. She states, "We could not defend the Lord and His Power by explaining away the criticism nor by attempting to silence it . . . Nor can we take one step away from the silence and broken speech that must descend over us when we stand before the saints, afflicted by God."[45] She refuses to explain the affliction of the just either in terms of the injustice caused by the world's fallen condition, or in terms of God's efforts through his beloved people to overcome the world's injustice. She holds that by trying to explain the suffering of God's beloved people as justifiable, we open the door to the abuser's blaming of the victim for the abuse. God's people are defenseless against God's absolute Power, and so God would be placed in the abuser's role. We must therefore remain

42. Ibid., 235.

43. Ibid., 239. Even so, we can testify to the fact that in our brokenness, we have been borne, we have been held, held and carried in the unspeakable "Silence that is His own Word, carried into death" (ibid.). Our brokenness may leave us speechless, without any ability to explain things, but for Sonderegger it never leaves us without God's consolation, embrace, and Promise.

44. Ibid., 240.

45. Ibid., 241.

silent about the reason for God's wounding of the faithful, at least insofar as we are not permitted to offer an "explanation" or justification.[46]

Is Sonderegger correct that "we simply do not know what to say about the dereliction that is Job's or Jeremiah's, the trial and great testing that some must undergo in their encounter with the Lord God and His awe-ful Subjectivity"?[47] In what follows, I explore the question of what can be said about the suffering and death of God's beloved by turning to the book of Job. I focus on Job because his personal suffering cannot be blamed upon the context of sin. In the cases of Jeremiah and Jesus (as well as Moses), God's beloved suffer in their obedience to God, but they do so insofar as they freely choose to stand as representative of the people to God and as the representative of God to the people. Their suffering, then, is directly related to the sinful context in which they find themselves. By contrast, Job's friends are condemned for trying to explain his suffering as the result of sin. Indeed, the book of Job portrays Job's suffering as having its origin in God's agreement to allow Satan to test Job's fidelity. If the good God torments his beloved children, then certainly we cannot speak theologically about it. The book of Job therefore is a test case for whether or not we must remain silent on this topic. I will argue that Job should be interpreted not as being about whether Job's suffering comes from God, but about whether God could justly have made any human being for everlasting annihilation.

II. God and Job's Suffering

The Book of Job as a Parable

When read as historical reportage, the first two chapters of Job are mis-read. The opening phrase, "There was a man in the land of Uz," already

46. Although we cannot offer an *explanation* that justifies God, Sonderegger adds that we can in faith point to "the pattern of exile and return, of death to Life, as confirmation of the Goodness that is Divine Power" (ibid., 243). We cannot explain or justify the suffering of Jeremiah or Jesus, but we can point to the actual return from exile and the actual Resurrection as compelling evidence that, in fact, God's Power is Good. We can see that in God's endless gifts to his people, preeminently in his gift of his own "Life for others," there is a "gracious exchange"; whereas in abuse, "there is no exchange, no living relationship, but all is defined, all said and determined by the abuser, and there is no remedy," since nothing counts but the power of the abuser (ibid., 244–45).

47. Ibid., 229.

indicates the parable-character—rather than historical character—of this text.[48] In the second sentence of the book of Job, we learn that Job has "seven sons and three daughters" (Job 1:2), and these symbolic numbers are echoed in the next sentence's observation that Job also had "seven thousand sheep" and "three thousand camels" (Job 1:3). The parable-character of the story similarly informs the description of the heavenly court. Job 1:6 states, "Now there was a day when the sons of God came to present themselves before the Lord, and Satan also came among them." In God's dialogue with Satan, God and Satan are like two powerful men arguing about whether a slave can perform with the grace that his master attributes to him.[49] This argument is important for setting the scene for the testing that Job undergoes, but it should not be taken, of course, as a literal description of God's attitude toward Job. Job is a "blameless and upright" man "who feared God and turned away from evil" (Job 1:1). Since Job also has a wonderful family and significant wealth, the obvious question is whether Job performs pious actions toward God out of love of and gratitude for his own earthly prosperity, rather than out of love for God. Many humans have done precisely this, as the storyteller well knows! The dramatic tension of the parable, therefore, is whether when Job loses every earthly thing, he will still worship God. Since God's

48. I recognize that, as the activist-theologian Daniel Berrigan, S.J. observes in his commentary on Job, "The text of Job is a daunting thicket of what experts call 'variant readings'" (Berrigan, *Job*, xix). All books in the Bible have places where the manuscript tradition is simply unclear, but this is true to a particularly significant extent for the Book of Job. See also Pope, *Job*, xxxix: "The Book of Job is textually the most vexed in the Old Testament, rivaled only by Hosea." I employ here the Revised Standard Version.

49. In his introduction to his translation of the Book of Job, Stephen Mitchell remarks, "Compared to Job's laments (not to mention the Voice from the Whirlwind), the world of the prologue is two-dimensional, and its divinities are very small potatoes . . . The author first brings out the patient Job, his untrusting god, and the chief spy/prosecutor, and has the figurines enact the ancient story in the puppet theater of his prose. Then, behind them, the larger curtain rises, and flesh-and-blood actors begin to voice their passions on a life-sized stage. Finally, the vast, unnameable God appears . . . [T]he god of the prologue is left behind as utterly as the never-again-mentioned Accuser, swallowed in the depths of human suffering into which the poem plunges us next" (Mitchell, "Introduction," xi–xii). In Mitchell's view, moreover, the Book of Job ends up embracing annihilation as a good: "Job's comfort at the end is in his mortality. The physical body is acknowledged as dust, the personal drama as delusion. It is as if the world we perceive through our senses, that whole gorgeous and terrible pageant, were the breath-thin surface of a bubble, and everything else, inside and outside, is pure radiance . . . The very last word is a peaceful death in the midst of a loving family. What truer, happier ending could there be?" (ibid., xxviii, xxx).

providential power is unquestioned by the storyteller, Job can only lose his earthly goods if God permits it to happen. In the story, God does not directly cause the evil that befalls Job, but he permits it.

Beginning in Job 1:13, four disasters are reported to Job in quick succession: the killing of all of Job's oxen and asses, and some of his servants, by Sabean marauders; the killing of all of Job's sheep, and some of his servants, by lightning; the killing of all of Job's camels, and some of his servants, by Chaldean marauders; and the killing of all of Job's sons and daughters by a great wind that blew down the house in which they were eating. In each of these four devastating events, furthermore, exactly one servant escapes to tell the tale to Job. The afflictions next shift to Job's own person. Job comes down with a case of "loathsome sores from the sole of his foot to the crown of his head" (Job 2:7) and goes to sit "among the ashes" (Job 2:8). His wife tells him to "Curse God, and die" (Job 2:9) and his three friends simply weep and lament at the sight of him. Having lost everything, Job, who is "blameless and upright" (Job 1:1), says things that confirm his righteousness: "Naked I came from my mother's womb, and naked shall I return; the Lord gave, and the Lord has taken away; blessed be the name of the Lord" (Job 1:21); and "Shall we receive good at the hand of God, and shall we not receive evil?" (Job 2:10). The narrator approves Job's righteousness in both instances: "In all this Job did not sin or charge God with wrong" (Job 1:22); and "In all this Job did not sin with his lips" (Job 2:10).

Job's Insistence upon His Innocence

In chapter 3, however, Job pours forth a lengthy curse against the day of his birth. His friend Eliphaz the Temanite reprimands him for not seeing the good pattern of divine providence: "Think now, who that was innocent ever perished? Or where were the upright cut off? As I have seen, those who plow iniquity and sow trouble reap the same. By the breath of God they perish, and by the blast of his anger they are consumed" (Job 4:7–9). Eliphaz goes on to point out that Job, in his claim that he is righteous before God, is being sinfully presumptuous. Eliphaz claims to have heard a voice in a dream that said: "Can mortal man be righteous before God? Can a man be pure before his Maker?" (Job 4:17). The point is that Job is being reproved and chastened by God for his sins. Eliphaz urges Job to respond sensibly: "Behold, happy is the man whom God reproves;

therefore despise not the chastening of the Almighty. For he wounds, but he binds up; he smites, but his hands heal" (Job 5:17–18). If Job repents, promises Eliphaz, Job will have many descendents and a long life.

Job refuses to listen to Eliphaz's rebuke, again claiming his own righteousness before God. Bildad the Shuhite therefore tries a turn at reasoning with Job. He points out to Job that if, indeed, "you are pure and upright, surely then he [God] will rouse himself for you and reward you with a rightful habitation" (Job 8:6). The key point is that God does not "pervert justice" (Job 8:3). Bildad then argues that if Job is charging God with iniquity in bringing Job low, Job is in the wrong, since "the hope of the godless man shall perish" (Job 8:13) and "God will not reject a blameless man, nor take the hand of evildoers" (Job 8:20). If Job is indeed innocent, Job has nothing to fear, and certainly nothing to slanderously blame God about; God "will yet fill your mouth with laughter, and your lips with shouting" (Job 8:21).

Job responds that in trying to make his case before God, God's over-bearing power will ensure that the judgment goes God's way. Job knows that he is innocent, but Job complains that he cannot fairly make his case because God is so dominant.

Zophar the Naamathite now takes his turn at answering Job. Zophar accuses Job of babbling nonsense and mocking God. It is not surprising, Zophar says, that Job claims to be "clean in God's eyes" (Job 11:4), since the wicked often persuade themselves that they are pure. Zophar concludes that since God sees far more deeply than Job can see, Job can be sure that "God exacts of you less than your guilt deserves" (Job 11:6). Zophar urges Job to repent immediately: "If you set your heart aright, you will stretch out your hands toward him. If iniquity is in your hand, put it far away, and let not wickedness dwell in your tents. Surely then you will lift up your face without blemish; you will be secure, and will not fear" (Job 11:13–14). Job responds forcefully against Zophar, accusing him and the other two friends of being "worthless physicians" who "whitewash with lies" (Job 13:4). Job then appeals directly to God.

Eliphaz, however, does not allow things to stop there. He condemns Job in stark terms. He tells Job that "you are doing away with the fear of God, and hindering meditation before God" (Job 15:4). He warns that Job has forgotten that all humans are sinners. Job's presumptuous insistence upon his own innocence in the face of the calamities that have befallen him shows, Eliphaz says, that Job's tongue has been carried away by "iniquity" and that Job's spirit has turned "against God" (Job 14:5, 13).

When Job responds once more, this time in a more despairing vein (although without giving in to his friends), Bildad chimes in against Job by insisting that calamities come justly to the wicked. Again Job bemoans his fate, only to have Zophar repeat and amplify Bildad's description of the calamities that befall the wicked, and that have now befallen Job. Job replies with exasperation. After noting the way in which the wicked often enjoy long and prosperous lives, he asks his three friends: "How then will you comfort me with empty nothings? There is nothing left of your answers but falsehood" (Job 21:34). Eliphaz now turns upon Job with strong condemnations suited to the sorry state in which Job finds himself: "Is not your wickedness great? There is no end to your iniquities" (Job 22:5). Eliphaz lists a large number of extremely grave sins that he attributes to Job, and then at the end of his discourse he once again urges Job to repent: "Agree with God, and be at peace; thereby good will come to you . . . For God abases the proud, but he saves the lowly" (Job 22:21, 29). But Job merely repeats his innocence and accuses the all-powerful God of not caring about the just while sustaining the life and prosperity of the wicked. When Bildad again urges Job to recall that all humans are sinners before God, Job responds by repeating his lamentations at even greater length: "God has cast me into the mire, and I have become like dust and ashes" (Job 30:19). The section concludes, "So these three men ceased to answer Job, because he was righteous in his own eyes" (Job 32:1).

At this stage, Elihu the Buzite, a man younger than both Job and Job's three friends, intervenes. Elihu "was angry at Job because he justified himself rather than God" (Job 32:2). Disgusted with the inability of Job's friends to persuade Job, Elihu asks why Job complains that God will not hear him. God speaks in various ways, says Elihu. One way that God works to "cut off pride from man" (Job 33:17) is to allow disease to afflict us; but the man who prays to God, and who finds an angel or mediator to intercede for him, can recover from a mortal disease. Such a man, when recovered, will proclaim in the hearing of his neighbors: "I sinned, and perverted what was right, and it was not requited to me. He has redeemed my soul from going down into the Pit" (Job 33:27–28). By contrast, Elihu points out, Job has insisted upon his own righteousness and has made clear that he considers God to be unjust. Job is therefore a scoffer who is getting what his sins deserve. Elihu emphasizes the justice of God: "Of a truth, God will not do wickedly, and the Almighty will not pervert justice . . . For his eyes are upon the ways of a man, and he sees all his steps" (Job 34:12, 21). Elihu deems that when Job complains that God does not hear him, it is because Job has not cried out in repentance to God but instead has continued to rely upon his own righteousness. Job has not given true praise to "the wondrous works of God" (Job 37:14) and has not adequately reckoned with the fact that "God is great, and we know him not" (Job 36:26). Elihu concludes that God, who utterly transcends us, "is great in power and justice, and abundant righteousness he will not violate" (Job 37:23).

Job's Justified Lament: Human Annihilation Is Not Just

The basic debate should be clear: is God just toward Job, who is enduring unspeakable sufferings, or has the righteous Job merited nothing of this suffering? God answers in favor of Job. Speaking to Eliphaz, God says, "My wrath is kindled against you and against your two friends; for you have not spoken of me what is right, as my servant Job has" (Job 42:7). God does not mention Elihu, but Elihu had not said anything particularly different from what the three friends said. God proclaims that Job has gotten the best of the debate. Job is therefore innocent and does not deserve the suffering that came upon him.

Yet, God also asks Job rhetorically, "Will you even put me in the wrong? Will you condemn me that you may be justified?" (Job 40:8). It is clear that God finds this to be laughable: Job cannot put God in the wrong. Job replies with repentance: "I have uttered what I did not understand, things too wonderful for me, which I did not know . . . I had heard of thee by the hearing of the ear, but now my eye sees thee; therefore I despise myself, and repent in dust and ashes" (Job 42:3, 5–6). If God affirms that Job has spoken rightly about God (by contrast to the three friends who have spoken falsely), this seems to justify Job's bitter complaints against God. But if so, why does God deny that Job can put him in the wrong? God approves Job's laments, and yet Job ends up repenting of his laments. Is this not an obvious contradiction?

I hold that Job's justified lament has to do with the problem of annihilation. In my view, his being stripped of everything at the outset of the parable signifies the beginning of his descent into death and ultimately into everlasting nothingness, where he will be stripped of absolutely everything. Job's truthfulness about his innocence removes the justification of death on the grounds of sin, a justification to which his friends have recourse in their efforts to reason with him. Having removed this justification, the Book of Job can probe the deeper issue, namely (abstracting entirely from sin) whether annihilation is fitting for any rational creature. Job argues that it is simply not right that the process of dying should result in the everlasting destruction of a human being made by God for communion with God. The kind of beings that we are could not justly have been made for annihilation, and so in justice God should give us more life. Being stripped of everything forever is wrong given the kind of creatures that God created us to be.

To appreciate the centrality of dying-as-annihilation for the parable of Job, consider Job's cursing of the day of his birth (and also of the night of his conception). He urges that complete darkness and oblivion swallow up that day and night, and he wishes that he had never known anything. He asks, "Why did I not die at birth, come forth from the womb and expire?" (Job 3:11). Had he died at birth, then without regretting anything, he could have been dead. Job complains that "the thing that I fear comes upon me, and what I dread befalls me" (Job 3:25). His situation is not solely one of physical suffering; it is also one of mental agony caused by approaching death. He states, "My days are swifter than a weaver's shuttle, and come to their end without hope. Remember that my life is a breath; my eye will never again see good" (Job 7:6–7). This apprehension of annihilation stands at the very heart of his complaint to God.

Against the notion that he selfishly or egotistically wants to exist, he describes his coming death in terms of the sudden ending of all interpersonal communion: "The eye of him who sees me will behold me no more; while thy eyes are upon me, I shall be gone" (Job 7:8). His death will affect more than himself alone; those who love him will never again be able to interact with him. They will see only his corpse, because he will never again know or interact with anyone. The descent to "Sheol" constitutes a permanent ending. This fact drives Job to deep anguish and complaint. If this is what life is, then life must be rejected. Why does God bother with humans, if God is simply going to allow humans to be annihilated? A God who creates humans to be annihilated could not really care about what humans do in their lives. Job challenges God: "If I sin, what do I do to thee, thou watcher of men?" (Job 7:20). Soon, says Job, "I shall lie in the earth; thou wilt seek me, but I shall not be" (Job 7:21). Doomed to move quickly from life to a state of everlasting non-existence, Job does not believe that God truly cares about him.

Job grants that God exists and that no one can contend against God. In his power, God has made everything to be as it is, and no one can stop God when God "snatches away" life (Job 9:12). Job knows that God's power is such that no argument with God can be won by a creature. Even though God "destroys both the blameless and the wicked" (Job 9:12)— as Job says, "if it is not he, who then is it?" (Job 9:24)—Job admits that "though I am blameless, he [God] would prove me perverse" (Job 9:20). God's power is such that no creature can argue successfully against him, and yet in the fact that all humans go quickly into everlasting death means that goodness and wickedness in life are "all one" in the end (Job 9:22). Job himself can do nothing but move swiftly toward annihilation: "My days are swifter than a runner; they flee away, they see no good. They go by like skiffs of reed, like an eagle swooping on the prey" (Job 9:25–26). It is quite clear that he is not merely complaining here about suffering. His fundamental complaint against God has to do with his inexorable slide toward death. Job's accusation centers upon his fast-approaching annihilation: "Thy hands fashioned and made me; and now thou dost turn about and destroy me. Remember that thou hast made me of clay; and wilt thou turn me to dust again?" (Job 10:8–9).

Not only is the Creator destroying forever the man Job—the Creator's own creature—but also, as Job points out, the Creator had shown him great love. Making and preserving Job was no easy thing. Job states, "Thou didst clothe me with skin and flesh, and knit me together with bones and sinews. Thou hast granted me life and steadfast love; and thy care has preserved my spirit" (Job 10:11–12). But now God is hunting Job so as to obliterate him. This action makes no sense, since it would seem that the creation of a human being, to whom God shows "steadfast love," should lead not to death as annihilation but to an enduring mutual relationship of love. Job again cries out that if this is what life is—to be destroyed by the God who has loved one into existence and whom one has loved—then "[w]ould that I had died before any eye had seen me" (Job 10:18). He again tells God, who has betrayed him, to leave him alone while he lives out his brief remaining days. The emphasis here remains firmly upon death as an entrance into everlasting non-existence. Job speaks of his remaining days of life as being "before I go whence I shall not return, to the land of gloom and deep darkness, the land of gloom and chaos, where light is as darkness" (Job 10:21–22). This is the "land" where human consciousness turns dark and goes off forever, never again to be restored.

As he continues with his complaint, Job adds that he can hardly believe that matters have come to such a grim conclusion. After all, he previously enjoyed a relationship with the One who is now working to annihilate him: "I, who called upon God and he answered me" (Job 12:4). Job is well aware that every living thing is in the hand of God, and that God wills a finite lifespan for everything on earth. God does not allow any human or any nation to endure for long, since human strength and pride are as nothing in comparison with God's strength. Job knows all this, and yet he makes clear to God that it is unjust that he (and all humans) should merely waste "away like a rotten thing, like a garment that is moth-eaten" (Job 13:28).

Job 14 makes an especially important contribution to understanding Job's complaint against the injustice of dying, assuming that death means personal annihilation.[50] Here Job first compares human existence to that of a flower that quickly withers and to a shadow that flees away. He then points out that God, having determined to give humans such a short existence, should not punish humans on earth for their sins, since humans will soon enter into non-existence anyway. In this situation, says Job, human life is more pitiful than that of a non-rational tree. A non-conscious tree can have "hope" to live again, since even if its roots grow old and its stump dies, nonetheless its shoots can come forth again from the ground. By contrast, "man dies, and is laid low; man breathes his last, and where is he?" (Job 14:10). A dead human is like a dried up river: the same river will never flow again. Job paints a portrait of terrifying annihilation: "man lies down and rises not again; till the heavens are no more he will not awake, or be roused out of his sleep" (Job 14:12). The imagery here does not portend a day on which the dead man will awake, since the implication is that the heavens will always exist. Job then puts the matter into interpersonal terms that are deeply moving. He tells God that he would be glad if God would place him in Sheol, if only this were not an everlasting annihilation. He wishes that God would "appoint me a set time, and remember me!" (Job 14:13). He wants to be remembered by the God who created him, and he wants to be restored to the interpersonal relationship with God that he has only just begun to enjoy: "If a man die, shall he live again? All the days of my service I would wait [in Sheol], till my release should come. Thou wouldest call, and I would answer thee; thou wouldest long for the work of thy hands" (Job 14:14–15). This is a

50. As Marvin Pope comments on Job 14:13–15, "Job here gropes toward the idea of an afterlife. If only God would grant him asylum in the netherworld, safe from the wrath which now besets him, and then appoint him a time for a new and sympathetic hearing, he would be willing to wait or even endure the present evil" (Pope, *Job*, 102).

depiction of a God who truly loves what he has created. Job would respond with joy and love to the God who calls him. The yearning of Job for relationship would be met by the Creator's yearning, rather than being suppressed through everlasting annihilation.

Such a God would mercifully not allow death to be the destruction of the human person. Human finitude would not bring a total end to the dying person's interpersonal communion. Humans would not know and love for a fleeting period only to be everlastingly destroyed. Again, Job does not doubt that God exists. It is God's goodness that Job challenges. Job compares the way God treats humans to the way that running water washes away soil. In time, each human "falls and crumbles away" (Job 14:18) and in this way, says Job, "thou [God] destroyest the hope of man" (Job 14:19). God destroys us as though he did not care about us. Job uses the image of sending away a friend forever: "Thou prevailest for ever against him, and he passes; thou changest his countenance, and sendest him away" (Job 14:20). Our countenance turns to stone, and we no longer know anything. Since the dying person will never know what happens to others after his death, Job suggests that the dying person becomes totally self-focused; "[h]e feels only the pain of his own body, and he mourns only for himself" (Job 14:22).[51] What kind of God would treat his beloved in this way, or allow his beloved to come to such a state? God is unjust because he is uncaring. God does not care that our finitude means that we cease forever to exist and that we have utterly no share in what happens after our death.

After a pause for a response by one of Job's friends, Job continues his attack upon the injustice of death as annihilation. Criticizing his three friends, Job complains that God has worn him out and shriveled him up. Worse, Job observes, God "has torn me in his wrath, and hated me; he has gnashed his teeth at me" (Job 16:9). God has shown himself to be not a loving Creator or a faithful God, but an enemy who desires the destruction of the human being who loves God. Job had been in good health, but now God attacks and breaks Job. Describing this attack vividly (and building upon the poignancy of Job 14), Job states that God "slashes open

51. I may be misinterpreting this, since Pope argues that what Job means in 14:21–22 is that "[a]lthough man is deprived of knowledge by death, he is still subject to pain" (Pope, *Job*, 105). Against Pope's interpretation, note Job 14:12's statement that "man lies down and rises not again; till the heavens are no more he will not awake, or be roused out of his sleep." This certainly appears to be a complete lack of consciousness, and therefore no conscious bodily suffering or pain would be possible for the dead person.

my kidneys, and does not spare; he pours out my gall on the ground. He breaks me with breach upon breach; he runs upon me like a warrior" (Job 16:13–14). Although Job is innocent and he weeps piteously, God does not care. Job argues that God should have a law preventing God from killing man, just as God has a law that man must not kill man. Job expresses deep despair about his coming death. He has nothing to look forward to, because death will extinguish him forever and so his future is nothingness. He complains about the humiliation of his situation, about the "mockers" (Job 17:2) that lord it over a dying man. There is nothing to hope for in Sheol: "My days are past, my plans are broken off, the desires of my heart. . . If I look for Sheol as my house, if I spread my couch in darkness, if I say to the pit, 'You are my father,' and to the worm, 'My mother,' or 'my sister,' where then is my hope? Who will see my hope? Will it go down to the bars of Sheol? Shall we descend together into the dust?" (Job 17:11, 13–16). The answer is that the pit and the worm, total darkness, obliterate all hope.

God created Job to have hope, but now God is going to crush Job's hope. The injustice of this situation—made clearer by taking sin out of the parable—is the fundamental complaint of Job. Having created humans for interpersonal communion, for hopes of the future, how can God justly annihilate them? Such a God is a brutal hunter. Job states that God has "closed his net about me. Behold, I cry out, 'Violence!' but I am not answered. I call aloud, but there is no justice. He has walled up my way, so that I cannot pass, and he has set darkness upon my paths" (Job 19:6–8). Job's words nicely portray the existential standing of a human being confronting his or her own death (understood as annihilation).[52] The future is "walled up"; the path is utterly dark. God the hunter has trapped Job, given Job no escape, and will soon kill Job, despite Job's desire for interpersonal communion. By leading Job into annihilation, God has acted as though Job were a mere animal, as though Job was not a unique and unrepeatable center of consciousness reaching out for God. The glory of Job was Job's ability to give free worship to God, to seek for and love God. Now God crushes Job as though Job were an enemy or a mere animal. As Job puts it, "He [God] has stripped from me my glory, and taken the crown from my head. He breaks me down on every side, and I am gone, and my hope he has pulled up like a tree" (Job 19:9–10).

52. Pope suggests that Job is complaining simply about his "cruel sufferings" (Pope, *Job*, 131) but I think that it is death (understood as annihilation) that Job has primarily in view.

God has created a glorious creature, able to know and love and able to plan and hope, but death utterly destroys that creature as though the human being were a mere animal.

Zophar had proclaimed that God ensures that the wicked suffer during their earthly lives for their sins. Job knows that this is often not true. He insists that many thrive who make clear that they have no interest in God or God's ways. Even in this context, however, Job returns to his fundamental concern regarding annihilation: both the wicked and the good "lie down alike in the dust, and the worms cover them" (Job 21:26). All are obliterated. Job knows that he himself has obeyed God and has lived righteously: "My foot has held fast to his steps; I have kept his way and have not turned aside. I have not departed from the commandment of his lips; I have treasured in my bosom the words of his mouth" (Job 23:11–12). Despite Job's obedience to God's law, God will annihilate Job. It is God, therefore, who terrifies Job, because God unjustly intends to destroy forever even those who love God. Job complains that "the Almighty has terrified me; for I am hemmed in by darkness, and thick darkness covers my face" (Job 23:16–17). This darkness is the darkness of utter annihilation. According to Job, God treats both the poor and the wealthy in the same way that we treat "heads of grain" (Job 24:24). Heads of grain serve us, we consume them without thinking twice about it, and they never exist again.

Again, Job is not concerned about questions of whether God exists or whether God is all-powerful. He has no doubts on such matters. It is precisely because God is so powerful that Job challenges him. Having created Job, God appears to unjustly will his annihilation. Job states that God "has taken away my right" (Job 27:2). There is no hope for anyone "when God takes away his life" (Job 27:8). Even one who wishes to "take delight in the Almighty" (Job 27:10), as Job does, loses existence forever at the moment of death. It seems that God does not care about those who wish to delight in him; God coldly destroys them. In this way, what once was a beautiful relationship with God in wisdom and understanding has now been turned to nothing. Job cries to God but God makes no answer. God is tossing Job "about in the roar of the storm" (Job 30:22) in preparation for bringing Job "to death" (Job 30:23).[53] Although Job obeyed God and God once gave Job his favor, now God is like a faithless friend who

53. Pope capitalizes "Death" here and argues that the word should here "be taken as the proper name of the ruler of the infernal region, Mot" (Pope, *Job*, 196). I think that Job simply has in view everlasting destruction or unconsciousness.

spurns Job. Indeed, God wills that Job become dirt forever. Job details all the ways in which he has obeyed God by avoiding lust, falsehood, adultery, vengeance, reviling, hypocrisy, and greed, and by caring for justice, for the land, for the poor, for sojourners and strangers, and for widows and orphans. Yet God has now abandoned him to everlasting death, and Job insists that this is a profound injustice. God owes a far better destiny to a person who once enjoyed "the friendship of God" (Job 29:4) and who should still enjoy that friendship or protection.[54]

The complaint of Job, then, does not at its root have to do with theodicy's question of why the innocent suffer, although Job's complaint is not unrelated to this question, since suffering leads to death. Instead, Job presses deeper, to the issue of how God could justly will to annihilate those who have been close to him. Job's innocence in the story functions as a way of undermining the easy answer that death justly punishes sinners. How could a good God forever destroy rational creatures whom he created for communion and who yearn to delight in God? In creating a creature that enjoys unique and unrepeatable consciousness, how is it just that God should condemn such a creature to the utter darkness of everlasting death, so that the person who dies will never know or love again? How can such a thing be bearable for a person, let alone be just? The book of Job confronts the unbearable darkness of death, and challenges God to defend it.

God's Defense against Job's Charge

Toward the end of the book of Job, God answers Job. How does God defend himself against Job's charge regarding the injustice of human death (understood as annihilation)? God's fundamental answer to this charge is to present himself as the giver of existence and life. He begins by posing a series of rhetorical questions to Job, the first of which has to do with the moment of creation: "Where were you when I laid the foundation of the earth?" (Job 38:4). God is the one who ordered the earth so that it could sustain life, by giving bounds to the sea (which would otherwise have swallowed everything in chaos). God also asks what Job really knows about death: "Have the gates of death been revealed to you, or have you

54. I am not trying to overemphasize the word "friendship." Pope's translation of this verse reads: "As I was in the autumn of my life, when God protected my tent" (Pope, *Job*, 184).

seen the gates of deep darkness?" (Job 38:17). Job knows nothing about the governance of the universe, of the snow and rain or of the courses of the stars. Job cannot sustain the life and strength of animals, nor does he understand how the variety of wild animals and birds comes to be. In describing all these natural things, God lays emphasis on the fact that the wisdom that sustains non-rational things comes from without. He asks, for example, "Who has put wisdom in the clouds, or given understanding to the mists? Who can number the clouds by wisdom?" (Job 38:36–37).[55] Likewise, he asks, "Is it by your wisdom that the hawk soars, and spreads his wings toward the south?" (Job 39:26). God also lays emphasis on his power, which is obviously greater than even immensely powerful created things. God describes "Behemoth" and "Leviathan," two creatures—perhaps the hippopotamus and the crocodile—whose power far overshadows human power.

When God first established the universe, he tells Job, "the morning stars sang together, and all the sons of God shouted for joy" (Job 38:7). One can see why they would do so; creation is so magnificent. God notes that he alone is the giver of such a good thing. All creatures belong to God: "Who has given to me, that I should repay him? Whatever is under the whole heaven is mine" (Job 41:11). God alone has the wisdom and power to understand the existence, energy, and life that we find in the cosmos. Job cannot understand these things. In reply to God, Job admits that "no purpose of thine can be thwarted" and that "I have uttered what I did not understand, things too wonderful for me, which I did not know" (Job 42:2-3).

Why, however, does Job conclude that God has made a sufficient answer to the charge of unjustly annihilating humans? God points Job back to the wisdom and power of the original creation, and to the joy with which it was greeted. God reminds Job that Job does not really know anything about "the gates of death" (Job 38:17). God is wise, but Job is ignorant. God gives and sustains existence, life, and strength, and does so in a wise manner that Job cannot fathom. It would seem, then, that God suggests to Job—without resolving the mystery in any way—that to die is to fall into the hands of the Giver of life, and that God can be counted upon to wisely order things.[56] The Creator, as the Giver of life, should

55. The meaning of the Hebrew words here translated "clouds" and "mists" is uncertain, but the basic point seems clear nonetheless.

56. Contemporary exegetes tend to emphasize the arbitrary divine power entailed by God's response and Job's submission. See Pope, *Job*, lxxv; Clines, *Job 38–42*,

be trusted to sustain Job's life after death rather than annihilating Job; but Job will have to take this on trust. This amount of hope seems to be enough for Job, especially since God has taken the trouble to respond to his entreaties. God does not unveil the mystery of human death, but God gives Job enough hope to make death bearable.

The final narrative portion of Job seems to promise, symbolically, even more. Job, who previously was on the very point of death, now recovers and has his earthly goods restored twofold. God "blessed the latter days of Job more than his beginning" (Job 42:12). One might interpret this as the Lord making up for "all the evil that the Lord had brought upon him" (Job 42:11), and it certainly is not less than that. But in the context of the story (or parable), it is also a sign that God is always a God of blessing and a God of life. The moral is not the mere fact that no matter how sick one is, God can restore one's health and fortunes. Job has already deconstructed that hope by pointing out that one will simply die later (as indeed Job does as "an old man, and full of days" [Job 42:17] in the last line of the story). Rather the moral is in the pattern of movement from tribulation and death to blessing and life. Knowing God, we can hope that death will not be the last word for us, but that our communion with God will continue on because God truly cares for his beloved. Put otherwise, God's wisdom and power will not let death be the last word for his beloved. The injustice of flowering into consciousness and communion only to face everlasting death and nothingness stretching out endlessly consists in the fact that humans, while mortal, are created for communion with the infinite God. The book of Job suggests that God will ensure that annihilation is not the final truth about his human creatures.

Because of the unsolvable difficulties with understanding the meaning of the Hebrew for Job 19:25–27, I have saved mention of this brief passage until now, rather than placing too much weight upon it.[57] The RSV translates Job 19:25–27 as follows: "For I know that my Redeemer lives, and at last he will stand upon the earth; and after my skin has been thus destroyed, then from my flesh I shall see God, whom I shall see on my side, and my eyes shall behold, and not another." The "Redeemer" is often thought to be a kinsman who will avenge Job against God at some

---

1214–15. See also, however, Pope, *Job*, lxxvii.

57. Marvin Pope comments about Job 19:25–27 that "these lines are extremely difficult, the text having suffered irreparable damage. It is clear that Job expects to be vindicated, but it is not certain whether he expects his vindication to come in the flesh or after his body has disintegrated" (Pope, *Job*, lxxi–lxxii).

future point. Likewise, Job's hope that "from my flesh I shall see God" can be taken to mean that although an avenging kinsman will come after Job's death, Job still hopes to see God before he dies. Against this line of interpretation, it seems more probable to me that Job is speaking of his hope of seeing God after death, which he expects to be coming soon.[58] If so, then in 19:25–27, we find an insertion of hope that contrasts with the general focus of Job's challenge to God to preserve him, in justice, from the annihilating consequences of death. On this view, 19:25–27 anticipates the hope that we observe in the concluding sections of the book of Job.

III. Conclusion

Katherine Sonderegger argues that in the face of the terrible suffering that some of God's most beloved people endure out of obedience to God, theologians must remain silent rather than trying to offer an explanation for how God could will that they endure such suffering in relating to him. Her contention is that otherwise theologians would become like Job's friends, trying to offer an explanation for what in fact cannot be explained. Job's friends try to defend God against Job's accusations. Likewise, when people accuse God of not being good because of the suffering that he wills that some of his most beloved people endure, it is tempting to offer a defense of God's goodness. Sonderegger urges us to rise above this temptation.

Sonderegger is right to insist that God's Presence need not be consoling; it can burn and make excruciating demands upon us, including the demand that we trust God during humanly inexplicable experiences of loss and desolation. In the case of Jeremiah and Jesus, their witness of sacrificial love was one of utter self-emptying for the sake of the sinful people of God: and this suffices for explaining why God willed that they freely suffer. But Job's sufferings tell us something different, and require a different explanation. Job's fundamental issue has to do with whether

---

58. Although Marvin Pope recognizes that Job 14 (among other passages) makes clear that "the only prospect is extinction" and that there is no consciousness after death (ibid., xvi), he nonetheless also thinks that Job 19:25–27 shows that "Job never completely gives up his conviction that justice must somehow triumph. Even if his flesh rots away and his body turns to dust, in his mind's eye he sees his ultimate vindication and expects to be conscious of it when it comes, though it be beyond this life in the dust of the netherworld" (ibid., lxxii).

humans have been created in such a way that human death, if it is an annihilation, is unbearable. Humans reach out toward God and seek to obey God; and God shows marks of creative love and fellowship toward humans, who rational powers enable them to relate to him. Yet, humans face death in such a way that it feels like an annihilation, like standing on the brink of oblivion and then stepping into everlasting darkness and nothingness from which there will never be an escape.

Job's complaints are deeply moving: "Behold, I cry out, 'Violence!' but I am not answered; I call aloud, but there is no justice. He has walled up my way, so that I cannot pass, and he has set darkness upon my paths. He has stripped from me my glory, and taken the crown from my head" (Job 19:7–9). As Job says, dying seems to be nothing less than God killing Job, God stripping Job of all the regard that God had shown for Job, without the slightest care for Job's loving obedience to God. In dying, Job can look forward to no future: he is trapped within a rapid and humiliating descent to nothingness. Job says that "my hope he has pulled up like a tree" (Job 19:10), and he—a human being—wishes that he could be even a mere tree, since "there is hope for a tree, if it be cut down, that it will sprout again" (Job 14:7). Job fantasizes about a God who truly loves him, a God who might place Job for a time in the darkness of death, but who would then revive him by calling him to return to relationship with God: "Thou wouldest call, and I would answer thee; thou wouldest long for the work of thy hands" (Job 14:15). Can God truly be good if God turns his back for ever upon a rational creature who desires communion with him? God has created humans to thirst for communion with God, and Job makes clear that it is cruel and unjust for God to obliterate those who love him. This is the core problem that Job raises.

Job's story is a parable of human suffering in the face of death viewed as annihilation. The story challenges God: if death is annihilation, then God is abandoning and killing the very ones who, by his own invitation, obey, know, and love God. How could this be a just situation? The foolishness of Job's friends consists in their inability to apprehend the impossibility of annihilation being a just situation for humans who love God. Job's friends continually bring up the context of sin and argue that God punishes sinners and rewards the just during their earthly lives. But Job's point is that for God to create a human person who yearns for relationship with God, and then to draw that person into such a relationship only to abandon and annihilate the person, would be radically unjust. God approves of Job's challenge, and in response God emphasizes his creative wisdom and power. God makes clear, in other words, that Job is in the hands of a wise God who has the power to give life; and God reminds Job that he does not know what death is. The ending of Job also confirms the pattern of exile and return, and thereby suggests that Job will not be abandoned to everlasting death. The contested text of Job 19:25–27 seems also to indicate that Job will "see God" after dying.

Sonderegger aptly concludes about God: "To be Omnipotent, for the True God, is to burn with Blessing. From Him, pours out Generation and Gift, Life Itself; and behold, It is Good, and altogether Very Good."[59] A good God, however, cannot have created humans simply for annihilation. Job's struggle with God is not a mystery of theodicy in the face of which we can speak a little but must ultimately remain silent. Rather, Job's struggle with God requires us—and Job's friends—to speak firmly and decisively against the surd of everlasting death. We must call to mind the God who creates wisely and who gives life powerfully; we must call to mind that even if death looks like annihilation, we are not wise enough to know what death is unless God reveals it to us. If human death were annihilation, then God would not and could not be good, since God would be turning his back upon and killing those whom he had made to be his people in an intelligent and loving communion. With Job, we must cry out against such a view of death, and we must insist that no amount of justice in this life—no amount of blessings in this life—could comfort us when we face the reality of such death. We are created for more than everlasting death, and God would be cruel and unjust not to grant us the good for which, out of love for him, we yearn.

This is a problem in the face of which we must not be silent, both to cry out with Job and to rejoice in Jesus Christ's fulfillment of the pattern of exile and return, the pattern with which the book of Job ends. In the encounter with God, we will be seared and emptied, both because of our sin and because of the divine demand that in love we must give our lives for the sake of others so as to be configured to Christ and to the Father in the Holy Spirit. But at the same time, with Job, we must urgently cry out for what God has willed from creation to give those who love him: eternal life. As he does to Job, the all-powerful and all-loving God will respond.

59. Sonderegger, *Systematic Theology*, 326.

BIBLIOGRAPHY

Berrigan, Daniel. *Job: And Death No Dominion*. Franklin, WI: Sheed & Ward, 2000.

Clines, David. *Job 38–42*. Grand Rapids: Zondervan, 2011.

Levenson, Jon D. *Resurrection and the Restoration of Israel: The Ultimate Victory of the God of Life*. New Haven: Yale University Press, 2006.

Mitchell, Stephen. "Introduction." In *The Book of Job*. Translated by Stephen Mitchell, vii–xxxii. New York: HarperCollins, 1992.

Newman, John Henry. *Apologia Pro Vita Sua*. London: Longmans, Green and Co., 1893.

Pope, Marvin H. *Job*. Garden City, NY: Doubleday, 1965.

Sonderegger, Katherine. *Systematic Theology*. Vol. 1: *The Doctrine of God*. Minneapolis: Fortress, 2015.

Chapter 2

"What Have I Become, My Sweetest Friend?"

Death and Its Passions in the Early Church

MICHEL RENÉ BARNES

A preferential option for the mortal

HUMAN LIFE IS BOUNDED by two catastrophes: the inevitability but un-predictability of death; and the serendipitous character of birth.[1] Some ancients and moderns, pagans and Christians, focus upon the former; some ancients and moderns, pagans and Christians, focus upon the latter. That being said, it is typically modern to focus upon the problem of the serendipities of birth—think Marx—and to solve problems (or "injustices") produced by such serendipities through the remedy of a *predictable death*: "predictable" because consciously applied as class-extinction, genocide, or some other radical form of negative eugenics. Despite periodic claims upon the instrumentality of death by modern states and enduring tribes,[2] most of us live within the horizon of "*death as*

1. Seneca wrote that he expected death to be the same as pre-birth—the nonexistence of any consciousness—and in this way linked birth as the beginning of uncontrollable existence and death as the last experience *not in our power.*

2. If one were to write a "history of death" using the typical categories of "pre-modern", "modern", and "post-modern", it would become quickly clear that most of us are insufficiently modern in our sensibilities towards death and our perception of the

41

existentially[3] *inevitable but personally unpredictable"*. Within this specific horizon grief hovers *en potentia*: not a few of us will—through disease, serious injury, or genetic failure—experience our own bodies as IEDs to which we are unbreakably bound, just as we will have witnessed others taken away by radical failures of their bodies. Even when death is voluntary for a great good, those left behind grieve nonetheless. *Good men, the last wave by, crying how bright/ Their frail deeds might have danced in a green bay.*

When I was in the Masters of Divinity program in Toronto, I chose as my Clinical Pastoral Education (CPE) unit to be a chaplain at Toronto General Hospital. Each student was assigned hospital wards and shifts: mine was the ward for general surgery. Once a month we each took a rotation to be on call for the forty-eight hours of a weekend. For that time we lived at the hospital, and calls came at any time—but especially just before dawn, which is when the weak often die. One Sunday afternoon I responded to a "code blue" cardiac arrest alarm: in TGH chaplains were part of the cardiac arrest response team. The patient was a young woman in a high risk post-op ICU. She died: she was twenty-four. The day before she and her twenty-six year old husband, and their two young children, had been watching a football game on television in their home in Thunder Bay, Ontario. She had a headache and went to lie down. She never woke up. Thunder Bay quickly transferred her to Toronto by helicopter, and at TGH she was operated on for a cerebral hemorrhage. She survived the surgery, but later went into cardiac arrest, and died. Her husband was there in a little waiting room, as were her parents. I spoke with the husband; the other chaplain spoke with the young woman's parents. The doctors announced the outcome, and left. I remember walking round the rectangle of corridors with the husband, almost entirely silent, while

---

phenomenon: we have forgotten (if we ever knew) the multitude of ways in which the intended death of thousands and millions has been a preferred modern instrument for removing godless uncertainties over our daily bread.

3. I will use the word "existential" for what we experience or do because we are human, and "personal" for what we experience or do because *we are each ourselves and only ourselves* ("me" or "my"). The categories are used heuristically, without any conscious (on my part) debt to any philosophy or psychology (excepting, of course, the fact that I know the word "existential" through philosophical sources). The boundaries of the categories are soft, and in some cases are debatable: in one sense "fate" is an existential fact, because we are made up of atoms following mathematical rules; in another sense "fate" is personal, because *that guy is Oedipus who is the son of . . .* I use the words descriptively, not to carry the burden of any argument.

occasionally he talked. Although nominally a chaplain, I was reduced to offering biological explanations: a long time ago, when his wife was still gestating in her mother's womb, a blood vessel in her brain had failed to form with the proper strength. No one knew that this was true: she lived a normal life for twenty-four years. Then Saturday afternoon the blood vessel broke—as hydrodynamics would have predicted that, inevitably, it would. There was no warning, no escape, no remedy, no explanation. It was fate, it was what life in a body was like. It was "death's dread dominion".

The Apostle Paul says that if Christ was not raised from the dead then Christians are the most pitiable of all people.[4] Paul does not say that if Christ was not of a greater election than Moses, or if He was not wiser than Solomon, or even if He was not freed from death like Enoch or Melchizedek, then Christian faith is empty. The truth of the faith lies squarely in the Passion narrative, from the cross to the empty tomb, or it lies nowhere at all. It is true that the resurrection demonstrates that God has glorified Christ as His Son, but if that glory does not spill upon the dead bones of humanity then the most we can say is "Good for Him". If Christ was not raised from the dead then Christians live deceived lives, unaware of the end that awaits them: our hope is false, and our grief is only a shadow of what it would be—should be—if we knew our true fate: that dead is dead, and there will be no rising.[5] A great difference between Christian and Pagan reflections on grief and death lies in the fact that Christianity, as already in Judaism, presumes a discrete beginning to the fact of death among us, and offers if not quite an unequivocal end to death then at least a reversal of the phenomenon. The existential question in Christianity has fairly consistently been how and to what extent

---

4. "Pitiable" here translates ἐλεεινότεροι.

5. I find myself reminded of an analogy from my adolescence: in the first volume of the *John Carter of Mars* series much is made of a funeral ceremony in which the deceased is placed in a small boat on a sacred river, and, with his more valuable and most personal possessions around him, set into the river's current to carry him away to the land of the dead. Edgar Rice Burroughs obviously based his fictional ceremony on Viking or Native American funeral practices. The sentiment that death is a "sailing away" is a widely used device: recall, e.g., Tolkien's "sailing west" trope. With the unexpected financial success of what Burroughs wrote as a "stand alone" novel, he wrote a second John Carter of Mars novel—in which the plot turns on the discovery that some distance downriver was a nation of cannibals who received the funeral boats as bountiful gifts from their gods! Sometimes fantastic fables function better to reveal what otherwise cannot adequately be set in words.

the promise of recovery—i.e., a future resurrection—should figure in the present experience of death.

The "Vietnamization" of Our Life: Cicero on Grief[6]

In the year 45 BCE, Cicero's only child, his daughter Tullia, died during child-birth. Cicero was devastated, and retired [some speak of this as an "exile"] to the countryside for isolation and in search of the means by which he could successfully cure himself of the spiritual "disease" of grief. Cicero's self-administered cure had two parts: first, reading from previous works of *Consolatio*—many of which are unknown or lost even when we know the titles—Cicero wrote a book of *Consolation* to himself, the earliest known case of such a project. His research for this book of consolation involved his reading works by numerous philosophers of different schools: all this research is put to use in Book III of his *Tuscalan Disputations*, which is devoted to the problem of grief. Grief is a problem because it is regarded as a passion: it painfully disrupts the tranquility of reason and results from the mourner's assenting to propositions that are false or ignorant. Grief represents the breakdown of the mind's watch over the effects of our experiences and the impulses they trigger. As Seneca will shortly later put it:

> For the mind is not a member apart, nor does it view the passions merely objectively, thus forbidding them to advance farther than they ought, but it is transformed into the passion . . . Passion and reason are only the transformation of the mind toward the better or worse.[7]

Cicero identifies the following five philosophical options as proffered remedies to the malady of grief; that Cicero identifies them does not mean that he believes them all equally to be true, possible, or effective:

6. The phrase "the Vietnamization of our life" is taken from Banks, *The Sweet Hereafter*, introduced in chapter two by the character Billy Ansel, after the death of his wife followed a year later by the deaths of their two children: " . . . there was death, and it was everywhere on the planet and it was natural and forever; not just dying, perversely here and merely now." (Page 67; see also pp. 51–55 for the origin of the term for Billy.) A more contemporary term derived through analogy would be "The Falluyahization of our Life" or "The Khandaharization of our life". The statement is existential, not political. One is tempted to sum up Billy's insight as "Everything, everyone, every part of us, is an IED" except that there is nothing *improvised* about these "explosive" devices.

7. Seneca, *On Anger* I.viii.2–3, p. 127.

- First, *an expected loss hurts less than an unexpected loss:*[8] therefore we should always remember that we are weak, short-lived, mortals and expect death—for ourselves and for everyone we know.[9] To be human is to die.[10]

- Second, *recent deaths hurt worse than past losses*: knowing this we should await time's healing ways.[11]

- Third, *others have gone through this—or worse—and survived*: we should be encouraged by their endurance,[12] and—especially—we should recognize that the courage and endurance shown by some rose to the level of greatness, and these people should be our moral exemplars.[13]

- Fourth, *grief serves no purpose*—except if we regard the fact that experience hardens us to pain as a purpose.[14] Since grief serves no purpose it obviously cannot be "natural", but is rather the outcome

8. See *Tusculan Disputations* III.xxii.52 ff. "For we have this argument always at hand: that no evil should be unexpected." *Tusculan Disputations* III.xxiii.57. Cicero's discussion of grief and its remedies may be found in *Tusculan Disputations* Book III in the Loeb series of Cicero's works published in twenty eight volumes, of which the Disputations are in volume XVIII. In the comprehensive numbering of Latin works published in the Loeb series, the relevant volume is 141. The monograph Graver, *Cicero on the Emotions*, 25–37, contains Graver's translation and excellent commentary on the relevant passages.

9. "Some people suffering grief are said to have borne it worse after being told that everyone suffers, everyone dies: that we are born under such conditions as make it impossible for someone to be free from suffering." *Tusculan Disputations* III.xxiv.59.

10. "But the necessity of bearing what is the common condition of humanity reminds you that you are human, which lessens grief." *Tusculan Disputations* III.xxxii.77 f.

11. "It is because we have suffered loss *recently*, and not because we have suffered loss *unexpectedly*, that makes the loss seem greater." *Tusculan Disputations* III.xxii.54.

12. *Tusculan Disputations* III. xxiv: "Enduring misfortune is made easier by the fact that others have suffered the same, and the fate of others causes what has happened to us to seem less important than it has been previously thought. What was imagined to be the greatest evil is not so great as to defeat the happiness of life. Anyone suffering may be induced to bear what he observes many others have previously borne with tranquility and moderation." See *Tuscalan Disputations* III.xxxiii.

13. "Any bodily pain, let it be ever so grievous, can be endured where there is hope of some greater good."

14. "What is more effective at dispelling grief than realizing that it serves no purpose, and has been undergone to no account? Therefore, if we *can* get rid of it, we feel it because we didn't get rid of it." *Tusculan Disputations* III.xxvii.64–xxviii.67.

of an opinion or a judgment,[15] and such judgments are within our power—they are "up to us".[16]

- Fifth, *we are thus under no moral obligation to mourn*, there is no virtue to it, only social expectations and pressures.[17]

The consolation that *an expected loss hurts less than an unexpected loss*—an observation attributed to Euripides and Chrysippus—Cicero regards as failing to be remedial, and not universally true in any case. The fact that painful feelings fade with time Cicero acknowledges as true, but it has no force as a consolation because the torment of the loss—the power of grief—is so great that the possibility of future peace cannot break through present pain.[18] The judgment that *grief serves no purpose* Cicero expects—or rather, wants—to be the decisive realization that will enable us to withhold our assent to the impulse to feel grief. If grief serves no purpose, it accomplishes nothing but emotional pain, and can impede processes which do serve a purpose (ranging from eating to governing). If grief falls under the category of "passions we allow" then it also clearly falls under the category of "passions we can disallow."[19] The fifth and last argument Cicero critiques is that *we are under no moral obligation to mourn*. The social expectation for melodramatic and irrational states of grief after the death of a loved one must have been strong in early Roman culture, just as it must have been two or three centuries before in Greece where such reactions are commonly offered in theater and epics as motivations for the tragedy that follows (as in the case of the *Oriestea* trilogy).

Tullia's death was not simply "a death in the family" such as we all endure: Tullia's death was a public event as it made a spectacle of the conflict between Cicero's behavior and his teachings as "the leading philosopher, theologian and theorist of his generation"[20] at a time of great

15. "All passions are nothing else but an opinion and judgment formed of a present acute evil."

16. "It must be acknowledged, then, that people take up grief willfully and knowingly." *Tusculan Disputations* III.xxvii.66.

17. *Tusculan Disputations* III. xxvi–xxviii.

18. As we shall see, the power of exemplarity looms large in Gregory of Nyssa's response to his sister Macrina's death.

19. Something of the idea that the "uselessness" of grief has survived in the twentieth century in the (apparently) popular admonition, "Doing/feeling this isn't going to bring her/him back!"

20. "It is now widely agreed among Classicists that Cicero was "the leading philosopher, theologian and theorist of his generation." See Cole, *Cicero*, 10, for multiple

turmoil in Roman culture (especially in Rome itself). If the great and wise Cicero could not deflect the force of the great passion of grief, what chance was there for the rest of us, and—no less important—what was the point of all this philosophy anyway? Cicero was under considerable pressure to return to the city and be an exemplar himself of philosophical tranquility.

I said at the beginning of my treatment of Cicero that "Cicero's self-administered cure had *two parts*" of which the first part was his articulation of a philosophy of a consolation against grief. Now I turn to the second part of Cicero's "cure". He found such a solution in his decision to have his daughter divinized (ἀποθέωσις), that is, publicly recognized as a god. We must pause over this decision for at least one reason: although Cicero had been experimenting in his pre–45 BCE writings with the logic of human divinization, he had not, to that point, actually proposed such a case. In his writings after Tullia's death—which include most of his lengthier and more influential works—Cicero develops and proposes the prospect of merit-based posthumous divinity.[21] However, Cicero's proposal that Tullia be divinized and worshipped in her own temple was the first time the divinization of a human had ever been proposed in Rome.[22] The first actual carrying-through of divinization occurred in the months after Tullia died, when Julius Caesar was made Emperor and declared a "god" (whatever that meant).[23] As scholars we must be careful not to allow our popular entertainment-induced fantasies about "Roman 'political' divinization" and Roman "political religion" to function as historical verities.[24] (I want to stress that this warning against entertainment-induced fantasies applies as much to BBC productions as it does to

---

references. We should regard Cicero's role in defining western Roman culture in the same way as we regard Augustine's role in defining western post-Roman culture.

21. See Cole, *Cicero*, 12.

22. Cole argues that in the much earlier *Pro Lege Manilia* (66 BCE) Cicero was already taking the "initial steps toward introducing the divine honors that Pompey already enjoyed in the Greek east onto Italian soil." Cole, *Cicero*, 12.

23. For a careful corrective to our judgments about Roman religion, see Levene, "Defining the Divine in Rome," 41–81.

24. This point becomes relevant to our overall topic when contemporary scholars debate what Gregory's opinion on virginity really was since it could not have been literally what he said on the subject. Such readings consistently de-value Roman thought on the subject which, incidentally, deprive Gregory's theology of any intellectually serious context.

Hollywood productions.)[25] The point here is that Cicero's proposal that his daughter be divinized was, by his own admission, a recourse borne out of his need to fight off the "disease" of grief and the pool of pain into which he had been immersed. As Cicero puts it, "What is not only more wretched, but also more repugnant or more grotesque than a man who is shattered, enfeebled and laid low by distress?"[26]

This therapy by distraction seems to have worked—since after Cicero returns from his grief-induced "exile" over Tullia's death his writing grows in depth and number as he gradually ceases to obsess over the building of a temple to Tullia (which was to have been the first step towards achieving the acceptance of her *apotheosis*). The idea captured his attention and allowed time to heal his wound—one of the proffered remedies to grief in the *Disputations*. More importantly for history—though probably not for Cicero—is that Cicero introduces and provides the superstructure for the post-Republican Roman religious/political practice of divinizing exemplary men and women. In Cicero's words, "let us assent to the wisdom of those people whose talents and discoveries we consider to have adorned our entire life and established it by laws and institutions. But if ever any living creature ought to have been consecrated, surely it was she"—"she" being Tullia, his daughter.[27]

A Death in the Family: Gregory of Nyssa on the Severity of Our Pain

It is undeniable that in major trajectories of thought in Christianity death was related to sexuality; in particular, to sexual reproduction. I am not referring here to encratite communities but to the theology represented by,

---

25. My comment here on BBC fantasies about Roman political religion is definitely intended to raise awareness of the paucity of our intellectual resources for imagining Roman life at very nearly any period in its history (I trust Yosemite Sam portraying a Roman centurion as much as I trust "I, Claudius"). I also mean to bring to mind the bemused patronization (if not contempt) of Roman religion that has been endemic to the study of Latin Classics for the last two centuries in Germany and England. (I believe it sufficient to call out only these two countries because virtually every "history" of modern Scripture studies is content to discuss only these two countries.) The English upper class read the Latin classics in order that they might be gentlemen, but that didn't mean anyone thought the Romans actually believed all that rot.

26. *Tusc Disp.* IV.35, see Erskine, "Cicero," 36–47.

27. Cole, *Cicero*, 1.

e.g., Methodius of Olympus and Gregory of Nyssa.[28] Looking at Gregory in particular, the fiercest ravages of the experiences of death are reserved for husbands, wives, parents and children. Monasticism—"virginity" or celibacy—offered a life sheltered from this radical vulnerability: it offers a time of calm in a world otherwise constituted of a chaos of decay and dissolving. For Gregory this calm has a kind of "realized eschatology" character: the grief-free calm that the monk experiences is in continuity with the heavenly peace Christians will experience in the passion-free, death-free bodies that God resurrects.

Gregory's argument for virginity seemingly develops out of his own experience of married life.[29] This argument for virginity, which constitutes the majority of chapter three of On Virginity, is a distinctive one. Gregory argues that marriage is an extremely painful experience which virginity allows one to avoid or escape.[30] Gregory gives an honest, if one-sided, description of married life. A man falls in love and marries,

28. Some historical and literary context is needed for a better understanding of Gregory's thoughts on marriage, virginity, and death, and in order to provide an abbreviated synthetic account of the link between these three I draw from Eijk, "Marriage and Virginity," 209–235. Van Eijk traces ascetical judgments on marriage, virginity, and death from Plato to Gregory of Nyssa. For my present purposes the following facts are worth noting: first, that in the Acts of Paul and Thecla "resurrection is reserved to those who have practiced continence" (p. 212); in the Gospel of the Egyptians the Christian (= encratite) community has already experienced resurrection, and thus must refrain from sexual intercourse (following Luke 20:34–36), since procreation (characterized particularly as "the female" act) feeds death (pp. 214–16); that Methodius links virginity to "affinity with divinity" (p. 222); and that Basil of Ancyra (in the On Virginity traditionally attributed to Basil of Caesarea) emphasizes that sexual reproduction comes after the fall, and that the virgin "already lives in Paradise and already is incorruptible" and angelic (pp. 224–26). Ton van Eijk remarks that "Gregory takes up the view of [Gospel of the Egyptians] that marriage gives nourishment to death" (p. 234); he likewise repeats Basil's view on the origin of marriage and the status of virgins. Van Eijk does not remind the reader of the obvious fact that since Macrina's spiritual name is Thecla, Gregory is engaged with aspects of the asceticism expressed in the Acts of Paul and Thecla. In de Anima Res Gregory has clearly rejected the judgment that "resurrection is reserved to those who have practiced continence" but in the Life of Macrina it seems—if my reading is correct—that death is, in some special way, associated with those who have sexually reproduced: the decay of his parents' bodies does not bring Gregory to reflect upon their future resurrection.

29. Portions of the next several paragraphs have appeared before in my "'The Burden of Marriage,'" 12–19.

30. The pain-free state of virginity has an eschatological character, in which humans attain to the life of the angels, which is the life Gregory's sister Macrina attained on this earth, as he makes clear in his book the Life of Macrina, which I will consider in detail shortly.

and eventually his wife becomes pregnant. This occasion for joy contains sadness, however, for it is all too possible that the wife will die in child-birth. Perhaps she doesn't die, but the child may. Even if the mother and child survive childbirth, then it is all too possible that the child will die in infancy, and that the next pregnancy (or the one after that) will end in death for the woman. Gregory goes on: sometimes it is the woman whose bridal joy is swept away by the death of her husband, and "sud-denly she has to take the name of a poor lonely widow . . . Death comes in an instant and changes that bright creature in her white and rich attire into a black-robed mourner." This is, if nothing else, a sobering account of the married life. I want to make two points about Gregory's description of married life: the first point puts the argument in a general context, the second point develops—I hope—an insight into Gregory's theology.

The first point: the precedents and the contexts for Gregory's argu-ments for virginity as an alternative to marriage lie in the long-standing and carefully worked out debates among the Stoics. The most important philosophical authority on the question of the emotional vulnerability inherent in marriage and the family is the first-century Stoic, Musonius Rufus; one also finds the argument articulated clearly in the writings of Musonius's famous student, Epictetus. The Stoics are interested in what the life of the Stoic sage or wise person will be like: the conventions or expectations of society bring the Stoics a list of options that require choices. Can a woman be trained in philosophy? Must a father raise every child born to him? Can a true philosopher be married? Musonius Rufus's judgments have a certain optimism or courage to them that draws the contemporary eye, as one observes in Martha Nussbaum's *The Therapy of Desire*: Musonius answers yes to all these questions.[31] Musonius's student Epictetus, on the other hand, has different answers, and his argument that the true philosopher cannot marry has substantial points of contact with Christian sensitivities and vernacular. Marriage, according to Epictetus, involves a person in a permanent state of distraction. This long quotation from Epictetus will illustrate:

> But as the state of things now is like that of an army prepared for battle, is it not necessary that a true philosopher be without dis-traction, entirely attentive to the service of God? For, consider, there are some responsibilities due to the wife, [particularly responsibilities around childbirth]. [A]fter [marriage] the true philosopher is confined to the care of his family, and distracted

31. See Jagu, *Musonius Rufus*, 67–70.

> by making provisions for their support. [The philosopher] has
> to provide a bed and roof over their heads. Do you see how we
> deprive our philosopher of his kingdom?[32]

Gregory is not the only Christian to borrow the Stoic argument to support the vocation of perpetual virginity. A similarly intended account of the "burdens of marriage" appears in Ambrose of Milan's work from 375, *Concerning Virgins* (I.6.25), where Ambrose contrasts, for his sister's sake, the emotional peace of virginity with the distraction and turmoil of marriage. The chronological coincidence of these two appropriations of the Stoic argument is almost eerie, for here we have two texts not simply on the same subject written in the same century, or even half century, but two treatises on virginity, both using Stoic arguments, written in the same decade. Whatever literary debt Ambrose may later owe to Basil or Didymus, I cannot imagine Gregory's 371 text being a source for Ambrose's 375 text. Obviously, in the latter half of the fourth century two educated Christians from distant parts of the Empire both independently know an argument for celibacy based upon the emotional hardships of marriage. This argument is not a universal one: it does not appear, for example, in Methodius's *Symposium*, a work which sometimes seems to be a kind of catalogue of topical Christian opinions on virginity. At present one can decide either that the Stoic argument came into the tradition some time before Gregory and Ambrose, early enough that by the late fourth century it would be widely distributed geographically for their independent appropriation; or one can believe that a common educational background shared by Gregory and Ambrose allowed them independently to recognize the appropriateness of applying a Stoic argument to a Christian situation.

The appearance of the Stoic-based argument in Ambrose's *Concerning Virgins* does allow us, at last, to come to the second point I promised: namely, to derive some insight into Gregory's theology from recognizing the origins of his argument on the burdens of marriage. If we recognize Gregory's argument as his appropriation of a standing Stoic analysis of the virtuous life, then we can begin to ask how Gregory utilizes and develops the Stoic material to further his own theological point, or, in other words, Gregory's own spin on the received material can be better discerned in comparison to another Christian use of the same Stoic argument. We have this in Ambrose.

---

32. Epictetus, *Moral Discourses* III. 22.8.69–72, p. 155.

First of all, Ambrose's use of the Stoic material is much, much short-er than Gregory's: not unlike Epictetus, Ambrose gives it in two para-graphs, while Gregory gives it in three pages. Moreover, the emphasis in Ambrose's version more closely resembles Epictetus's than Gregory's does: Ambrose writes about distraction and emotional pain; Gregory writes almost exclusively about emotional pain. The comparative length of Gregory's treatment tells us, I think, of the importance the argument has for him; his emphasis on the painful—and not just distractive—char-acter of married life similarly reveals an important thread in Gregory's spirituality.

Gregory's thought is this: the original Stoic insight was that marriage is a way of life which fills one's mind with an explosion of responsibili-ties and distractions. Such distractions are in themselves morally neutral for the Stoics, but the suspicion was strong among them that marriage would sweep away most if not all people from the task of true philosophy. Gregory accepts the Stoic diagnosis of marriage as invasive and intrinsi-cally material, but supplies one other fact, a fact clear for Musonius Rufus but lost by Epictetus: marriage is in itself an occasion—or at least an op-portunity—for comfort and joy.

Occasionally throughout the book, Gregory uses terms and phras-ings borrowed from tragic literature, all justified by recognizing marriage as a "tragedy". The reality of marriage is this: sad, hurting; all the more sad and hurting—all the more "tragic"—because the expectation for comfort and joy is so great. At this point Gregory turns the Stoic description into a revelation: the human point of contact with the human hope for love is in fact the entryway into deep pain; an entryway into separation, not union. Looking at marriage, Gregory says:

> you would see there, if only you could do it without danger, many contraries uniting; smiles melting into tears, pain mingled with pleasure, death always hanging over the children that are born, and putting a finger upon each of the sweetest joys.[33]

Thus, according to Gregory, human existence itself is haunted by its own doppelganger, in which joy slides into sadness. We each exist, Gregory says in a famous passage, as moral doubles. Psychologically this double-ness means not simply that there are two opposite forces at war in us, but, more pointedly, that experiences of love—experiences of life and de-light—inevitably contain and dissolve into their opposite, the experience

33. Schaff, *On Virginity, Select Writings and Letters of Gregory, Bishop of Nyssa*, 346.

of abandonment—experiences of death and sadness. As anyone who has read Gregory's *On Perfection* or his *Fifth Sermon on the Beatitudes* knows, such dissolving opposition is at the heart of our conception and birth—our nature—which means that it is the guarantee of our death.[34] The point in *On Virginity* where Gregory reveals this fact is chapter three, where early into his account of the pain of married life Gregory says, "The very sweetness which surrounds the lives of lovers is the spark which kindles pain . . ." The Stoic account of the burdens of marriage chronicles very well the fact that experiences of life and delight dissolve into their opposites, the experiences of death and sadness.

Such instances of polarity figure deeply and repeatedly in the theology of *On Virginity*, as when Gregory says in the longer quotation I gave earlier that in marriage there are "many contraries uniting". Throughout the treatise, but especially in chapter three, Gregory uses one of his favorite categories for analysis: the co-existence of opposites. Indeed, to some extent *On Virginity* may be seen as a rumination by Gregory on the significance of opposites as a map of our existence.[35]

34. It is this resemblance between *On Virginity* and the two works, *On Perfection* and *Fifth Sermon on the Beatitudes*, which causes Gerhard May to date *On Virginity* as approximately 380, or contemporary to the two later writings. See his article "Die Chronologie ,"51–66.

35. In *On Virginity* Gregory brings forward a number of words based on the root εναντιος which are seemingly unique to him—"unique" to the extent that they do not appear in either Liddell & Scott or Lampe. Such words would be εναντιος, εναντιως, and εφναντιωσις. εναντιος, for example, appears in chapter twenty-two, when Gregory refers to what his physician friend taught him about the four elements which are opposite to one another. This clue to the source for Gregory's "opposite" vocabulary bears out, for two of the three words that seem peculiar to Gregory appear frequently in the medical writings of Galen. Moreover, εναντιος is used by Galen when he is quoting doctrines from the Stoics Chrysippus and Posidonius in ways which suggest that the term had a technical sense. εναντιος consistently has the meaning of an opposition which does not have the structure of being and lack of being. For example, the opposition between fire and water is not one of existence and non-existence, which is why the two can be said to be εναντιος. Another example to illustrate my point can be found in Galen: "women are opposite to men insofar as they have certain organs provided by nature for conception, and men do not. In one respect women are similar to men, in another they are opposite." In each case the Greek for "opposite" is εναντιος. Galen, *On the Common Doctrines*, 557.

The Life of Macrina: Everyone I Know
Goes Away In the End

I will quote several passages from *Life of Macrina*[36] and then cite from the
Ciceronian material I developed earlier in this essay. My point is to show
how Gregory employs, or rather, presumes, the philosophical arguments
summarized (not always sympathetically) by Cicero against assenting to
the impulse to grieve and thus being given over to the passion of grief.[37]
The theme of grief has been introduced into the story several times before we get to dealing with Macrina's own death. A younger brother dies
in a hunting accident; Macrina feels the urge to grieve, but holds it back,
and remains calm and helps her mother deal with the loss. Macrina deals
calmly with the early death of her brother, Basil, bishop of Caesarea.[38]
In Macrina's presence Gregory recalls Basil and breaks down—causing
Macrina to respond by talking Gregory out of his melancholy. In his description of Macrina's reaction to each of these deaths Gregory sets them
out as moral trials that Macrina withstood and emerged from victorious.
(Seneca would have said that she stopped the passions "at the gate" of the
city.)

> The high quality of her thinking was thoroughly tested by suc-
> cessive attacks of painful grief to reveal the authentic and unde-
> based nature of her soul, first by the death of her other brother,
> Naucratios, after this by the separation from her family, and
> third when Basil, the common honor of our family, departed
> from life early. So she stood her ground like an undefeated ath-
> lete, who does not cringe at any point before the onslaught of
> misfortune.[39]

36. *Life of Macrina* is easily available in English translations. I will refer here to
Kevin Corrigan's translation, *The Life of Saint Macrina*.

37. Other scholars have mined Gregory's *On the Soul and Resurrection* for his
theology of grief and his understanding of the passions generally; I will have nothing
to add directly to this conversation which started with Rowan Williams's "Macrina's
Deathbed Revisited" and developed further with a rejoinder by Warren Smith, "Macrina, Tamer of Horses"; and is most recently taken up by Hans Boersma in his article,
"'Numbed With Grief,'" and chapter four of his book, *Embodiment and Virtue*.

38. Basil died in 378. There is no universally agreed-upon date for Gregory writing
the *Life*, but most scholars tend towards a date soon after Macrina died (which was
379/380). While the death of her young brother Naucratios is a story from her youth,
the death of her brother Basil is fresh—which is why that death weighs upon Gregory.
(Note that these are all deaths *in the family*.)

39. Corrigan, *Life of Saint Macrina*, 33.

But when we finally come to Macrina's death, the sadness of this event—
even though fully expected[40]—brings those who are with her to a crisis.

> For, up to this point, they had continued to bear their suffer-
> ing in silence and kept in check the grief in their soul, stifling
> the *impulse* to cry out their sorrow . . . But when their suffering
> could no longer be contained in silence, and their grief was like
> a fire within them smoldering away at the souls, all at once a
> bitter, uncontrollable wailing erupted, with the result that my
> reason no longer maintained its proper balance . . . [and] I was
> swept away by sorrow.[41]

Gregory has several "grief-strategies" to choose from, which included "In
time we will look back at this . . ." (which is what Gregory the writer is doing—is his grief diminished by the interval?), "Grief serves no purpose,"
and "No one here is under any social obligation to give themselves over to
expressions of grief and mourning" (Cicero's *bête noir*). The basic Stoic/
Sceptic "Life is meaningless in any case"[42] was unacceptable to any Christian. He has "She has gone on to a better place," or a Platonic "At long last
she is free of this body, a body which bound her not only to its materiality
but to sickness"—which Ambrose[43] (Gregory's Latin contemporary and
social peer) probably would have employed.[44] Gregory's exhortation to

40. Recall that one of the philosophical accounts of grief is that it strikes us hardest
when the death is unexpected, and therefore (1) an expected death should be easier to
bear; and (2) we should maintain an awareness of the transitivity of human life and the
possibility that anyone can die at any moment. Cicero does not buy this reasoning—at
least the first conclusion—and sees this line of thought as a useless medicine for grief.
The anguished scene at Macrina's death (which Gregory emphasizes) proves Cicero
right.

41. Corrigan, *Life of Saint Macrina*, 43. The word *impulse*, which I have emphasized, is ὁρμή, *horme*, a technical term in Stoic moral psychology.

42. No wonder Albert Camus turned back to Greek myths—e.g., *Myth of Sisyphus*—to express the meaninglessness of life: some of their philosophers had already
laid out the narrative.

43. John Cavadini has extensively analyzed Ambrose's judgment that the parting of
the soul from the body at death is the soul's release from the influence and constraints
of the body: see "Ambrose and Augustine," 232–49.

44. Gregory has ruled out the "Platonic" comfort of mind-escaping-body: there
is no sign of that argument. Is this because Gregory has risen above a "Platonic" understanding of mind-body dualism, or because Gregory has pre-empted that dualism
through his recurring description of Macrina as having already achieved an angelic
state, in which the mass of her body no longer exerted a gravity upon her mind and
soul? The fundamentals of Macrina's life have already been described in protologi-
cal or prelapsarian terms —her birth while her mother slept [Eve from Adam] and

"Calm down! Just calm down!" is an argument from *exemplarity*: Macrina has herself given the example of how a Christian faces death, and we should try to emulate her virtue.

> Look at her and remember the precepts she taught you, that you conduct yourself in an orderly and graceful fashion in every circumstance.[45]

In the *Life* Gregory desires to present Macrina as a moral exemplar; the book scarcely has any other reason for existing. Within the overarching narrative of Macrina as moral exemplar for the reader is Macrina as moral exemplar to those who knew her and attended to her death. Gregory seeks to shame those in the room with him who have lost themselves to grief: the way that Macrina faced her own death ought to be the pattern for those who loved her to face her death, and that "pattern" is a calmness born out of the proper understanding of what was about to happen. Cicero summarized this philosophical tactic against grief when he said (I emphasize here the key line):

> Enduring misfortune is made easier by the fact of that others have suffered the same, and the fate of others causes what has happened to us to seem less important than it has been previously thought. What was imagined to be the greatest evil is not so great as to defeat the happiness of life. *Anyone suffering may be induced to bear what he observes many others have previously borne with tranquility and moderation.*

The last excerpt from the *Life* that I want to utilize here shows Gregory presenting a very similar argument as the previous "Macrina as moral exemplar", who faces her death serenely. The difference in nuance from the previous quotation is that here Gregory is pointing to Macrina's own motivations—*why* it is that she faced her own death without fear. Again, the emphasis is mine:

> For not even in her last breaths to feel anything strange in the expectation of death nor to fear separation from life, but with sublime thinking to philosophize upon *what she had chosen for this life*, right from the beginning up to her last breath.[46]

---

without pain to her mother [childbirth without the curse of "pain and travail"]—and it is clear that, to Gregory, Macrina already has one step in the next life. See, e.g., Corrigan, *Life of Saint Macrina*, 30.

45. Corrigan, *Life of Saint Macrina*, 45.

46. Ibid., 40.

The entire *Life* up to this point has presented Macrina as someone who chose the form of her life, as, for example, when she argued that she could not be betrothed to any (other) man. Macrina has been described as the most perfect of philosophers, in whom passion—which is to say the powers of her body upon her mind or soul—had never succeeded in winning the reins over her mind. Gregory has pushed the moral disjunction between her body and her mind even further, by describing it almost as "unnatural"—or by attributing her moral state to one who lived without the burden of a body: a kind of angel. The passage above continues: "Instead, it was as if an angel had providentially assumed human form, an angel in whom there was no affinity for, nor attachment to, the life of the flesh." But what angel did Christ ever call His "bride"? Macrina was free of bodily passions, but she was not free of love and spiritual desire: "[S]he seemed to me to be making manifest to those then present that pure, divine love of the unseen bridegroom, which she nourished secretly in the most intimate depths of her soul, and she seemed to transmit the desire which was in her heart to rush to the one she longed for."[47] Neither Cicero nor any other philosopher of the era (with the possible exception of Plotinus) allowed for a personal love "on the other side" though they did allow that love of virtue or love of nation could support the mind against fear of an evil consequence: "Any bodily pain," Cicero says, "let it be ever so grievous, can be endured where there is hope of some greater good."[48]

47. *Life of Macrina*, 49. If we accept the conventional dating of Gregory's writings, then in this relatively early text there arises the bubble of his later *Commentary on the Song of Songs*. I note in passing that by the fourth century the most common belief of Christians is that the immediate passage after death of the soul to heaven is a possibility for all Christians and not a spiritual outcome reserved for the souls of martyrs (with the souls of everyone else either "sleeping" or standing by until the Second Coming).

48. Two points may qualify my judgment that neither Cicero nor any other philosopher of the era allowed for a "personal love" on the other side of death. First, in Cicero's era (first century BCE) and into the third century CE easily there was a pagan fascination with love lost but waiting: Isis and Osiris may be the paradigm here. Second, in a time closer to Cicero than to Gregory we find in Hebrew Sophiology a strong eroticization of the figure of Wisdom, such as one sees in the Dead Seas Scrolls text of *Sirach* 51.

My Empire of Dirt: Augustine on Grief

Scholarly treatments of Augustine's thoughts on grief and death rightly focus on *Confessions* IV and *City of God* XIII: the episode in *Confessions* deals with grief in the face of the fact of human death; the "treatise" in *City of God* XIII deals with the moral status of death itself.[49] These scholarly judgments are altogether justified, but for my purposes here I begin my discussion of Augustine by recalling *City of God* XIV.7–8, where Augustine critically rehearses the Stoic doctrines on the emotion (passion) of grief within, as they see it, the set of other problematic feelings. It is here that Augustine defines "grief" and sets his understanding apart from the Stoic understanding; indeed, it is here that Augustine sets the *Christian* understanding of grief apart from the Stoic and Platonic understandings. Augustine begins by noting the different words for "love" and different types of love (good love, bad love) in the Bible (principally the New Testament) and in Stoic-influenced moral psychologies. He remarks, almost off-handedly, that he doubts whether a good sense of "grief" can be found in any of this literature; it is consistently something to be avoided, and

---

49. Cavadini speaks of Book XIII of the *City of God* as "what is in effect a short treatise on the subject of death." See his "Ambrose and Augustine" (already cited). The characterization occurs in the first sentence of the essay. Cavadini reveals the distance between Ambrose's judgment of death as a "good" (because the separation of the soul from the body is a good) and Augustine's judgment that death is not a good but a punishment: fundamentally an unnatural act. "Hence all Christians who truly hold the Catholic faith are agreed that even the death of the body was not inflicted on us by the law of our nature, since God did not create any death for man in his nature, but it was imposed as a just punishment for sin." *City of God* XIV.15, p. 524. Prior Christian teaching of the "naturalness" of physical death—everything put together falls apart, the center does not hold—may be found in Athanasius's *On the Incarnation*. Cavadini identifies and explains Augustine's profound difference of opinion on this matter from Ambrose's (his nominal mentor) in terms of the role a "Platonic" anthropology played in Ambrose's theology—an influence which by the time of *City of God* XIII was not there in Augustine's anthropology. ["Augustine's most resounding critique of this anthropology is his depiction of it as an ultimate incoherence, peering at us in a truly macabre way from the end of time and history." Cavadini, "Ambrose and Augustine," 238.] In his earlier work, *On the Nature of the Good* (viii), Augustine can locate death within the good of an ordered universe: "When things pass away and others succeed them there is a specific beauty in the temporal order, so that those things which die or cease to be what they were, do not defile the measure, form or order of the created universe." [Burleigh, *Augustine: Earlier Writings*, 328.] Whether Augustine's observation here owes to School Platonism, a rhetorician's fascination with the meaning created by spoken words successively coming into being and passing into silence (undeniably a trope that fascinated Augustine), or to Scripture—*Ecclesiastes* 3:1–8 ("Turn, turn, turn")—or to all three cannot be adjudicated with certainty.

indeed it is a feeling that the wise person succeeds at avoiding (or else s/he is not wise).[50] The Stoics, Augustine says,[51] find in the wise person "will instead of desire, gladness instead of joy, caution instead of fear. But they deny the possibility of any emotion in the wise man's mind answering to distress or pain, which I have preferred to call 'grief' [*tristitia*] to avoid ambiguity."[52]

The standard definition of "grief" is that it is—shall we say—the past tense of fear. Fear is the passion arising in expectation of an experience of something bad (i.e., injurious to the soul), and grief is the passion arising after the experience of something bad. But the Stoic sage has no fears, knowing that the only evil that can be experienced is to assent to an impulse and thus feel a passion: that is evil, and the experience is under our control (or "up to us").[53] "Caution" is the rational correlate to fear, but there is no *ex post facto* rational correlate to grief.[54] Augustine

50. The presence of grief in any one would be evidence of that person's failure to be a sage.

51. The translation is Bettenson's, *Concerning the City of God*, 558. Quas enim Graeci appellant eupatheias, Latine autem Cicero constantias nominauit, Stoici tres esse uoluerunt pro tribus perturbationibus in animo sapientis, pro cupiditate uoluntatem, pro laetitia gaudium, pro metu cautionem; pro aegritudine uero uel dolore, quam nos uitandae ambiguitatis gratia tristitiam maluimus dicere, negauerunt esse posse aliquid in animo sapientis.

52. This is not to imply that after he had announced this judgment in *City of God* XIV he always used *tristitia* over *aegritudo*. Also, perhaps Augustine preferred *tristitia* over *aegritudo* because *tristitia* had a strong Johannine and Pauline pedigree in the Latin New Testament.

53. See Seneca, *On Providence*, for a clear and substantial discourse on this reasoning. The same text provides a paradigmatic Stoic articulation of the judgment that "God allows evil and/or suffering to happen as a *test*—the way an athlete's opponent provides a "test" of one's training. Seneca's conclusion is that the sage experiences nothing evil—only challenges. The Stoics may have had a prosperous franchise on this doctrine, but they by no means held a monopoly—much less can they be held responsible for inventing the doctrine. It was a bad judgment widely held.

54. When, in *Oedipus at Colonus*, Oedipus and Antigone produce arguments for Oedipus's lack of guilt for those two fateful actions long ago (so that he might be allowed to stay in Athens), they speak of his ignorance, the justice of self-defense, the non-negotiable fate he was made part of, and so on: Oedipus never says to King Theseus, "I am truly sorry for what I did; I have spent each day repenting and accepting the punishment due to me." He never thinks to express remorse over what he did, and no one asks him to. When Ham is exiled for seeing his father Noah "uncovered" *we* supply the argument that Ham had not intended anything bad but in fact was acting to save his father's dignity. That Ham is punished offends *our* sense of justice, but there is nothing to suggest that Ham or his brothers regarded him as anything but defiled.

quotes 2 Cor 7:8–11: "And so I am glad, not because you were grieved, but because your grief led to repentance"[55] and then criticizes the Stoic failure to imagine or appreciate the existence of a virtue-building regret. This "grief"—remorse, contrition—is not the "grief" presently at hand: the grief that is bereavement in the wake of losing a loved one.

Confessions IV is dominated by Augustine's account of his shattering sense of loss at the death of a close friend. In this recollection Augustine provides as vivid a description of the piercing and overwhelming emotional pain of grief as one might find in all of classical Latin literature. Augustine is uninhibited in his description of the devastation he felt and his inability to escape it. The recent excellent analysis by James Wetzel of grief in *Confessions* IV is unlikely to be bettered in the foreseeable future.[56] I limit my own observations to just one: Augustine's retrospective "solution" to the problem of his own grief—given that he is writing perhaps as much as two decades at a remove from his friend's death—is to remind himself (and the reader) that we will always be vulnerable to such emotional devastation so long as we love improperly—that is, if our love is (as Carol Harrison puts it) "disordered" (though Harrison focuses on Augustine's plea to God to "*order* his love").[57] Augustine's diagnosis of his own young emotional catastrophe is that he loved his created and mortal friend with a love properly reserved for the spiritual and eternal.[58] Such a diagnosis is not rare in Christian literature of the time, or in any pagan literature influenced by Stoic prescriptions: if one loves the temporary as though it were permanent one will inevitably experience a profound

---

Gregory's fear at opening the tomb in *Life of Macrina* is rational and just to Gregory at least.

55. Augustine's Latin for the New Testament passage is: "Nam laudat apostolus Corinthios, quod contristati fuerint secundum Deum. Sed fortasse quis dixerit illis apostolum fuisse congratulatum, quod *contristati* fuerint paenitendo, qualis tristitia, nisi eorum qui peccauerint, esse non potest. Ita enim dicit: Video quod epistula illa, etsi ad horam, *contristauit* uos; nunc gaudeo, non quoa *contristali* estis, sed quia *contristati* estis in paenitentiam." Tristitia—my emphasis—is "grief."

56. Wetzel, "Book Four," 53–70.

57. Harrison, *Beauty and Revelation*, 247–253. See Augustine's *Sermon* 37.21–24, for a succinct Augustinian expression of the theme Harrison develops.

58. Two quotations from *Confessions* IV will illustrate this point, I think: "The reason why grief had penetrated me so easily and deeply was that I had poured out my soul on to the sand by loving a person sure to die as if he would never die." IV.viii (13); "Things rise and set: in their emerging they begin as it were to be, and grow to perfection; having reached perfection, they grow old and die. Not everything grows old, but everything dies." IV.x (15). Translation by Chadwick, *Confessions*, 60–61.

loss when the object of that love dies. A Stoic would say nothing can properly be loved like that; Augustine will say, of course, only God can—and should—be loved with such an unconstrained love. One might judge that the distinctly Christian content of Augustine's prescription is that such a love ought properly to have God and only God as its object—and that judgment would not be wrong, but it might be incomplete. There are analogies here between Augustine's reflections in *Confessions* IV and Gregory's in *On Virginity*: a postulated desire in us for the ever-present (that is, a need for a permanence of presence) and that God answers that need and fulfils that desire and need as God alone can. Gregory seems to confine this shelter from the storm to monasticism, a life lived in freedom from temporal love. Gregory stresses monasticism as a God-given (*via* the Church) escape from a life of pain (which, as is typical for Gregory, is largely equal to a life of *family*).[59]

I would like to point to another engagement by Augustine with the unique way *death in the family* discloses the congenital (or existential) hole in our hearts which is to be found in *City of God* (*Civ Dei*) XIX, where it occurs under the rubric of the question "What is the state of virtue that we can reasonably expect as a possibility in this life?" In the classical context the question could just as well be stated, "What is the degree of happiness (beatitude) that we can reasonably expect as a possibility in this life?"[60] In Book XIX the significance of death is laid within

59. Largely, but not entirely: see my "Snowden's Secret," 107–122. Macrina lived most of her life surrounded by her family, and yet their deaths do not wipe away the stability she derived from her devotion to God and the sense of order in which her life—all life—has been disposed. This is also an appropriate moment to point out a little mystery and a big mystery in *Confessions* on this topic (mysteries to me, at least): in the *Confessions* Augustine mentions the death of his father retrospectively, as a way of dating the events he is recounting ("... my father had died two years earlier ...") but he does not mention his father's death at the proper point in his autobiographical narrative (e.g., "It was then that my father died"). The "big mystery" is this: Augustine mentions the birth of his son, but he does not mark—much less *describe*—the death of his son.

60. I point out that *again* questions of family, virtue, and death are interlocked (or: that discourse on the three subjects of family, of virtue, and of death turn out to be interwoven). Is this simply Roman? Is this the continuing unfolding of a revelation dramatized in the Scriptural facts that the first two human sins occur with a family: Eve tempts Adam (and is punished by henceforth producing children—family—in great pain), and Cain kills Abel, inadvertently producing civilization? See, for two completely different constructions on this overlap, the novel *A Death in the Family*, by James Agee, and the critical anthropology in *Bloodlust: On the Roots of Violence from Cain and Abel to the Present* by Russell Jacoby (not to mention Aeschylus's *Orestria*

the intimacy of family and within the structure of "familia," i.e., the cities: in both cases the fact of family death unseats claims to the possibility of present-world happiness.[61] Augustine's engagement here with the "death in the family" *topos* is not as elaborate as Ambrose's in *On Virginity*, much less Gregory's, but he attaches no less significance to this species of emotional pain.[62] However, Augustine's engagement with the *topos* is not for the purpose of undermining the devastating emotional force of family death—as one could claim is the goal of engagements such as those of Ambrose and Gregory. On the contrary, Augustine understands the diminishing of grief as part of the Stoic project which renders one inhuman (a monster) and, at the same time, locates one squarely within the City of Babylon. The Stoics seek to remove grief and all other emotional vulnerabilities by dismissing the significance of—indeed, the reality of—such feelings. From Augustine's point of view, the Stoics remove us from the reality of our suffering—emotional as well as physical suffering—and thus offer a false, premature happiness. The happiness they offer turns out not to be very different from the happiness the drunkard achieves in *Confessions*. Book XIX is shot through with the question of "happiness": the Cities are distinguished by the kinds of *eudaemonia* they each value. The great evil Augustine seeks to overcome in *Civ Dei* XIX is false, premature happiness: any happiness which is presently "whole": "What a life of bliss that seeks the aid of death to end it!"[63] All true beatitude is

trilogy; the Oedipus trilogy by Sophocles; *The Martyrdom of Perpetua and Felicity*; Shakespeare's *Hamlet*; Freud; and any origin story of Batman). Paul Connerton has a provocative analysis of the *Orestria* trilogy as a parable on "progress" in *The Spirit of Mourning*, 4–12. From Rousseau to Marx to R. D. Lang, all proposed social utopias—that is to say, all political communities intended to bring about virtue and happiness for all its inhabitants—have required the abolition of the biological family.

61. In *City of God* XIX.4 Augustine cites, among other authoritative precedents, Cicero's grief over the death of his daughter, Tullia.

62. Given the way in which the Roman "familia" serves in *City of God* Book XIX as the fundamental metaphor for ordered human relationships, any family dynamic is going to be determinative of its analogous political (*civitas*) application. I take it that part of a critique of a Book XIX-centered Augustinian political theology involves this *familia* paradigm—John Rist has already criticized Augustine from this very perspective: see *Augustine*, 210–16.

63. *City of God* XIX.4, p. 855. It is in *City of God* XIX.4 that Augustine points to the deep sadness that we are liable to experience through the family (i.e., through the death of a loved one). Recall Gregory's grief over the loss of his brother Basil, and, of course, his grief when his sister Macrina dies. Every death in *The Life of Macrina* that might trigger the passion of grief is a death within the family—with the possible exception of the "sisters" gathered around Macrina's deathbed.

deferred until the eschaton. Happiness in this world, even the happiness of a Christian saint, is partial and ultimately equivocal—the word "happiness" is used in such cases with an inherently limited understanding.[64] It is in *On the Trinity* XIII that Augustine lays out as fundamental the challenge the reality of death makes to any earthly happiness.

Heaven is a Place Where Nothing Ever Happens: De Trinitate XIII

In chapter 2 of book 13 of *On the Trinity* Augustine cites or quotes a Roman comedian, the poet Ennius, Cicero, Epicurus, Zeno the Stoic, and Cicero again.[65] He begins chapter 3 by quoting the Carthaginian-born Latin playwright and slave Terence.[66] All these authors are cited to one effect: with equanimity, everyone wants to be happy; with something considerably less than equanimity, that only virtue can make one happy. A variety of philosophers have argued for a variety of "virtue"—"virtue" here being unmasked as "the life I want to live." People strongly endowed with a keen sense of "the life I want to live" can fight their way through much hardship and pain in the hope that one day the life they want will be a reality. (The twentieth century revealed that people strongly endowed with a keen sense of the life they want to live can move through humanity inflicting on others much pain and death in the hope that one day the life they want will be a reality.) Augustine remarks that someone who waits with faith for the happy life he wants is "happy in hope"—the person who has no such hope may endure great pain but he is only *bravely unhappy*, a phrase any number of twentieth century authors (e.g., Camus) could have written—and proselytized for. The bravely unhappy person unflinchingly endures what he or she would have preferred never to experience, much less to endure. Continued unflinching endurance becomes their object of desire, their "what they will", as we see in the case of prisoners who are deprived or tortured: they desire to endure whatever is inflicted upon them. Now Terence is apt: "Since what you will can never be, will what

64. Connections may be made with the intricate and paradigmatic role(s) grief plays in our conversion/call, and with Augustine's theology of lament: see Brian Brock, "Augustine's Incitement," 183–203.

65. All translations of *de Trinitate* are taken from *The Trinity*, Edmund Hill, O.P., trans.

66. "Chapters" are the products of editors, but they here serve my purpose as a symbol on the map for navigating *On the Trinity*.

you can do"—but this saying only objectifies their unhappiness, since what they want can never be and they know that fact so well that if they have any hope left it is only a hope never to hope.

At this point Augustine introduces a notion unexpectedly: that no one can have what they want unless they are immortal because to have what one wants "is not for this mortal life; it will only be when there is immortality" (Hill, 351). Why is it that *to have what one wants* is not for this mortal life? Augustine is not saying "Happiness requires immortality because what everyone wants is not to die"; he is saying "getting what you want requires immortality." The argument seems to be slipping towards the conclusion that death is a bad thing we all want to avoid, and living forever—without dying—would remove the single greatest "that which I do not want" and thus the single greatest impediment to our happiness. But I think Augustine's argument is different than that: I think his argument depends upon a logic expressed in Plato's *Symposium*: happiness, it turns out, is to want what one does not have—not in the sense of "I want a billion dollars," or "I want my hair back," but in the sense of "I want this good thing to continue in the future,"[67] and we do not have—cannot have—the future or anything it provides because we are not immortal. Someday our future(s) will end; we will not be able to keep what we want and may even have, or to keep wanting what we want hopefully. In order to keep having what we want to continue to have we must be immortal, but we are not. "All people then want to be happy; if they want something true, this necessarily means they want to be immortal. They cannot otherwise be happy . . . But as long as they despair of immortality, without which true happiness is impossible, they will look for, or rather make up, any kind of thing that may be called, rather than really be, happiness in this life" (Hill, 351).[68] Desiring with the proper strength the right thing to continue requires time which continues forever.[69] *Desiring with the proper strength the right thing to continue requires immortality.*

"Was there no other way available to God of setting us free from the unhappiness of our mortality than by desiring His only Son to become

67. *Symposium* 200d–e; see also 208. As may be said, "When this kiss is over it will start again. It will not be any different, it will be exactly the same" (From the song "Heaven," written by David Byrne and Jerry Harrison. Talking Heads, "Fear of Music," Sire Records, 1979).

68. Nineteenth-century Germany?

69. *Desiring*, with the *proper strength* the *right thing* which *continues without end* are all part of the definition(s) of virtue in the dialogue, *Meno* (e.g., 78b–c).

human, and being human to be mortal, and being mortal, to die?" Leibniz, the man who invented "Theodicy" asked. It is not simply a matter of another way," Augustine replies, but what was the best way (XIII.4.13). I personally must be clear and not evade: Augustine does talk about the grace won by Christ (XIII.4.14); Augustine does talk about the power of Christ's blood, the blood which justifies (XIII.4.15), and he does talk about fulfilling but overturning the "justice" by which we were held captive to death (XIII.4.16): ". . . when Christ was killed. That is when this blood of His, of one who had no sin at all, was shed for the remission of our sins . . ." (XIII.4.19, Hill, p. 358). It is possible that some or all of these goods could have been accomplished another way. Augustine's answer (at XIII.4.13) begins with what I will characterize as a non-denominational, directly existential, and very personal reason that the economy of the Incarnation was the best and the necessary way to set us free from the unhappiness of our mortality. What was required was a remedy for our grief at our own deaths: it was our grief all along.

> Nothing was more needed for raising our hopes and delivering the minds of mortals, disheartened by the very condition of mortality, from despairing of immortality, than a demonstration of how much value God put on us and how much He loved us. And what could be clearer and more wonderful evidence of this than that the Son of God, unchangeably good, remaining in Himself what He was and receiving from us what He was not, electing into partnership with our nature without detriment to His own, should first of all endure our ill deserts without any ill deserts of His own.[70]

The conclusion that it is our grief over our own deaths—and over the deaths of those we identify with ourselves (e.g., family)—that calls specifically for a divine physician allows me to pivot onto my last point. I do not think that the Romans found the idea unthinkable that a group of people would regard someone from out of their community as a god. (Philo occasionally came perilously close to "divinizing" Moses.) Nor would they regard as inconceivable the belief that someone arose from

70. Hill, trans., *On the Trinity* XIII.4.13, pp. 253–54. One cannot help but catch the sampling of Romans 5:6–8 (to follow), and I note that *On the Trinity* XIII.4.14 (i.e., the next paragraph) contains quotations of Romans 5:5, 6, 8, 9, 10, RSV: "While we were still weak, at the right time Christ died for the ungodly. Why, one will hardly die for a righteous man—though perhaps for a good man one will dare even to die. But God shows his love for us in that while we were yet sinners Christ died for us." Another resource would be to follow Augustine's exegesis of Romans 5:7–8.

the dead or was taken up into heaven; the scholarly understanding (or presuppositions) that supported previous "obvious" explanations for Roman hostility survive with the same vigor as eight-track.[71] *Acts of the Apostles* 1 is not conspicuously different from Livy's *The History of the Roman People* 1. This is *Acts* 1:9–11:

> [9] And when he had said this, as they were looking on, he was lifted up, and a cloud took him out of their sight. [10] And while they were gazing into heaven as he went, behold, two men stood by them in white robes, [11] and said, "Men of Galilee, why do you stand looking into heaven . . ."

This is Livy's *History* 1:16:

> [A]s the king [Romulus] was holding a muster in the Campus Martius, near the swamp of Capra, for the purpose of reviewing the army, suddenly a storm came up, with loud claps of thunder, and enveloped him in in a cloud so thick as to hide him from the sight of the assembly; and from that moment Romulus was no more on earth.[72]

71. This is not a reference (oblique or otherwise) to Candida Moss's cited-to-death (!) book, *Myth of Persecution*.

72. Livy, *History of Rome*, 57. See also Plutarch, life of Romulus in his *Lives*, 175: "He disappeared on the Nones of July, as they now call the month which was then Quintilis, leaving nothing of certainty to be related of his death; only the time, as just mentioned, for on that day many ceremonies are still performed in representation of what happened. Neither is this uncertainty to be thought strange, seeing the manner of the death of Scipio Africanus, who died at his own home after supper, has been found capable neither of proof or disproof; for some say he died a natural death, being of a sickly habit; others, that he poisoned himself; others again, that his enemies, breaking in upon him in the night, stifled him. Yet Scipio's dead body lay open to be seen of all, and any one, from his own observation, might form his suspicions and conjectures; whereas Romulus, when he vanished, left neither the least part of his body, nor any remnant of his clothes to be seen. So that some fancied, the senators, having fallen upon him in the temple of Vulcan, cut his body into pieces, and took each a part away in his bosom; others think his disappearance was neither in the temple of Vulcan, nor with the senators only by, but that, it came to pass that, as he was haranguing the people without the city, near a place called the Goat's Marsh, on a sudden strange and unaccountable disorders and alterations took place in the air; the face of the sun was darkened, and the day turned into night, and that, too, no quiet, peaceable night, *but with terrible thunderings, and boisterous winds from all quarters*; during which the common people dispersed and fled, but the senators kept close together. The tempest being over and the light breaking out, when the people gathered again, they missed and inquired for their king; *the senators* suffered them not to search, or busy themselves about the matter, but *commanded them to honor and worship Romulus as one taken up to the gods, and about to be to them, in the place of a good prince, now a propitious god.*

What brought discredit to the Christian account of the resurrection (and in Acts, the assumption) was the fact that Jesus died publicly punished as a criminal—which was a social and legal recognition that Jesus possessed no special virtue (*virtus*), but was a man without conspicuous moral quality. His life up to that point did not recommend him as a role model or moral exemplar. Jesus lacked even the ascetic credentials of John the Baptizer (who was himself arrested and executed as a criminal). The fact that Jesus was known to have associated with social low-lifes (e.g., tax-collectors, Samaritans) seemed to reinforce the opinion one took away from his execution. The stories that count to Jesus' special virtue were the miracles and the parables and stories he told. Even the apostles had trouble believing they could *imitate* Jesus in his wonder-working,[73] and while many of Jesus' parables were understood typologically after the resurrection, at the time they were taken as fables, some of which had obvious moral applications, but others of which were just obscure and more like "mystery" initiation stories. Despite what nineteenth-century liberal Protestant Germans tried to make of him in their prolific *Life of Jesus* genre, Jesus was not an obvious paradigm of virtuous behavior (or of the virtues of the German *Volk*). If Jesus had possessed some virtue to the degree that it seemed he personified it, then his apotheosis would have made sense to the Romans. (His exclusive worship would have remained, in Pagan eyes, irrational.)

All of this changes if one believed that Jesus was the Christ that he had given up the form of God to take on the form of a servant. As God everything Jesus did was virtuous and revealed God's presence (including changing water into wine). Philippians 2:7 and most of John 14 speak to a shared understanding of a profound mystery of the one who came down so that he might go up. Recognized as God Jesus revealed the (new) divine trait of a self-humbling love. As an analogy any act of self-humbling love we performed was incommensurate with what Jesus had done; as an act of similitude, of imitation, even our acts of self-humbling love could suggest the original. (As the Incarnation was once explained

---

The multitude, hearing this, went away believing and rejoicing in hopes of good things from him; but there were some, who, canvassing the matter in a hostile temper, accused and aspersed the patricians, as men that persuaded the people to believe ridiculous tales, when they themselves were the murderers of the kin." Emphasis added. Note the reference to conspiracy as an explanation offered by sceptics and political opponents; conspiracy theories will be offered by pagans and Jews as counter explanations of the Christian claims to Jesus' resurrection.

73. The story of Simon Magus is relevant here.

to me, "When you're stuck in the mud, you need someone to come along who isn't afraid to get dirty.") The love He showed in the Incarnation was unique and could not be duplicated: the love could be given perfectly in common, but it could not be duplicated.

There are two forms of Christian grief: the one we feel for each other because death was not meant to be, and the grief God feels for us—for the same reason. We should grieve for one another because He grieves for us.[74]

BIBLIOGRAPHY

Augustine. *Augustine: Earlier Writings*. Edited by John Burleigh. Philadelphia: Westminster, 1963.

———. *Concerning the City of God against the Pagans*. Translated by Henry Bettenson. London: Penguin, 1972.

———. *Confessions*. Translated by Henry Chadwick. Oxford: Oxford University Press, 1991.

———. *The Trinity*. Translated by Edmund Hill. Brooklyn: New City, 1991.

Banks, Russell. *The Sweet Hereafter*. New York: HarperCollins, 1991.

Barnes, Michel René. "'The Burden of Marriage' and Other Notes on Gregory of Nyssa's *On Virginity*." *Studia Patristica*, vol. 37, edited by M. F. Wiles and E. J. Yarnold, 12–19. Leuven: Peeters, 2001.

———. "Snowden's Secret: Gregory of Nyssa on Grief and Death." In *A Man of the Church: Honoring the Theology, Life and Witness of Ralph Del Colle*, edited by Michel Barnes, 107–122. Eugene, OR: Pickwick, 2002.

Boersma, Hans. *Embodiment and Virtue in Gregory of Nyssa*. Oxford Early Christian Studies. Oxford: Oxford University Press, 2013.

———. "'Numbed With Grief': Gregory of Nyssa on Bereavement and Hope." *Journal of Spiritual Formation & Soul Care* 7 (2014) 46–59.

Brock, Brian. "Augustine's Incitement to Lament, From the *Enarrationes in Psalmos*." In *Evoking Lament*, edited by Eva Harasta and Brian Brock, 183–203. Edinburgh: T & T Clark, 2009.

Cavadini, John. "Ambrose and Augustine—*De Bono Mortis*." In *The Limits of Ancient Christianity*, edited by William E. Klingshirn and Mark Vessey, 232–49. Ann Arbor: University of Michigan Press, 1999.

Cicero. *Tusculan Disputations*. Translated by J. E. King. Loeb Classical Library 141. Cambridge, MA: Harvard University Press, 1945.

Cole, Spencer. *Cicero and the Rise of Deification at Rome*. Cambridge: Cambridge University Press, 2013.

74. Many readers will recognize that my title and one section heading are taken from the song, "Hurt," written by Trent Reznor (1994) but better known through the cover version by Johnny Cash. Another section title is borrowed from "Heaven" by David Byrne (1979). The last line of the very first paragraph—*Good men, the last wave by, crying how bright / Their frail deeds might have danced in a green bay*—is a stanza from the poem "Do Not Go Gently Into That Good Night" by Dylan Thomas.

Connerton, Paul. *The Spirit of Mourning: History, Memory and the Body*. Cambridge: Cambridge University Press, 2011.

Epictetus. *Discourses, Books 3–4. Fragments. The Encheiridion*. Translated by W. A. Oldfather. Loeb Classical Library 218. Cambridge, MA: Harvard University Press, 1928.

Erskine, Andrew. "Cicero and the Expression of Grief." In *The Passions in Roman Thought and Literature*. Edited by Susanna Morton Braund and Christopher Gill, 36–47. Cambridge: Cambridge University Press, 1997.

Galen. *On the Common Doctrines of Hippocrates and Plato*. Edited, translated, and commentary by Phillip de Lacy. Corpus Medicorum Graecorum 4,1,2. Berlin: Akademie-Verlag, 1980.

Graver, Margaret. *Cicero on the Emotions: Tusculan Disputations 3 and 4*. Chicago: University of Chicago Press, 2002.

Gregory of Nyssa. *The Life of Macrina*. Translated by Kevin Corrigan. Eugene, OR: Wipf & Stock, 2005.

Harrison, Carol. *Beauty and Revelation in the Thought of Saint Augustine*. Oxford: Clarendon Press, 1992.

Jagu, Amand. *Musonius Rufus Entretiens et fragments*. New York: Georg Olms Verlag Hildesheim, 1979.

Levene, D. S. "Defining the Divine in Rome." *Transactions of the American Philological Association* 142 (2012) 41–81.

Livy. *The History of Rome*, vol. 1. Translated by B. O. Foster. Loeb Classical Library 114. Cambridge, MA: Harvard University Press, 1919.

May, Gerhard. "Die Chronologie des Lebens und der Werke des Gregory von Nyssa. In *Écriture et culture philosophique dans la pensée de Grégoire de Nysse*, edited by M. Harl, 51–66. Leiden: Brill, 1971.

Plutarch. *Lives*, vol. 1. Translated by Bernadotte Perrin. Loeb Classical Library 46. Cambridge, MA: Harvard University Press, 1914.

Rist, John. *Augustine—Ancient Thought Baptized*. Cambridge: Cambridge University Press, 1994.

Schaff, Philip, et al., ed. *Nicene and Post Nicene Fathers*, Second Series, vol. V: *Select Writings and Letters of Gregory, Bishop of Nyssa*. Peabody, MA: Hendrickson, 1999.

Seneca. "On Anger." In *Moral Essays*. Vol. 1. Translated by John W. Basore. Loeb Classical Library 214. Cambridge, MA: Harvard University Press, 1958.

Smith, J. Warren. "Macrina, Tamer of Horses and Healer of Souls: Grief and the Therapy of Hope in Gregory of Nyssa's *De Anima et Resurrectione*." *Journal of Theological Studies* 52 (2001) 37–60.

Van Eijk, Ton H. C. "Marriage and Virginity, Death and Immortality." In *Epectasis—Melanges Patristique Offerts au Cardinal Jean Danielou*. Edited by Jacques Fontaine and Charles Kannengiesser, 209–235. Paris: Beauchesne, 1972.

Wetzel, James. "Book Four: The Trappings of Woe and Confession of Grief." In *A Reader's Companion to Augustine's Confessions*, edited by Kim Paffenroth and Robert P. Kennedy, 53–70. Louisville: Westminster John Knox, 2003.

Williams, Rowan. "Macrina's Deathbed Revisited: Gregory of Nyssa on Mind and Passion." In *Christian Faith and Greek Philosophy in Christian Antiquity: Essays in Tribute to George Christopher Stead*. Supplements to Vigilae Christianae 19. Edited by Lionel R. Wickham et al., 227–46. Leiden: Brill, 1993.

Chapter 3

Growth towards Final Freedom

Gregory of Nyssa on Death and Eternal Life

BRIAN E. DALEY, S.J.

IN THE MID-1950S, THE distinguished Swiss New Testament scholar Oscar Cullmann published a small monograph—really an expanded version of an article he had written for a collection commemorating Karl Barth's 70th birthday—entitled, *Immortality of the Soul or Resurrection of the Dead? The Witness of the New Testament.*[1] Writing with his customary sense for the broad theological implications of Scriptural texts, Cullmann begins by drawing a sharp contrast between the central Christian hope for resurrection at the end of time, attested in various passages of the New Testament, and the "Greek" belief in the immortality of the soul, as set forth by Plato in his *Phaedo*, his *Republic*, and other dialogues. Plato's hope for immortality, and that of many in the Greek philosophical tradition after him, was based, Cullman argues, on the assumption that the center of the human person is an immaterial, indestructible soul, which is the seat of intellectual activity, desire, and choice. In our present existence, the soul is both dependent on the body and hampered, even imprisoned by, its needs. Death, in which it is separated from the body, is for the soul of a virtuous person who has practiced philosophical inves-

1. The original version, in French, appeared in *Mélanges offerts à Karl Barth à l'occasion de ses 70 ans* (Basel: Reinhardt, 1956). Cullmann also delivered a form of the treatise, in English, as the Ingersoll Lecture on the Immortality of Man, in the Andover Chapel of Harvard Divinity School, on April 26, 1955.

tigation—for someone, say, like Socrates—a liberation, allowing it to be fully united to the world of deathless, intelligible realities and aesthetic and moral norms: the world it has sought out previously in this present realm of limited intelligibility and goodness.

Although many Christians, from late antiquity until today, have knowingly or unknowingly allowed this Platonic idea of immortality to be substituted for the hope held out by the Apostolic witnesses to their faith, Cullmann protests that biblical and Greek philosophical hopes for existence after death are radically different expectations:

> If we want to understand the Christian faith in the resurrec-
> tion, we must completely disregard the Greek thought that the
> material, the bodily, the corporeal is bad and *must* be destroyed,
> so that the death of the body would not be in any sense a de-
> struction of the true life. For Christian (and Jewish) thinking
> the death of the body is *also* destruction of God-created life.
> No distinction is made: even the life of our body is true life;
> death is the destruction of *all* life created by God. Therefore it is
> death and not the body which must be conquered by the resur-
> rection . . . Resurrection is a positive assertion: the whole man,
> who has really died, is recalled to life by a new act of creation
> by God. Something has happened—a miracle of creation! For
> something has also happened previously, something fearful: life
> formed by God has been destroyed.[2]

Consequently, in Cullmann's view, the New Testament does not offer any vision at all of a life directly after death for the conscious part of the human person, but hints rather at a "sleep"—marked by the closeness of the dead to the crucified Christ, by their being "grasped" by the Holy Spirit—which will only be broken when all humanity is formed anew, in the likeness of the risen Christ, at the end of history.[3]

Whatever one thinks of Cullmann's thesis about the origins of the Christian belief in an immortal soul—whether it is "Greek" or "Jewish," "Platonic" or "biblical," or something more complex than these black-and-white alternatives—he is certainly right that there is little clear emphasis in Christian writing on this hope for the soul's continuing life after death until the Greek apologists of the second century.[4] Tertullian, in the

2. Cullmann, *Immortality*, 26–27.

3. Ibid., 48–57.

4. See, for example, Justin, *Dialogue* 5; 105; *I Apology* 18; 20; Athenagoras, *Plea* 31; *On the Resurrection* 13.

early third century, develops an elaborate picture of the lives of souls after death in Hades, awaiting resurrection;[5] and Origen, a few decades later, insists against the Middle Platonist apologist Celsus that the soul—which is itself immaterial, like God—still longs after death for re-integration with its body.[6] Nevertheless, it was not until the second half of the fourth century—after the general integration of Christians into the political and cultural life of the Empire, and the emergence of a few generations of highly educated Christian leaders in Church, state and letters—that the Greek philosophical tradition of affirming the soul's distinct life and immortality, in contrast with and in relation to the life of the material body, came to be seen as central to both Christian anthropology and eschatological hope. Key representatives of this new emphasis were Ambrose and Augustine in the Latin West, and the so-called "Cappadocian Fathers" in the Greek East: Basil of Caesaraea, his younger brother Gregory of Nyssa, their friend and colleague Gregory of Nazianzus, as well as their associates Amphilochius of Iconium and Evagrius of Pontus. A new, more fully articulated Christian vision of life beyond death had emerged.

Although a number of common themes and approaches to thinking through the Christian biblical tradition appear in all these writers, it was Gregory of Nyssa—the most overtly "philosophical" of the Cappadocian Fathers as well as the one most interested in what we would think of as questions of "natural science"—who has written the most surviving works directly expressing a Christian understanding of death and eternal life. Summarizing Gregory's thought on these issues is not always easy. For one thing, he is not a systematic writer, but has mainly left us an array of short essays—addresses, homilies, letters, occasional pieces—mostly intended for particular audiences and dealing with particular questions in a way those audiences might easily accept. So his emphases in these works, to the modern systematizer of Patristic thought, can appear inconsistent, even contradictory. Secondly, with a few exceptions, it is almost impossible to *date* Gregory's works in a way that is more than simply conjecture, and so to construct a reliable chronological scheme for the

5. *De Anima* 55–58.; *Adv. Marcionem* 4.34; *De resurrectione carnis* 17.

6. *Contra Celsum* 8.49–50. In his *Dialogue with Heracleides*, apparently a transcript of a conference Origen gave to a gathering of bishops somewhere in Palestine or Arabia, Origen spends a good deal of time discussing whether belief in the immortality of the soul is or is not compatible with Christian faith, and in the process of his remarks—apparently to the surprise of some of his hearers—defends the idea as fully biblical: see *Sources chrétiennes* 67, 10.15 – 28.20.

development of his ideas. Attempts by scholars in recent decades, such as Jean Daniélou and Gerhard May, to work out such a chronology usually depend largely on that scholar's judgment of what kind of thinking, on Gregory's part, is less or more "mature," and on perceived similarities of theme or treatment to the relatively few works that can be dated more securely.[7] Such attempts usually end by being largely based on arbitrary assumptions: that Gregory's theology, for instance, and more particularly his eschatology, developed in a consistent way, which reveals itself stage by stage, in all the works of a given period in his life; or that he "progressed" (as Augustine is sometimes thought to have done) from being largely philosophical in his interests, to being more directly concerned with Scripture and church doctrine, and finally to being more focused on a "mystical" vision of faith. Such assumptions tend to reveal more about the modern reader than they do about Gregory.

Our knowledge of the shape of Gregory's life and theological career, in fact, remains somewhat sketchy. He is thought to have been born between 335 and 340, one of the younger children in the large Christian Cappadocian family of a rhetorician named Basil and his wife Emmelia. Coming from a well-to-do economic background, all the children in the family seem to have received a thorough humanistic education, although we do not know whether Gregory, like his oldest brother, Basil the younger, received any of that training abroad—in Athens, or in some other prominent educational center. He seems himself to have worked as a teacher of rhetoric, and clearly was well trained in the rather flowery and complicated style of Greek oratory known as the "Second Sophistic." He was also unusually well-informed in matters of anatomy and physiology, zoology, botany, astronomy, and other specialized branches of knowledge of the natural world, and he was obviously well acquainted—as most well-educated Christians now were—with the long Platonic tradition of philosophy. By the early 360s, Gregory was married,[8] the father of a daughter, and apparently also was an ordained lector.[9] In 371 or 372, his

---

7. For a helpful summary of the opinions that have been advanced on the chronology of Gregory's writings, arranged according to the volumes of the modern Jaeger editions, with full bibliography of scholarly conjectures on Gregory's dating, see Maraval, "Chronology," 152–69.

8. See his treatise On Virginity, 3.

9. See Gregory of Nazianzus, Ep. 11, addressed to Gregory, which criticizes him for abandoning this career in the Church to work simply in the "secular" realm as a teacher of rhetoric.

older brother Basil—now metropolitan bishop of the provincial capital
Caesaraea—ordained him bishop of a newly-created see, the provincial
town of Nyssa, as part of Basil's attempt to build a strong pro-Nicene
majority among the bishops of the province of Cappadocia, and so to
resist the policy of the "Homoean" (non-Nicene) Emperor Valens. In 375
or 376, Gregory was accused by members of the new church of Nyssa of
financial mismanagement, and spent two or three years in exile. But he
continued to write, and took an increasingly active part in the theological
debates of the decade over the reception of the theology of Nicaea, affirming both the full, substantial divinity of the Son and the equal divinity of
the Holy Spirit. In this role of Nicene apologist, he became a close associ-
ate of Meletius, the veteran bishop in the divided Church of Antioch, as
was his family friend, the humanist bishop Gregory of Nazianzus.

At the accession of Theodosius as Emperor in the East in 378—a
Latin speaker from Spain, a successful general as well as a devout Nicene
Christian and a committed reformer—Gregory and his friends, led by
Meletius, suddenly found themselves political insiders rather than out-
siders: articulate representatives of a theological synthesis that would
become central to the emerging tradition of Christian orthodoxy. Gregory of Nazianzus was temperamental and over-sensitive, and after a few
months as the imperially recognized Nicene bishop of Constantinople—
and a few weeks as president of the Council of 381, after the sudden death
of Meletius of Antioch—retired in the midst of controversy to his family
estate in Cappadocia, to lead the life of a semi-monastic Christian *savant*.
But Gregory of Nyssa seems to have remained active in Church politics
and grew increasingly prominent, apparently acting as court preacher in
Constantinople for the first several years of Theodosius's reign, recognized widely both for his eloquence and for the comprehensiveness and
subtlety of his thought. In his decree recognizing the normative character
of the decrees of the Council of 381, Theodosius names Gregory of Nyssa
as one of eleven well-known bishops from the Greek world—three, including Gregory, from the political diocese of Pontus—whose faith might
serve as a standard for orthodox communion.[10] Around this time, too,
as we know from several of Gregory's letters, he traveled—doubtless
with at least the encouragement of Theodosius—to visit the Churches of
Arabia and Palestine, and to promote doctrinal and disciplinary reform
there, as envisaged by the Council of 381. Even though his older brother

10. *Codex Theodosii* XVII, 1.3 (trans. Pharr, *The Theodosian Code*, 440).

Basil came later to be named "the Great," and their friend Gregory of Nazianzus is known in the East as "the Theologian," Gregory of Nyssa was
clearly more celebrated than either, during his own time, as a thinker and
writer. Where he actually resided during the years following the Council
of 381—in the capital, in Nyssa, or elsewhere—is unknown; but it was
probably during this later period of his life that he wrote many of his
theological works. The date of his death is also unknown, although it is
usually assumed to be in the mid-390s.

Several of Gregory's works deal directly with the proper Christian
understanding of death and the promise of eternal life, within the context
of reflection on the wider Christian and philosophical understanding of
the human person, and on Scripture and the Christian Gospel of salvation. Since the chronology of his individual works, with a few exceptions,
is a matter of guesswork, as I have suggested, and since these works are
generally quite different from each other in their literary character and
their probable audience and occasion, it is difficult to form their contents
into a completely consistent picture, or to suggest clear lines of evolution
for Gregory's thought about death. Are their differences due to changes
in his own thinking over time, or due to the occasion, the addressee, and
the rhetorical form of each work? It is hard to say. Nevertheless, a number of important themes can be regarded as characteristic, anchored in
Gregory's underlying conception of human nature as created by God in
his image, and as redeemed by Christ in order to grow towards a new
perfection like his. However, before we attempt to identify these themes,
it seems important to characterize briefly main works that come into
question as sources for our knowledge of Gregory's eschatology.

1. One of Gregory's main thematic treatises on death in the context
of a theology of creation and redemption, is his discourse or essay *On the
Dead* (*De mortuis*): an apparently free-standing treatment, written in the
late antique style of a comprehensive lecture, but without a specific addressee or any suggestion of a particular occasion of composition.[11] The
ostensible purpose of the work is to persuade those who see death as the
ultimate human misfortune to change their minds. Gregory begins, how-

11. This work, hitherto untranslated into English, has been critically edited by
Günther Heil in *Gregorii Nysseni Opera* [GNO] IX/1, 28–68. A slightly revised publication of this edition, with Italian translation and commentary is Giuseppe Lozza, *Gregorio di Nissa: Discorso sui defunti* (Turin: Società internazionale editrice, 1991). For
thoughtful comments on the date, philosophical character, and rhetorical structure of
the work, see Alexandre, "Le *De mortuis*," 35–43. The translation I use here, from this
and other works of Gregory—unless otherwise noted—is my own.

ever, in strikingly philosophical fashion, by asking the question, "What is the ultimate, universal Good?" (cc. 1–4), and concludes that it cannot be identified with the present life, which is simply a process of "filling and emptying" our stomachs and our lungs! (5) Gregory argues that the true universal Good must be a life that is permanent, unchanging, and open to everyone; "the human soul moves on to this life from life in the flesh, receiving another level of life in place of the present one." (6) Such a life will be peaceful, effortless, and characterized by full freedom of choice; its activity will be nourished simply by knowledge of the divine nature." (6) In this context, physical death is to be seen as liberation (7–9).

This leads Gregory to reflect on what the human person most fundamentally is. He identifies the center of our identity as the *soul*, when seen as separate from its attachment to matter (8), as it recognizes itself to be made in the image of God: "immaterial and without shape, intellectual and incorporeal." (10) So Gregory suggests here, in arguments that clearly echo Plato's *Phaedo*, that the life of the embodied soul is always to some degree a life "in exile":

> For the matter of the body is truly an alien thing, foreign to the incorporeal nature; the mind is necessarily intermingled with it in this present life, and passes its time in wretchedness, sharing the fate of a different kind of life altogether. The shared relationship of elements woven together with each other has something forced and jarring about it . . . But the mind, which is mingled with these elements, not being composite, lives on in its simple and uniform nature in the midst of strange, foreign objects . . . Moving beyond them, it lives for itself, recovering in rest the strength it had lost for itself in its involvement with the body.[12]

Emphasizing that the whole human creature, soul and body, is always naturally equipped to grow and change (14–15), Gregory argues that this built-in dynamism is a preparation for the final healing of the human being, "our restoration to our original state, which is nothing else than likeness to what God is."(14) The purgation of the human composite begins now, in freely chosen ascetical practices (15), and is completed in the "purifying fire" of death itself (15).

But life beyond death will certainly include, eventually, a transformed body. The human problem, after all, is not embodiment, Gregory insists here, but the *use* we choose to make of our bodily existence (16).

---

12. *On the Dead*, 11.

"Let not the body, then, be vilified by thoughtless people," Gregory writes; after this life the soul will be adorned by a body that is transformed into a more divine state through regeneration . . . " (18) The risen body, as Paul assures us in I Cor 15.51, will be "changed"—*different* from the present body in form and quality; it is possible, he suggests, that sexual differentiation into male and female will be a thing of the past, but in this work he remains explicitly agnostic about this (20). The main assurance Scripture gives us about the risen body is that "our nature will be transformed into something more divine, and the human person will be given shape by his or her character" (20). In the end, "one and the same grace will appear to all," for all will be transformed into the image of God, as God himself originally intended (20). So a consciousness of our future, Gregory suggests, is able even now to "purify our grieving" when a loved one dies, by reminding us of the blessings promised to us all.

2. Another treatise of Gregory's that deals with death and the promised afterlife is his essay addressed to Hierius, "On Infants Taken Away before their Time."[13] A formal, rhetorically fulsome work, the essay begins with elaborate praise of Hierius's virtue and simplicity of life. In chapter 5, however, Gregory begins to discuss the central subject of the work, which presumably his addressee has posed for him as a troubling question: how can the death of infants be reconciled with the idea of a just and provident God? If death leads to God's judgment on a person's deeds, followed by reward or purgative suffering, how should we understand the deaths of those who have not lived long enough to act freely on their own? (5) Would it be just, if God were to call such infants to full beatitude, along with those whose virtue has been tested by a long life? (6) The question, then, is as much one of theodicy as of eschatology, and may well grow out of Hierius's personal experience of losing a child.

---

13. This work, edited critically by Hilda Pollack in GNO III/2, 61–99, appears in an earlier English translation by W. Moore and H. A. Wilson, in *Nicene and Post-Nicene Fathers*, Series 2.5, 372–82. The identity of Hierius, the addressee, is not certain. However, a letter of Gregory to "the prefect Hierius" (Ep. 7) suggests this treatise may be addressed to the same person, who was the prefect (=Roman governor) of Egypt: a Christian, who is characterized as cultivated, philosophically well-read, and modest in his way of life. If the addressee of the treatise is this same Hierius, it is interesting to see here an added confirmation that Gregory became well connected with the imperial apparatus in Constantinople after the accession of Theodosius in 378, and was even a kind of court theologian in the mid-380s. This, in turn, would suggest a date in the 380s for this treatise.

After acknowledging that this is indeed a great mystery (7), Gregory begins his response by arguing that the goal of God's creation is to allow creatures to share in God's life through contemplation (8–10). Alienation from God, in our present state of ignorance and freely chosen evil, must be healed by God's restoration of our nature, bringing us completely into his presence. So what we call the "beatific vision" is not so much a reward of virtue as the "necessary consequence of our natural disposition" (10).[14] Even so, it is clear that someone who dies in early infancy will not be able, right away, to enjoy the vision of God as fully as someone whose capacities have been developed by choice and experience; the soul will still have to grow, "until, made mature inwardly by a nourishment appropriate to contemplation, it comes to be able to receive more, and shares as much as possible in the rich abundance of what is real" (12). Intellectual and spiritual growth, he believes, do not end with death.

Gregory then goes on to ask the more troubling question: *why* does God allow infants to die before they have acquired this level of experience and freedom in the world? Admitting his share in our common human ignorance, Gregory cautiously elaborates the thesis that God, who is always just and who brings good out of evil, may do this with some newly born humans because he foresees that in a life of normal length "they would have engaged themselves in vice in a still more damaging way than each of those who have been notorious for wickedness while they lived" (21). Like a watchful host at a dinner party, God may simply be escorting a guest out of the room who, he foresees, will get drunk and disgrace himself if he remains at table (17–19). In permitting the death of infants, it may be that "God forecloses the indiscipline of vice from those who are inclined to live in this way" (23). Whatever the explanation, the implication of this work is that all human beings who have been conceived will eventually, by purification and growth either before bodily death or after it, come to enjoy the vision of God.

3. A third essay treating life after death is Gregory's treatise, "On the Text, 'Then the Son Himself will be Made Subject to the One who Has Subjected All Things to Him' (1 Cor 15:24–28)."[15] This work, ap-

---

14. Gregory seems to see our eschatological fulfilment here less as a gift of God's grace than as the terminus of our natural and moral transformation, made possible through Christ's mediation.

15. The Greek text of the work referred to here is the critical edition by J. Kenneth Downing, in GNO III/2 (Leiden: Brill, 1987) 3–28. The standard earlier edition appeared in PG 44.1303–1326. The translation I use is my own, and for convenience in

parently addressed to an unnamed individual who has requested it (as
suggested by the use of the second person singular in the last sentence),
is less of a formal set piece than the essay directed to Hierius. It begins
as a discussion of a passage in 1 Corinthians 15 that was apparently used
in the fourth century, by Marcellus of Ancyra, to justify what was widely
criticized as his "modalist" or "Sabellian" understanding of God: the suggestion that the Son's personal distinction from the Father within the divine Mystery is, in fact, only a contingent part of the history of salvation,
and that the Son, along with those who adhere to him, will eventually be
"subjected" or reabsorbed into the single, infinite Mystery of God.[16] After
pointing out that Paul's reference to "being subject" can be understood in
a variety of ways (2–3), Gregory quickly gets to his christological point:
insisting that since the Son is eternally generated from the Father within
the divine Mystery, this text of Paul cannot refer to any eventual termina-
tion of his status and mission (4–5). In its context, Gregory argues, Paul's
saying is clearly ecclesial and eschatological in intent: it is about the final
salvation of "those who belong to Christ" (1 Cor 15:23) (6–7).

Gregory then goes on to develop this interpretation of the passage
in Paul, first by stating clearly what he takes to be its doctrinal intent,
then by showing exegetically how this is implied in Paul's own words. The
doctrine, as Gregory sums it up, is this:

> It is that at some point the nature of evil will be transformed
> into non-existence, completely made to disappear from reality,
> and pure divine goodness will contain all rational nature within
> itself; nothing of all that has come into being from God will fall
> outside the boundaries of God's Kingdom. But when all the evil
> that has been mingled with existing things is consumed, like
> some material impurity, by the melting-process of purifying fire,
> everything will become just as it was when it had its origin from
> God—as it was when it had not yet come to share in evil. (8)

In the incarnation of the eternal Word, Gregory goes on to explain (9),
God entered history and "mingled himself" into fallen human nature,
now tinged with death, "as a kind of first fruit of the mixture that will

---

reference, I have numbered the sections of the text myself.

16. See especially Marcellus, Frags. 113, 115, 117. See also Lienhard, *Contra
Marcellum*, 64–67; Marcellus argues that the Kingdom of Christ referred to by Paul is
simply the earthly phase of Christ's saving rule.

include us all" (9). In Christ's person, "the entire nature of evil has been annihilated" (9).[17]

> So evil has begun to disappear, death to be destroyed, with him as its starting-point; and then a sort of succession has been extended, in a kind of ordered series, to include everything that comes to exist . . . And surely this is the goal of our hope: the point where nothing opposed to the Good is left, but divine life permeates all things . . . When, then, all of us come to be outside the realm of evil, in imitation of our "first-fruit," the whole mix that is nature, blended in with the first-fruit and becoming one body in its solidarity, will receive within itself the rule of the Good alone; so with the whole body of our nature mingled with the divine, immortal nature, that subjection here ascribed to the Son will become reality through us, as subjection is brought to fulfillment in his Body and is referred to him who works in us the grace of submission. (10)

The "subjection" of the Son to the Father that Paul mentions is thus, in Gregory's view, to be understood of the Church, now taken broadly as "the whole of human nature" (12–13). So he insists that "there will be nothing outside the realm of what is saved" (13). Understood this way, Gregory argues—appealing to a number of passages in John's "last supper discourse" as well as to Rom 5:10—that "what [Paul] calls 'subjection' [in 1 Cor 15] he there [in Rom 5:10] names 'reconciliation,' signifying by both terms the one idea, which is salvation" (17).

4. Besides these three occasional essays, Gregory deals with the Christian hope for eternal life in a number of his homiletic works. The most elaborate of these doctrinally is his principal sermon for the feast of Easter, known as *In sanctum Pascha* or *In Christi resurrectionem* III.[18]

17. For Gregory's understanding of the sinless, unified person of Christ as the cause and mode of human transformation to a life of moral virtue and physical immortality, see my articles, "Divine Transcendence and Human Transformation: Gregory of Nyssa's Anti-Apollinarian Christology," and "'Heavenly Man' and 'Eternal Christ': Apollinarius and Gregory of Nyssa on the Personal Identity of the Savior." The image of Christ as the "first-fruit" of a future harvest of materially and morally transformed humanity appears in a number of his works, particularly in his anti-Apollinarian treatises, which can be dated to the late 380s. This may suggest a similarly late date for the present treatise.

18. This sermon, edited critically by Ernst Gebhardt, appears in Greek in GNO IX/1.245–270. Of the other Easter sermons attributed to Gregory, the "first," sometimes called *De Tridui Spatio*, deals with the question of understanding Jesus' time in the tomb as "three days," and the short "fourth" homily is usually taken to be its

This work, which has been dated variously to 379 or 382[19] and which was given to unknown hearers at an unknown location, begins with an evocation of the Paschal festival (1, cf. 4) as a day of unity, joy and rest for all Christians. The Christ who rose triumphantly is the same one who will come again as king and judge; his triumph is also a promise of our own salvation and purification. After briefly evoking the story of Jesus' passion and death, as the full acting-out of the Son's association with our mortal nature, Gregory then turns to the main project of this oration: an apologetic explanation of how bodily resurrection is conceivable and even plausible, given what we understand about the natural world. He describes the admittedly "miraculous" process of the material reassembling of decomposed bodies, and then reminds his hearers that God has surely formed the human person, "so wise and godlike" as each of us is, for more than ultimate disintegration (7). Gregory then describes the original creation of the human person in a way calculated to evoke wonder at God's power and wisdom (8–9). If God can create so wonderfully, he suggests, God can surely re-create more easily still.[20] He then turns to consider parallels in nature: the marvel of human gestation (11), and of the growth of a full ear of wheat from a small grain (12–13); the changes shown by trees through the seasons (13), the behavior of snakes awaking from hibernation (14); the lifelong growth and development of the human person (14), the difference in our own experience between sleep and waking (15). Gregory then points out that the human body does not completely disappear after death, but is simply broken down into its smallest parts.

Gregory turns then to the moral importance of resurrection: "for if there is no resurrection, there is no judgment; and if judgment is removed, fear of God will be eliminated with it" (17). The soul alone should not be the recipient of God's judgment, since the body has labored with it, both for good and for ill, during the present life; both must take some responsibility for human actions. After evoking a few key biblical passages—Ezekiel 37 and 1 Cor 15:52—Gregory concludes the sermon by emphasizing, in Paul's words, that "we shall be changed" (21), yet in a

---

concluding section. What appears as Gregory's "second" Paschal homily in the PG is in fact Severus of Antioch's Homily 77; the "fifth" is now thought to be a work of the "other Cappadocian," Amphilochius of Iconium, who was Gregory Nazianzen's cousin.

19. See Maraval, "Chronology," 162 for references.

20. Gregory's argument here recalls the apologetics of a number of second-century writers.

way that testifies to the personal continuity between the present life and the life to come. In this sermon, as in the dialogue *On the Soul and the Resurrection*, Gregory's emphasis is not explicitly on the final salvation of all humanity, but on how it might be conceivable, even likely, that whole persons—the God-man Christ and each of us—will be restored intact after undergoing death.

Three other homilies of Gregory's have come down to us that deal directly with death and Christian hope: memorial discourses, artfully constructed according to the rhetorical canons of funeral speeches (*epitaphioi logoi*), but nevertheless laying primary emphasis on Christian hope and using inspiring biblical parallels. A widely-used handbook of the rhetorical forms and techniques to be used in "epideictic" or "display" oratory, the third-century AD work attributed to "Menander Rhetor,"[21] lays out the customary structure of such an address, which may be delivered some months after the death of its subject. One should begin, "Menander" suggests, with emotional acknowledgements of the difficulty of making such a speech adequately, then turn to praise the family of the deceased, as well as his or her birth, education and career. Next, one should lament the cruelty of fortune in taking away such a person before the time, and conclude with words of consolation, reminding those closest to the dead person that he or she is now in a place of happiness and rest. Gregory's memorial homilies do follow this general outline in their development, yet also make frequent use of Scripture as he reminds his hearers of the specific details of Christian hope.

The first of Gregory's funeral homilies is his oration on the death of his friend and mentor, Bishop Meletius of Antioch, who came to Constantinople to preside at the ecumenical Council summoned—probably at his urging—by Theodosius in May of 381. Meletius died suddenly during the Council's first week. Gregory's address,[22] possibly delivered at a

---

21. See Russell and Wilson, eds., *Menander Rhetor* 2.11 [418.6–422.4] 170–179. The two treatises constituting "Menander's" work may in fact be by different late Hellenistic authors. In his brief article, "Rhetorik und Theologie in den Grabreden Gregors von Nyssa," Andreas Spira, the modern editor of Gregory's funeral homilies, argues that they belong to the slightly different genre of "consolations" (*monodiai*), which lack direct reference to the body and the funeral ceremonies of the deceased (see *Menander Rhetor* 2.16 [434.10–437.4]; Russell and Wilson, 200–207). This seems not to fit Gregory's three works so well, especially since the *epitaphios logos*, according to Menander, usually also contains a final section of consolation.

22. The Greek original of this work that I have used is the critical text edited by Andreas Spira, in GNO IX/1 (Leiden: Brill, 1967) 441–457. It is significant that of all

liturgical celebration in which the dead bishop's body is being sent back
from Constantinople to his home city, predictably evokes the sadness and
drama of that scene. Following the classical form of such orations, he begins by underlining the challenge of speaking on such a tragic occasion.
With frequent references now to biblical parallels—Joseph and his brothers sending Jacob's body back to Palestine, as well as a variety of prophetic
models for Meletius's own virtues—Gregory then to the grief that will
soon descend on Meletius's "family," the church of Antioch, when it hears
of the death of its beloved leader (paragraphs 3–4). Gregory goes on to
recognize the heroic shape of Meletius's conflicted career (5–7), stressing
his prophetic stance and his kind and gracious demeanor. He concludes
with a reflection on the bishop's present state as priest along with Christ,
that curiously echoes Plato, along with the Letter to the Hebrews:

> "But wipe away my tears . . . The bridegroom has not been taken
> away from us, but stands in our midst, even if we cannot see
> him. The priest is in the sanctuary; he has entered within the
> veil, where Christ the forerunner entered on our behalf (Heb
> 6:19–20). He no longer offers worship in the pattern and shadow
> of heavenly things (Heb 10:1), but gazes on the very archetype
> of the things themselves . . . The trap is broken, and the bird has
> flown away (Ps 123:7 [LXX]). He has left Egypt, and life here
> in the mud; he has crossed not that Red Sea, but the dark and
> cloudy sea of life. He has entered into the land of promise, and
> on the mountaintop he leads the philosophic life before God. (8)

Meletius is now alive in the fullness of Christian fulfillment, Gregory insists, and so remains present invisibly in the midst of his Church.

Gregory also has left us a moving oration on the death of the imperial princess Pulcheria, daughter of Theodosius and his wife Flaccilla,
who died in the summer of 385 at the age of six.[23] His address here also
follows the customary rhetorical shape of funeral addresses—his shock
and sense of inadequacy, the contrast between this present "earthquake"
and the anniversary of an earthquake in nearby Nicomedia some thirty

---

the 150 or so bishops who had assembled from around the Middle East for the Council, it was Gregory of Nyssa—not his friend Gregory of Nazianzus, for instance, also
a celebrated rhetorician and Meletius's successor as president of the Council—who
was asked to deliver this memorial address. Was this due to a superior reputation as
a thinker and speaker, to his connections among the other bishops present, or to the
special patronage of the Emperor?

23. For the Greek text, see the critical edition of Andreas Spira, GNO IX/1
(Leiden: Brill, 1967) 461–472.

years earlier, commemorated the previous day.[24] But his emphasis here, even more than in his homily for Meletius, is on the child Pulcheria's present life with God. Citing Jesus' saying, "Let the little children come to me" (Matt 19:14), he addresses her parents:

> So, then, even if this little one has gone away from you, she sure-ly has run away to the Lord. As far as you are concerned, she has closed her eyes, but she has opened them to the light of eternity. She has departed from your table, but has joined the table of the angels . . . How beautiful is that eye, which now gazes on God! How sweet the mouth, beautified by heavenly hymns! (4)

After drawing parallels between the present grief of the imperial couple and the way Abraham, Sarah, and Job dealt with the loss of their own children, Gregory concludes by making use of an image that he also employs in his *Catechetical Oration*,[25] pointing to the close connection between the salvation given us in Christ and the purifying process of our death and resurrection:

> Since, then our nature was created from the beginning by the God of all things as a vessel capable of receiving good things, but the enemy of our souls has deceitfully poured evil into us, so that the good has no more room, for this reason—so that the evil instilled into us might not remain forever—the vessel is shattered by death for a time by a beneficent providence, so that the evil might flow away and the human might be shaped anew and be restored, unmingled with evil, to the life it had in the beginning. For this is the resurrection: the formation of our nature once again in its original condition. (10)

Consoling reminders to the child's parents that she lives now with God are inserted into a larger affirmation of what seems now to be the wide-spread Christian conviction that the present reality of death is but the prelude to a final resurrection.

Gregory's third extant funeral oration was probably delivered some six months later, mourning the death of Theodosius's first wife, the

---

24. Gregory's apparent allusion to the Nicomedia earthquake suggests a date for this homily of August 25, 385.

25. This important work, dealing broadly with the Christian understanding of salvation and the worship of the true God, is usually dated to the mid- or late 380s. The image of death and resurrection as the breaking and reshaping of a clay vessel that has been maliciously filled with lead is in c. 8 (ed. Ekkehard Mühlenberg; GNO III/4 [Leiden: Brill, 1996] 29.13 – 31.21).

empress Flaccilla, who herself died, aged 30, while seeking a cure at a spa named Skotoume in Thrace.[26] Gregory again generally molds the shape of his words on the classical form of the *epitaphios logos*: evoking the difficulty of the occasion (1), pointing to the general grief of the population in the imperial capital (2–3, 4), emphasizing the Christian virtues of the late Empress—her devotion to her husband (3–4), her humility (4–5); her wide, self-effacing generosity to the poor (9–10); her resolute Nicene orthodoxy (10–11)—and movingly evoking the scene of her body's final reception in Constantinople (5–6). But in the midst of this vivid portrait of a strikingly Christian woman, Gregory again emphasizes that her soul is, even now, in a blessed state:

> Do you seek our Empress? She lives now in a royal palace. But do you yearn to see this with your eyes? It is impossible. . . Our Empress's home is in an ineffable place; you will see it yourself only when you, too, emerge from your body—for it is not possible to come within the Empress's dwelling in any other way than by removing the veil of the flesh. . . (7)
>
> What is there to mourn, then, if the blessed one is released from the evils of life, and casting off the filth of the body like a smudge in the eye, moves on with purified soul to the uncontaminated life: where deceit is not practiced, slander is not believed, flattery has no place, lies are not mingled with speech—where pleasure and pain and fear and rashness and poverty and wealth and servitude and lordship, and all the inconsistency of this life is removed as far as possible from that life to come? "Mourning and sorrow and groaning," as the Prophet says, "have fled from there!" (Isa 35:10). And what will take their place? Freedom from suffering, blessedness, removal from all evil, familiarity with angels, contemplation of invisible things, a share in God, joy that has no end. (8–9)

The understanding of the human condition evokes Plato, once again, but the terms of the hope held out by Gregory are explicitly biblical.

5. Undoubtedly Gregory of Nyssa's most famous treatment of death and Christian hope, however, as well as his longest, is his dialogue *On the Soul and the Resurrection,* datable to sometime in the 380s. The dramatic framework of this Platonic dialogue—clearly modelled on Plato's *Phaedo* as a Christian counterpart—sets it late in 379. Gregory says that on hearing of the death of his brother Basil (usually dated on January 1, 379,

26. For the Greek text of this oration, see the critical edition by Andreas Spira, GNO IX/1 (Leiden: Brill, 1967) 475–490.

but possibly a few months earlier), he travelled to the family estate in Annesoi, in the mountains of Pontus, to bring the sad news to his older sister, Macrina, who along with Basil had always served as the family's conscience and ascetical model, even (as here) as his "Teacher". When he arrived, Gregory tells us, he discovered that Macrina, too, was mortally ill. But she strictly forbids him to mourn, and so begins a long and detailed conversation with him about the meaning of death, embedded in a broader discussion of what constitutes the human person. As their conversation ranges, Macrina first offers a definition of what the human soul is: it serves as the steering presence, the "architect," of our life in the world; it is created in time, "an essence which has a beginning; it is a living and intellectual essence, which by itself gives to the organic and sensory body the power of life and of the reception of sense-impressions, as long as the nature which can receive these impressions maintains its existence."[27] Although not visible or measurable empirically, the soul's dynamic presence can be discovered in the human body in a way analogous to our finding God in the world: each gives life, maintains order, steers and continually shapes a complex *kosmos* without being a material part of it.[28] We know of its existence, like that of God, only by its effects. In this sense, it is most properly the *soul*, in Gregory's understanding, that is said by Genesis 1:26–27 to be made "in the image of God".[29] But Gregory has Macrina insist here—in a way decidedly different from Plato's thought— that even though soul and body are substantially distinct, they are also permanently, even teleologically related:

> Therefore, even when the elements in the body are resolved into themselves, the bond is not destroyed which united them through the activity of life. While the compound of the elements still holds together, each element receives life, because the soul enters equally and similarly into all the members which constitute the body . . . Consequently also when the compound is dissolved and has returned again to its proper elements, it is quite plausible to suppose that the simple and uncompounded nature remains with each of the members even after the dissolution. That which has once been united in some ineffable manner to the compound of the elements will also remain forever with those elements with which it was mixed, without being in any

27. *On the Soul and the Resurrection*, PG 46. 29 B 10–14; 37–38.

28. PG 46. 25 B 1–28 C 15; 33–34.

29. PG 46. 41 B 9–44 A 7; 45.

way separated from the union which happened to it once and
for all.[30]

Soul and body can be separated, as happens in death, but they are permanently oriented to union with each other and to common, dynamic
activity. Gregory's emphasis here is remarkably different from the more
Platonic, soul-centered description of the treatise *On the Dead*.

In its present condition, after the fall, which Gregory frequently
refers to by the image of Gen 3:21 as the state of being "clothed in garments of skin,"[31] the soul finds itself inordinately attached to the material things its body needs, and so is hampered and bound by "passions,"
or unhealthy fleshly desires; but after ascetical practice, as well as death
itself, has purified those desires, and possibly after even a post-mortem
spiritual purgation, the soul will be reunited in resurrection with the scat-
tered material elements of the body that still are its own, marked with its
distinctive stamp; when that occurs,

> it will go back to itself and see clearly what is in its nature, and
> through its own beauty it will look upon the archetype as if in a
> mirror and an image . . . And when it has passed beyond fleshly
> desire (*epithumia*), [and] has entered into that towards which
> it was previously being raised by desire, it no longer gives any
> place in itself either to hope or to memory. It has what it was
> hoping for . . . Thus it imitates the superior life, being conformed
> to the properties of the divine nature, so that nothing else is left
> to it but the disposition of love, as it becomes attached in its
> nature to the beautiful.[32]

This state of union with God as its source will confer on the re-embodied
soul the freedom and virtue which allow it to resemble God most fully:

> Freedom consists in becoming like that which has no master
> and is under its own control. This likeness was given to us by
> God at the beginning, but it has been veiled by the shame of our
> debts. Virtue has no master. Therefore everything free will be in
> virtue, for that which is free also has no master. But indeed the
> divine Nature is the source of all virtue. Hence those who are

---

30. PG 46. 44 C 4–D7; 46.

31. See also *On the Dead*, 15.

32. PG 46. 89 C 9–13; 93 B 8–C 5; 78–80.

released from evil will be *in* the divine Nature, so that, as the Apostle says, "God may be all in all."[33]

What this re-created human nature will look like, how its graced virtue and freedom will be expressed in the restored organism of soul and body, is beyond our present knowledge. All we can say with certainty is that resurrection will be "the restoration (*apokatastasis*) of our nature to its original condition," its coming to be a "divine sort of thing (*theion ti chrēma*)" free from all the disordered attraction to self that is, in the biblical narrative, the root of mortality.[34] Until the resurrection happens, like people in the night awaiting the dawn, we can only look forward in hope to a life that will both fully realize what we humans naturally are, and yet be wholly unlike anything we have known.[35]

After this rapid survey of what seem to be the main points in Gregory of Nyssa's most extensive reflections on the mystery of death and eternal life, we can certainly begin to ask ourselves, with Cullmann, how adequately Gregory captures the hope of the Gospels and Paul. Is his personal eschatology simply late Hellenistic thought garnished with Scriptural quotations? Has he abandoned the full promise implied for humanity in the news of Christ's resurrection? Is Gregory truly confusing Paul with Plato, so that in his writings, as Cullmann put it, "I Corinthians 15 has been sacrificed for the *Phaedo*"? I would certainly argue "No," and suggest instead that what Gregory is doing here, in a strikingly individual way, is what theology always does: he is meditating on the gospel message from the perspective of the most sophisticated scientific and philosophical thought of his day, trying to present the Word of Scripture in the logical and rhetorical dress of his own culture's best efforts at rational, persuasive thought, while holding the Christian faith's central Mystery undiminished as a source of life for the world of his time. In a way that may seem foreign to us in our post-Enlightenment culture, what he offers here is "faith seeking understanding," as a learned Greek humanist of the fourth century might go about that challenging task. The more important question seems to be: how do *we* understand *him*?

Let me suggest a few general conclusions:

1) As someone highly educated in the linguistic, dialectical, and scientific culture of his time, as well as a bishop highly respected by his

33. PG 46.101 C 13–104 A 10; 86 (emphasis mine).

34. PG 46.145 A 1 – 9; 113.

35. PG 46.145 B 15 – C 7; 113.

peers and leaders among the contemporary Christian faithful, Gregory is quintessentially Greek as well as quintessentially Christian. Although his writings on death and eternal life vary considerably in their emphasis and content, as in their literary character, still all seem to be centered, as in a refrain, on Paul's insistence in 1 Cor 15:20 that indeed "Christ has been raised from the dead, the first-fruits of those who have fallen asleep." *Resurrection*, not simply bodiless immortality, is the promise of faith as Gregory understands it; the pressing question was how this promise could be made intelligible to people educated in the science and philosophy of his time. Gregory's meditations on the structure and activities of *the human person*, as an intricate and mutually coherent interplay of intellectual and material components, of soul and body, of self-motivating freedom and pre-given determination, are really all in service of making more intelligible the challenging promise that we, too, shall be "raised incorruptible" with Christ.

2) A constant theme in these writings is that Christian hope is directed towards both continuity and transformation: at the end of history, Christians believe that God will *restore* the human race and its world, including every individual human who has lived, to *what God intended them to be* at the beginning, but to a hitherto unguessed degree. "If anyone is in Christ," Paul writes, "he is a new creation; the old has passed away, behold, the new has come" (2 Cor 5:17). So, besides the risen Christ, the clearest clue to our final form is the account of *creation* in Genesis 1–2, in which a world still free of humanly caused pain and violence was given its present shape, in a negative way, by the free activities of the human pair who had been created in God's image.

3) *Salvation*, as the restoration of this original state of innocence and beauty, will include everyone who has ever existed, Gregory frequently insists. If it parallels creation, it must also be *universal*. To hold otherwise would be to ascribe to evil a substance and power parallel to that of God, which Gregory insists is impossible. In Gregory's view, evil is a power which will come to an end, which is what Paul meant in promising that "God will be all in all" (1 Cor 15:28).

4) Salvation is therefore a process of *transformation* rather than simply election: the restoration of the weak and vulnerable creature to its original robust health, of the ignorant to discernment and wisdom, of people held down by the shackles of habitual vice and passion, trapped in their clumsy "garments of skin," to freedom and virtue. This *healing process* has already begun in the person of *Christ*: fully human while fully

God, sharing our vulnerabilities yet utterly virtuous, transforming and transformed. It is revealed in his life and miracles, in his obedient gift of himself on the cross, and in his resurrection from the dead. From him it spreads to us.

5) The *ontological key* to this hope for transformation, in Gregory's view, seems to be his belief in the immortality and immateriality of the human *soul*. The soul is clearly a creature, Gregory has Macrina insist in *On the Soul and the Resurrection*; thus it has a beginning in time, is no eternal aeon or spirit. But it cannot be destroyed, because it is made to be akin to God. We only know the soul indirectly, by what it does. So it acts and is known within the human "microcosm" in a way analogous to the way God's activity within the "great world" acts and is known: by ordering, activating, holding a complex material reality together. It is made to be the unifying force in a body with sense-organs, a body that interacts with the larger material world outside; its distinctive identity is "imprinted" on every atom, every minuscule fragment, of its body's material constitution. So the soul knows its own physical "bits," and when the body has disintegrated in death, the soul—being non-spatial—remains transcendentally present to all of them: capable of re-forming them, when the event of resurrection comes, into a new, dynamic organism that is recognizably the person himself. It is the soul, in its non-material, non-spatial continuity and life, in other words, that makes bodily resurrection thinkable. Without the survival and continuity of human souls, the "new creation" promised by Paul (and hoped for by Cullmann) would be the creation of a different human race, not the salvation of this one.

6) The reality of sin and disordered affections in our present life demands moral *purification* if the person is to be renewed for life with God. This either takes place during the present life, by our freely-chosen attempts at disciplining our drives and focusing our desires on God—which is the meaning of ascetical practice, the "philosophic life"—or it will happen (in a way Gregory seems reluctant to speculate on further) in and after bodily death. Purgation is an unavoidable part of our transformation.

7) Gregory's argument for the intelligibility of the Gospel of salvation and transformation is thus also centrally a *moral argument*: if humans are to be *accountable* for their present actions, created freedom must be taken seriously; there must be a *judgment* of human actions; sin must be purged and healed. But divine judgment and human guilt cannot be separated from God's intended activity of rehabilitation, if God's

ultimate goodness is to triumph over creaturely resistance. The final goal of providence must be the voluntary "subjection" of all living beings to God, in union with Christ the savior.

8) Despite some resemblances to *Origen's* earlier efforts to integrate the teachings of the gospel with the learned "wisdom" of his time, and despite his own undenied admiration for Origen's exegetical and theological brilliance, Gregory makes clear efforts to distance himself from those themes ascribed to Origen (rightly or not) which were meeting strong resistance in the church of his day. So in *On the Soul and the Resurrection* he expressly denies the possibility that souls ever existed independently, before the formation of the living body; he also rules out the possibility of the "transmigration" of the soul to a body different from its original one.[36] These were both ideas Origen had toyed with as possibilities in *De Principiis* III. But Gregory's understanding of the risen body, in contrast with that of Origen, emphasizes its materiality as well as its spirituality, even though he admits ignorance as to its particular features, including sexual differentiation. And he now conceives of the divinity of the Son and the Spirit within the life and activities of God—along with his fellow Cappadocians—in a fully Trinitarian way, and carefully distinguished this from both a subordinationist model (like that of Origen) and a modalist one (like that ascribed to Marcellus). If he is to be thought of as an Origenist, it is only at the end of a long trajectory.

9) Gregory's use of *Scripture* certainly recognizes its normativity for faith, but also shows a freedom of interpretation, especially in dealing with certain passages, that can surprise us. So in *On the Soul and the Resurrection* he offers an extensive interpretation of Jesus' parable of the Rich Man and Lazarus, seeing it as especially applicable to questions of psychological attachment and worldly passions, that seems to move well beyond its possible original meaning in Luke's gospel. Some of this is clearly due to a pre-modern hermeneutic, which easily finds figural and moral senses in Scriptural texts where moderns tend to see none. But it also reminds us that for Gregory and his contemporaries, the core of

36. Origen proposes the hypothesis of the pre-existence of intelligences or souls in *De Principiis* I, 8.4 and III, 1.22, and their subsequent rebellion and "fall," as a way of explaining the radical differences in condition presently experienced by conscious creatures. For the suggestion that Origen also hinted at the possible transmigration of souls to other living beings, after the present life, see Justinian, *Epistula ad Menam*, Frag. 17b. It is not clear that Origen himself ever held this.

faith is still the Word of Scripture, as it is proclaimed in the community. Philosophy stands simply in service of this interpretation.

10) Central to Gregory's anthropology, as to his eschatological vision, is his conviction that the *life of created intellects is always in flux*, always changing and growing. In the present historical order, this can mean change in both a negative and a positive direction—growth towards or away from God our end, movement towards our real identity as creatures or rebellious refusal. The work of *grace*, however, as achieved through Christ, is the growing transformation of the whole human race united with him as an interconnected body: towards the free choice of the Good by each of us, towards the virtue that reflects God's life, towards the perfection of finite human nature, which—as Gregory memorably writes in the *Life of Moses*—is "always to want to have a greater share of the Good,"[37] which is God. So he writes of the soul, later on in that same work:

> And if no higher being prevents its movement upwards, (for the nature of the Good draws to itself all things that gaze up towards it), surely it always comes to a higher place than where it was, "reaching out beyond what lies behind" in its yearning for heavenly things, as the Apostle says (Phil 3:13), and always winging its way upwards. For because of what it has already received, it yearns not to abandon what is higher and lies above; so it makes its way ceaselessly towards higher things, always renewing its energy for the flight upwards from what it has already achieved. Activity directed towards virtue, after all, is the only thing that nourishes its powers by effort—never flagging in its strength because of the work it has already done, but only increasing in it.[38]

It is a vision of human life and fulfilment which is both fundamentally Hellenic and radically biblical—a way of reading Paul that flows from the heart of Gregory's own understanding and practice of faith.

BIBLIOGRAPHY

Alexandre, Monique. "Le *De mortuis de Grégoire de Nysse.*" In *Studia Patristica* 10, 35–43. Berlin: Akademie-Verlag, 1970.

37. *Life of Moses*, "Preface," 9 (Gregory of Nyssa, *La Vie de Moïse,* Jean Daniélou, trans. Paris: Cerf, 1987). This work is generally thought to be one of Gregory's latest, dating from the late 380s.

38. Ibid., 225–226.

Cullmann, Oscar. *Immortality of the Soul or Resurrection of the Dead? The Witness of the New Testament*. London: Epsworth, 1958.

—. *Mélanges offerts à Karl Barth à l'occasion de ses 70 ans*. Basel: Reinhardt, 1956.

Daley, Brian E. "Divine Transcendence and Human Transformation: Gregory of Nyssa's Anti-Apollinarian Christology." *Modern Theology* 18 (2002) 497–506.

—. "Divine Transcendence and Human Transformation: Gregory of Nyssa's Anti-Apollinarian Christology." In *Studia Patristica* 32, 87–95. Peeters: Leuven, 1997.

—. "Divine Transcendence and Human Transformation: Gregory of Nyssa's Anti-Apollinarian Christology." In *Re-thinking Gregory of Nyssa*, edited by Sarah Coakley, 67–76. Oxford: Blackwell, 2003.

—. "'Heavenly Man' and 'Eternal Christ': Apollinarius and Gregory of Nyssa on the Personal Identity of the Savior." *Journal of Early Christian Studies* 10 (2002) 469–88.

Gregory of Nyssa. *Gregorii Nysseni Opera III/2, Opera dogmatica minora*. Edited by J. Kenneth Downing et al. Leiden: Brill, 1987.

—. *Gregorii Nysseni Opera III/4, Opera dogmatica minora*. Edited by Ekkehard Mühlenberg. Leiden: Brill, 1996.

—. *Gregorii Nysseni Opera IX/I, Sermones*. Edited by Günther Heil et al. Leiden: Brill, 1967.

—. *Gregorio di Nissa: Discorso sui defunti*. Translated with commentary by Giuseppe Lozza. Turin: Società internazionale editrice, 1991.

—. *On the Soul and the Resurrection*. Translated by Catherine P. Roth. Crestwood, NY: St. Vladimir's, 1993.

—. *La Vie de Moïse ou Traité de la Perfection en Materiè du Vertu*, 4th ed. Translated by Jean Daniélou. Sources Chrétiennes 1 bis. Paris: Cerf, 1987.

Lienhard, Joseph T. *Contra Marcellum: Marcellus of Ancyra and Fourth-Century Theology*. Washington D.C.: Catholic University of America Press, 1999.

Maraval, Pierre. "Chronology of Works." In *The Brill Dictionary of Gregory of Nyssa*, edited by L. F. Mateo-Seco and G. Maspero, 152–69. Leiden: Brill, 2010.

Russell, D. A., and N. G. Wilson, eds. *Menander Rhetor*. Oxford: Oxford University Press, 1981.

Spira, Andreas. "Rhetorik und Theologie in den Grabreden Gregors von Nyssa." In *Studia Patristica* 9/3, 106–14. Berlin: Akademie-Verlag, 1966.

The Theodosian Code and Novels, and the Sirmondian Constitutions. Translated by Clyde Pharr. Princeton: Princeton University Press, 1952.

Chapter 4

Two Ancient Christian Views of Suffering and Death

JOHN C. CAVADINI

> He had no form or comeliness that we should look at him,
> And no beauty that we should desire him.
> He was despised and rejected by men,
> A man of sorrows, and acquainted with grief.
> ....
> Surely he hath borne our griefs,
> And carried our sorrows;
> yet did we esteem him stricken,
> smitten by God, and afflicted.
> But he was wounded for our transgressions,
> He was bruised for our iniquities,
> Upon him was the chastisement that made us whole,
> And with his stripes we are healed.
> ....
> And they made his grave with the wicked . . .
> Though He had done no violence,
> And there was no deceit in his mouth.
> ....
> Yet he bore the sin of many,
> And made intercession for the transgressors.
> (Isa 53:2–3, 4–5, 9, 12; RSV)

As familiar as these biblical images of suffering may be, they seem to pose, rather than to answer, a question about suffering: is death, and the suffering to which mortality makes us heir, in any way good?

If "by his stripes we are healed," and if "the Lord was pleased to crush him," and take him from the land of the living to bear our sins, then surely *these* stripes are precious if any are, and of *this* death the Psalms can say most accurately that it is "precious in the eyes of the Lord" (Ps 116:5). But this does not necessarily mean that the suffering and death of the Servant in the Song, *qua* suffering, or *qua* death, were themselves something good. The evident pathos of the passage would argue against the idea. What is happening to the Servant is evil. And yet again, his suffering was the occasion of patient, loving endurance. One might argue that, at least to that degree, it was a good, or at least insofar as it was *his* death and *his* suffering. The question is further raised, are death and suffering necessarily connected? In this passage from Isaiah, corresponding, I think, to our own experience, it is the fact that the suffering is endured with death ominously on the horizon that seems to make it so much worse. But is the connection necessary?

The problem is exacerbated, of course, when we turn to the lives of ordinary persons. On the one hand, it seems to be common sense that some suffering, even when it involves facing death as a possibility, is good for you. We tend to regard people who have led lives insulated from suffering as shallow, lacking in empathy, oblivious to other people's problems.

Nor is it just our common sense that finds some good in suffering. "Justice tilts / the scales to ensure that suffering / is the only teacher," the Chorus tells us in a famous passage of the *Agamemnon*. They continue:

It was Zeus who set
Men on the path to wisdom
When he decreed the fixed
Law that suffering
Alone shall be their teacher.
Even in sleep pain drips
Down through the heart as fear,
All night, as memory,
We learn unwillingly.
From the high bench of the gods

> By violence, it seems, grace comes.[1]

Further, the stark contrast between gods and mortals that this passage invokes seems to indicate that death itself, the *terminus ad quem* of this and almost all other Greek tragedies, while not exactly good, is perhaps the unique burden of mortals, and this implies it is a kind of gift, a kind of modality for receiving wisdom, tragically, it is true, as here described by Aeschylus. Plato, as it is well known, goes the whole hog and declares, through Socrates in the *Phaedo*, that death is an unqualified good, because it liberates the soul from the body, its tragic prison (see for example *Phaedo* 66e–67a).

On the other hand, the glorification of suffering in certain kinds of Christian spirituality seems to border on, or even cross the border into, masochism, while, at times, and paradoxically, death can be trivialized, in quasi-Platonic fashion, to the point where it is not uncommon to hear a sermon at a funeral where death is envisioned simply as walking through the door to a new room in a house where your loved ones are waiting for you. On the other extreme, it would be offensive to claim that the Holocaust or any genocide, as a kind of suffering and systemic murder, was in any way a good for the victimized populations. We can recall, in this regard, Simone Weil's description of "affliction": "Affliction is an uprooting of life, a more or less attenuated equivalent of death, made irresistibly present to the soul by the attack or immediate apprehension of physical pain . . . At the very best, he who is branded by affliction will keep only half his soul. As for those who have been struck by one of those blows that leave a being struggling on the ground like a half-crushed worm, they have no words to express what is happening to them."[2] It would be hard to say that affliction, so described, is good for anyone, though it could be tempting to say that for one so afflicted death, on the other hand, would be.

So we are left with our original dilemma about the value of suffering and its relationship to death. I propose to contextualize this dilemma by identifying in ancient Christian tradition two strands of reflection on suffering, each of which is related to a particular view of death. The first is associated generally, though not exclusively, with ancient Eastern Christianity, and, in this paper, most especially with the second-century bishop and theologian, St. Irenaeus of Lyons and others in his lineage.

1. Aeschylus, "Agamemnon," 287–89, 200–210.
2. Weil, "The Love of God and Affliction," in *Waiting for God*, 118, 120.

The second is associated generally, but not exclusively, with Western Christianity, and, in this paper, with St. Augustine, who died in 429. These two strands of reflection, or models, are not "pure" in the sense that they never intersect or influence each other. Augustine, for example, until about 418, adhered somewhat tentatively to the earlier model, and so his legacy is divided, at least for the West. Nevertheless, there really are two quite distinct, if complementary, views of suffering entailed in each of these models. We run into trouble if they are unknowingly confused or when one is "read" with the lens of the other without realizing it.[3]

Irenaeus was a member of a church that had sustained a gruesome persecution in which the bishop, Pothinus, was martyred in 178.[4] Irenaeus succeeded to his position. Irenaeus's theology can be understood

3. John Hick has famously offered a theodicy which, he claims, is "Irenaean" and which he contrasts to an "Augustinian" theodicy that he claims is traditional but seriously flawed. See Hick, *Evil and the God of Love* (originally published New York: Harper and Row, 1966, recently reprinted, New York: Palgrave Macmillan, 2007; my citations are from the 1966 printing, which is still in many libraries and not replaced). My essay here covers some of the same territory that Hicks covered but it has no intention of addressing the basically philosophical problem of theodicy and is not constructed with this end in view. Hick spends much of his monograph detailing the "Augustinian" option in theodicy, which he regards as Neoplatonist and aesthetic in inspiration (see pp. 44–64, 76–90) and, for this reason and others, seriously deficient as a Christian theodicy. Hick almost completely ignores the christological dimension of Augustine's thought, almost as though it did not exist or was not relevant. Hick's treatment of Irenaeus is very brief (pp. 217–221), intended only as a springboard for a trajectory which he develops up to the 20th century and incorporates into his own proposal for a contemporary theodicy. The christological dimension of Irenaeus's thought is reduced to one sentence on p. 219, a passage cited from *AH* 4.38.2 without comment (though see p. 290, which contains a hint of Christocentrism). In general, I agree with the critique of Scott, "Suffering and Soul-Making," 313–34. He notes on p. 315n11, "Hick's initial move of polarizing Irenaean and Augustinian theology overlooks the salient points of intersection between these two pivotal theologians [and] . . . overstates their differences for his own constructive agenda." I agree, though in fairness to Hick, he does cite "points of hidden agreement" between the two types of theodicy (not necessarily between Augustine and Irenaeus) on pp. 264–66, yet these do not serve in any way to mitigate the thoroughgoing negative evaluation of Augustine. For the limitations of Hick's approach with regard to Irenaeus, see Scott's comments on pp. 322–23, though we must on the other hand note with appreciation Hick's desire to enter Irenaean insights into a contemporary discussion, even if the terms of that discussion remain largely contemporary and philosophical and for that reason, tendentious when it comes to Irenaeus. However, my overall point is that my essay is not intended as an engagement with Hick's essay, either globally or in contesting particular points. It is an independent reading with very different goals in mind.

4. Musurillo, *Acts*, 42–61.

in part as a defense of the martyrs and their suffering against the claims of those whom he refers to as "gnostic" Christians, who, he reports, denied that the suffering of the martyrs, or indeed their deaths, had any value as "witness" (see e.g., *Adversus Haereses* 4.34.9; 3.18.5). Their own position, more or less, was that life in the body was life alienated from its true source in God, and that the body and everything associated with it were an imprisoning illusion with at best the reality of a nightmare, from which one must awaken, and at worst an oppressive and degrading actual reality from which one must escape. In either case, the suffering associated with life in the body was meaningless, of no more significance than any other feature of bodily life. The gnostic Christian was one who had discovered the truth of his or her own condition as essentially a divine self alienated from the "Fullness" of divinity, and kept in this alienated state by the God of Creation.

From the perspective of the gnostics, the question may be asked, why, if the Creator is good, as Irenaeus following Scripture and its traditional interpretation, holds, why did he create beings who were capable of sinning and bringing destruction upon themselves, and why would he have subjected his own newly minted creatures to death in response to their sin? In response, Irenaeus elaborates a theology intended to uphold apostolic tradition regarding the goodness of creation and to vindicate the witness of his fellow church members who had preferred to suffer gruesome tortures and death rather than to deny their faith. Irenaeus sets for himself the task of developing and defending the idea of a *created good*, that is, something that is not divine, not uncreated, but nevertheless truly good.

> If, however, anyone say, "What then? Could not God have exhibited man as perfect from the beginning?" let him know that, inasmuch as God is indeed always the same and unbegotten as respects Himself, all things are possible to Him. But created things must be inferior to Him who created them, from the very fact of their later origin; for it was not possible for things recently created to have been uncreated. But inasmuch as they are not uncreated, for this very reason do they come short of the perfect. Because, as these things are of later date, so are they infantile; so are they unaccustomed to, and unexercised in, perfect discipline. (*AH* 4.38.1)[5]

5. All citations from Irenaeus's *Adversus Haeresies* are from the *Ante-Nicene Fathers*, accessed online.

A created self's perfection would not simply coincide with its existence, as is the case in God. Rather, the perfection of a created good would be a matter of growth and maturation, a kind of journey from an inexperienced infancy to a fully experienced adulthood.

> For as it certainly is in the power of a mother to give strong food to her infant [but she does not do so], as the child is not yet able to receive more substantial nourishment; so also it was possible for God Himself to have made man perfect from the first, but man could not receive this [perfection], being as yet an infant. (*AH* 4.38.1)

So, Irenaeus continues, "God had power at the beginning to grant perfection to man; but as the latter was only recently created, he could not possibly have received it" (*AH* 4.38.2), just as an infant could not receive filet mignon even if it did not cost $22/lb. In fact, it would be an abuse of God's power, a kind of violence, to try to force the spiritual filet mignon of perfection into the spiritual throats of us infants.

Irenaeus is trying to say that the gnostic critic has the wrong idea of God's power if he thinks it consists in shoving perfection into those who are not yet ready to receive it, that is, if he thinks it is in any way coercive. Against this, Irenaeus states flatly, "there is no coercion with God," because that would violate the "ancient law of human liberty" (4.37.1). The power of God is not the power imagined in the gnostic myths, a power of constraint and force—that is the way Satan works. The true God is actually powerful enough to make *freedom*, which exhibits itself first as a purely formal state, the ability to choose, needing exercise, growth, experience, and discipline to be able to choose the good. Otherwise, the good is not really one's own. More importantly, one's own very being really isn't one's own. One doesn't realize how good he or she is, speaking in terms of human nature and its created capacities, until those capacities are exercised enough so that the person discovers he or she can make consistently, and eventually heroically, loving choices, just as the martyrs did. If the good were imposed on a free creature, apart from his or her choice, Irenaeus comments,

> thus it would come to pass, that their being good would be of no consequence, because they were so by nature rather than by will, and are possessors of good spontaneously, not by choice: and for this reason they would not understand this fact, that good is a comely thing, nor would they take pleasure in it. (*AH* 4.37.6)

Corresponding to our status as untrained, inexperienced spiritual infants, God had a plan for bringing us into spiritual maturity. It's called the Incarnation. Irenaeus comments that God "might easily have come to us in His immortal glory, but in that case we could never have endured the greatness of the glory"—it would be a coercive, overwhelming imposition, like trying to feed a 6-course gourmet dinner to an infant—"and therefore it was that He appeared as a man, that we, being nourished, as it were, from the breast of His flesh, and having, by such a course of milk-nourishment, become accustomed to eat and drink the Word of God, may be able also to contain in ourselves the Bread of immortality, which is the Spirit of the Father" (*AH* 4.38.1). The Incarnation is not "Plan B," but rather it is Act II of Creation itself, and it reveals what kind of power created us in the first place, a power that is, as Irenaeus loves to put it, "long suffering," patient, willing to undertake the work of nourishment that generates freedom, willing to train us in this long-sufferingness, which is the essence of creative love, so that we may bear his Spirit unto immortality. The Incarnation was intended to reveal that, as Irenaeus loves to put it, God's *power is perfected in weakness* (e.g. *AH* 3.20.1, alluding to 2 Cor 12:9), something we would not imagine simply from reading the Creation story in Genesis alone. We see it by reading it in retrospect, from the story of the Incarnation. Creation is a project in creating freedom, and creative power more like the beginning of a relationship, where instead of the created member of the relationship already existing, the act of beginning a relationship establishes the existence of the created party. It is not an act of magic or caprice.

The image of what created freedom means is imaged quite decisively as well from the story of the Exodus. Irenaeus interprets the paradoxes of this narrative as the paradoxes of created freedom. Not even God can remove the element of struggle involved in "growing up" into the freedom God has given, for that would mean destroying the very freedom he created and/or the physical world in which this freedom is defined.[6]

6. Thus the Law, paradoxically, is a kind of bondage that is intended to teach freedom to people who had the desire to return to slavery in Egypt. The law is a beneficial bondage to God, training the people in the free obedience to God that is human flourishing. See for example *AH* 4.14.1. In *AH* 4.14.2 Irenaeus points out that this adaptation of God's longsuffering instruction in freedom for those whose hardness of hearts makes them want to reject the growth in freedom, which perfects human nature, is not restricted to the Jews, but to Christians too, whose hardness of heart required Paul to make certain adaptations to their condition, yet in all of this tempered bondage, God always preserves human freedom.

God can't choose for us, or make it so that there are no real choices to be made. God can and does change the exterior environment by miracles (such as the manna in the desert, *AH* 4.16.3), but not as dazzling displays of wonder to mesmerize and coerce, never to obviate, but only to call forth the struggle to be grown up, to be truly experienced, truly tested, seasoned and thus finally, free.

It is from this perspective[7] that Irenaeus reads the story of Adam and Eve, who commit a sin that is serious enough to deserve death as a punishment, but nevertheless a choice made in "infancy," the disobedience of inexperienced, untrained creatures who, precisely as inexperienced and untrained, are not as free as they would have been later when experienced, seasoned and grown up. Irenaeus interprets Adam's hiding from God as an indication of salutary repentance, and the fig leaves as a purposeful attempt at self-discipline, because, Irenaeus says, Adam realizes "he had lost his natural disposition and child-like mind." Irenaeus pictures Adam as saying, "Inasmuch as . . . I have by disobedience lost that robe of sanctity which I had from the Spirit, I do now also acknowledge that I am deserving of a covering of this nature, which affords no gratification, but which gnaws and frets the body." Apparently fig leaves are very scratchy. Be that as it may, Irenaeus continues, "And he would no doubt have retained this clothing for ever, thus humbling himself, if God, who is merciful, had not clothed them with tunics of skins instead of fig leaves" (*AH* 3.23.5). It is not politically correct these days, but it is certainly charming that God's mercy extends to replacing scratchy fig leaves with nice soft furs. "For God detested him who had led man astray, but by degrees, and little by little, He showed compassion to him who had been beguiled" (ibid.).

Paradoxically enough, this compassion includes the punishment of death, that is, of mortality, a severe punishment if ever there was one, but nevertheless a remedial measure. No good parent punishes without a remedial aim:

---

7. Irenaeus reads the story of Creation backwards from the story of the Exodus and subsequent dispensations. He learns what created freedom means from God's working with his creatures. This is why he takes up the question of what created freedom means in Book 4 (in the passages we examined from 4.37–38) only after a thorough examination of how and why God gave the Law, intending to show that God acted not out of need on his part, but freely for our benefit, to train us in freedom (see *AH* 4.14.2 for a good summary of God's dealings with humankind).

> Wherefore also He drove him out of Paradise, and removed him far from the tree of life, not because He envied him the tree of life, as some venture to assert, but because He pitied him, and did not desire that he should continue a sinner for ever, nor that the sin which surrounded him should be immortal, and evil interminable and irremediable. (*AH* 3.23.6)

Death is that which makes it so we are not left in a landscape whose only horizon is *sin*. Death reigns, paradoxically, so that God's creation is not undone, so that the possibility of an eternal life of never growing up, of always refusing to trust, is relativized. Death, as it were, is the occasion of re-presenting the original invitation to trust, only now as an ultimate choice such that we have the occasion to affirm that interminable life is not *in itself* a good, is not *in itself* the fulfillment of our being, but that trust in God is true life. Through death, God returns to us the possibility of freely choosing to trust that the very act of trusting God *is* life, and the loving obedience that results is the fulfillment of our nature, and the one that will grant the true incorruptibility that God had intended in the first place.

But death is only, one could say, the *formal* re-presentation of the original choice. God does not leave us alone to face this choice, without understanding it. In Irenaeus's system, the surprise is not that sin, as a *felix culpa*, calls forth a hitherto unexpected Incarnation, but rather that the Incarnation, which was always part of God's Plan A, as it were, happens anyway, despite sin. The amazing thing is that sin does not stop God's plan, even though it now will require facing death. God does not abandon his loving plan; if anything, it is even more revealing of God's love that the Word still becomes Incarnate in a world dominated by rape, violence, greed, fraud, and apostasy, and yes, as a kind of paradoxically necessary and merciful condition to preserve the possibility of freedom in the face of these—death. The Word's willingness to enter even this world, live under its conditions, face death, and still never make an unloving choice, shows us both that God's long-suffering love cannot be gainsaid by evil, and, correspondingly, that human freedom cannot be destroyed by evil:

> For as He became man in order to undergo temptation, so also was He the Word that He might be glorified; the Word remaining quiescent, that He might be capable of being tempted, dishonoured, crucified, and of suffering death, but the human nature being swallowed up in it (the Word), when it (the human

nature) conquered, and endured, and performed acts of kindness, and rose again, and was received up [into heaven] . . . For
when *strength was made perfect in weakness*, it showed the kindness and transcendent power of God." (*AH* 3.19.3; 3.20.1)

The awesome spectacle of a human being who even under torture and the
threat of unjust execution not only endures but performs acts of kindness, reveals the amazing beauty of what a comely thing a human being
is, reveals and vindicates the Creator's intentions in the first place, against
the gnostics. And note that, although *made perfect in weakness*, it is still
a feat—not of abstract, coercive power—but of *strength.* "For He fought
and conquered, for He was man contending for the fathers, and through
the obedience doing away with disobedience completely, for He bound
the strong man, and set free the weak, and endowed His own handiwork
with salvation, by destroying sin" (*AH* 3.19.6).

We can receive God's love gratefully, and gratefully act with the loving choices that constitute obedience to God the Creator and so, even
(and especially!) in the face of evil, perfect and fulfill our freedom. We
need not fear death. We can trust that it is the Father's beneficent provision of an opportunity, once again, to trust, with everything at stake once
again. The course of training is more grueling than it might have been
before sin, but created life is still essentially a kind of training, in which
God acts as a loving parent, nurturer, educator, teacher, to help us achieve
perfection, to learn that sin, not death, is the ultimate evil, empowering
us to the struggle that is still the *sine qua non* of created life. The point is
that this struggle is *preserved* for us, rather than allowing sin to negate it.
We could say that suffering under these conditions is a fallen version of
an unfallen good. No evil can utterly destroy human freedom, can finally
preclude or obviate a loving choice. Human nature cannot be destroyed
by evil. Yet another way of putting this is that our suffering is always
something truly and finally ours, it cannot be alienated from us, it always
presents itself as a locus of the self and of our freedom. In that qualified
sense, it is a good, and physical death, while not full stop and *per se* a
good, is not an evil either, *if* you can see it as a remedial, though punitive,
provision of a loving parent. Irenaeus, a Greek-speaking Christian who
came to Lyons from Asia Minor, would understand the sentiments of the
chorus in the *Agamemnon*.

And yet the vision is transformed from a tragic one to a comedy, if
we can accept Dante's later use of the word "comedy" as helpful also here.
The image painted by the letter of the Churches of Lyons and Vienne to

the Churches of Asia Minor, reporting the savage persecution that the church had sustained (the same one in which the bishop Pothinus was martyred), provide us with a picture which displays the victory of the martyrs as a victory of "endurance and kindness" (to use the words of Irenaeus just cited), as the martyrs not only refrain from hatred of their persecutors, but also refuse to demonize their fellow Christians who had apostasized. They thus depart leaving behind nothing to grieve their virgin Mother, the church.[8] Here is the wondrous, amazing beauty of human nature as the Creator intended it, as it is perfected in Christ, and the contrast is repeatedly drawn to the pagans who, by their persecution and torture of women, boys and old men have reverted to the subhuman status of raging beasts. There is no reason not to think that Irenaeus himself was not the author of the letter that describes the martyrs' victory in Christ as the pinnacle of human, and humane, achievement. We can note in passing that its *terminus ad quem* is not only individual achievement, but the loving communion of the church.

Although there is no time to discuss this here, Irenaeus's vision is received by no less a theologian than Origen, who famously conflates the tunics of skin as an act of God's mercy with the idea of death as a remedial punishment, such that mortal bodies are at once a punishment for sin and provide the locus for the training in Christ and so for growing in freedom, while Christ is also the "Great Wrestler," the stronger-than-the-strong-man.[9] God-become-man is God humble enough to be reduced to fighting, striving and struggling. In these theologies, struggle and wrestling for perfection is part of created nature. Anyone who wants to learn to play the piano has to practice, and no one can practice for you, nor can the divine teacher simply program (for example) the Chopin waltzes into our genes, because it is precisely the struggle to learn them that makes them "ours," that provides an interpretation, uniquely our own, that makes it moving to a listener and renders a performance an instance of self-expression. In this system suffering is not simply the result of the fall or of evil. In the world after the fall, what we recognize as suffering

8. Musurillo, *Acts*, 77, 85.

9. For Christ as the "Great Wrestler," see Origen, *Against Celsus*, 1.69 in *Ante-Nicene Fathers*, vol. 4: *Tertullian, Part Fourth; Minucius Felix; Commodian; Origen, Parts First and Second*, trans. Frederick Crombie, ed. Alexander Roberts and James Donaldson (Peabody, MA: Hendrickson, 1995), 395–669, at 428. For the coats of skins, see Crouzel, *Origen*, 91, 94. Whether or not Origen taught this directly, Gregory of Nyssa has certainly taken over the idea, for example, in *The Life of Moses* 2.22, trans. Abraham J. Malherbe and Everett Ferguson (New York: Paulist Press, 1978).

includes much that would not have been present in the unfallen world, yet the unfallen world would have included struggle, temptation, discipline and training and whatever "suffering," if that is the right word, these naturally entail. While we have no direct access to what that might have "felt like" in an unfallen world, it is fair to say that in this system, one can imagine an "unfallen" suffering, a suffering that is in some way, in itself, a good. Death in this system, is ultimately a good, though absolutely not because, as Plato thought, it liberates the soul from its prison in the body, but rather because it is God's way of restoring a true horizon for life in the body to be meaningful, so it can once again be the locus it was meant to be for the struggle for freedom against the real enemy, sin. Christ's loving endurance of death conquers it by conquering the real enemy, Satan. He it is who has left us with the legacy of sin, ultimately.

If we turn to Augustine now, it will seem at first that we are almost in another world. For Augustine, the fundamental starting point is the same, namely, the defense of a created good against a quasi-gnostic mythology, Manichaeism, which doubted the good of creation and thus the goodness of the Creator God of Genesis. But Augustine's treatment of the problem of death and suffering is dramatically different. In his interpretation of the Genesis narrative, unfallen humanity is not in a state comparable to infancy, but rather exists in the opposite state of complete freedom. What Augustine notices in the story is that human willing in the Garden of Eden was unchallenged by any internal or external exigency. The lives of Adam and Eve before the fall are not characterized by incipient struggle, but by freedom from struggle. Eden is a state of "ease and plenty," where the human couple "lived in the enjoyment of God, and derived their own goodness from God's goodness. They lived without any want . . . Food was available to prevent hunger, drink to prevent thirst . . . there was no trace of decay in the body, or arising from the body, to bring any distress to any of his senses. There was no risk of disease from within or injury from without . . . There was no sadness at all, nor any frivolous jollity. But true joy flowed perpetually from God . . . Between man and wife there was a faithful partnership based on love and mutual respect . . . Man was at leisure, and tiredness never wearied him, and sleep never weighed him down against his will" (*City of God* 14.26).[10]

In other words, there was no need that disobedience could meet that was not already met by obedience. God's commandment not to eat

10. All citations are from Augustine, *City of God*, trans. Henry Bettenson (London; New York: Penguin Classics, 2003).

of the fruit of one particular tree was therefore incredibly easy to keep. The disobedience of Adam and Eve was a choice made with a degree of freedom from constraint, passion and need that we can no longer even imagine. Far from being analogous to the fault of a child whose freedom was not fully developed, their disobedience was an act of perfect adult freedom, and therefore unambiguous, gratuitous malice. It is, in its very gratuity, completely irrational.

It is as though someone were to show up on one's doorstep and unexpectedly announce that he, the owner of New York City, was giving up the City to you, who answered the door, completely free of charge and with no obligation, except one, namely, in case this now former owner of the City ever wanted to visit, to keep the light on in his apartment on 75th and Park. Original sin in Augustine's view is as if, once the key to the City had been delivered, you chartered a helicopter to 75th and Park, entered the apartment and turned off the light. Why? Only because you will have the City, and in the analogy, your own being, on one's own terms, *not* as a gift. This is the sin of Pride in St. Augustine, the pretense that one's being is self-interpreting apart from any reference to its being a gift from God. But this is to render one's own being as incoherent, since it has no meaning apart from its character as a gift from God. In this scheme, death is not so much a penalty imposed from without by God, but is the result of freely willing to define our humanity by an incoherence, so much so that human nature is vitiated by this incoherence, and death is one of the features of this vitiation. Human freedom, abused in this way in its first and freest use, was permanently disabled, disfigured and "tilted" ever since towards the bad, because delivered by its own will into incoherence, and now powerless to freely will anything good unless healed by God's grace. This entails a disfigurement of human nature in general back towards the nothingness from which we were created. Mortal life as we know it, subject to death, old age, disease and infirmity—in a word, suffering—began.

In this scheme, all the suffering of mortal life, that is to say, all suffering, is post-fall, and Augustine after 418 has no doubt that there is no good in it. Decisively breaking with the whole of the Platonic tradition, and in particular as it was found in Ambrose's teaching, Augustine proclaims that death is *not* a good, even for the good. Ambrose had essentially accepted Plato's position that death is a good that liberates the soul, the essential self, from the body that is its extrinsic prison.[11] Ambrose's

11. See Cavadini, "Ambrose and Augustine," 232–49.

idea in embracing this position is to offer words of consolation to grieving Christians, but Augustine finally comes to reject the position of his
mentor, arguing that the body is part of the human being and so death
cannot be conceived of as the *good* of the liberation of the soul from the
body, but rather a disintegration of the human being that cannot possibly
be in any way good. It is simply part of the vitiated state of human nature
after the fall, and there is no good in this vitiation. Unlike in Irenaeus, the
punishment for sin has no remedial intent or effect because it is simply
part of the weakening of human nature intended by the malice of the
first human couple when they tried to opt for something better than having being on God's terms—when rejecting God's terms is rejecting one's
own being itself. Augustine thus emphatically rejects the idea that there
is anything good about death:

> The death of the body, the separation of the soul from the body,
> is not good for anyone, as it is experienced by those who are, as
> we say, dying. This violent sundering of the two elements, which
> are conjoined and interwoven in a living being, is bound to be a
> harsh and unnatural experience. (*City of God* 13.6)

Death is in no way simply a "passage," a *transitus*, in which the soul passes
from its bodily prison into liberation and freedom, as Ambrose pictured
it following Plato. Augustine's point is that to picture death that way is actually a denial of death. In fact, the whole of mortal life, as Augustine sees
it, is one extended act of dying. The violent sundering of the natural unit
of soul and body is not limited to the moment of death, as we commonly
understand that, but is felt in the sufferings, pains, sicknesses and gradual
dissolution that is all too familiar to ageing mortals, and there is nothing
good in any of it. "Death be not proud." It is all a mark of the incoherence to which we subscribed in Adam. There is nothing to romanticize
in any of this. The whole of mortal life is a kind of dying, a "race toward
death"; and death is not a "moment" of separation easily sublimated into
a metaphor of passage and so bleached of reality by a mere application
of words. You can't explain death away by words: "Death not only exists
but is so troublesome a reality that it can neither be defined by any verbal
formula nor avoided by any course of reasoning" (*City of God* 13.11).
Death, if truly faced, resists theorizing because to theorize it would be to
show how, in a way, it corresponded to rationality, how it was, in a way, a
good. There is no easy opposition between "death" and "life" as we know
it. Such is the legacy of the fall.

God does not abandon us, but he must take drastic measures. Although of course Augustine does not think the necessity of the Incarnation takes God by surprise, it is not something that would have occurred if we had not sinned. That does not exactly make it Plan B, as it was foreseen by God, but it was foreseen precisely as a response to the malicious act of Adam, not, as in Irenaeus, something that would have occurred without sin—hence the idea of the *felix culpa*, which is ultimately Augustinian. In the Incarnation of the Word of God, God himself comes to the rescue, comes to pay the price for sin that he has been prepared to pay from before the foundation of the world. he "empties himself" to live in hidden solidarity with us, under the conditions of fallen human life, as though he were a sinner himself, accepting the penalty of the solidarity with sinners which is death. Because he did not owe death as a penalty of sin, but chose it anyway, he, and he alone, could put it to use, something inherently unusable, with no *utilitas* of its own because it is not a good but an evil. He *used* it for our salvation, to demonstrate his love. Just as in Irenaeus, the martyrs also play a big role in Augustine's thought. Their faith in Christ, Augustine says, enabled them, too, to put death "to a good use," that is, to the use of witness to their faith in Christ's love.

Augustine is absolutely clear that this does not turn death, or any manifestation of mortality *qua* mortality for that matter, into a good. Faith in Christ does enable good to be drawn from these evils which remain evils. It is the true mark of God's work, to create good from nothing (and evil is a form of nothing, a vitiation of a good). Death and its attendant suffering cannot be redeemed as goods, and yet the virtues of patient endurance and of charity, which are the expressions of faith in Christ, are good.

To be clear, the essential good in this theology is neither suffering nor even virtue, primarily, but Christ. Augustine's point is that it is no true consolation to rationalize away death by saying it is just a passage, and to rationalize away suffering by saying it is a good in disguise. True consolation is to preach the conquest of death and evil in Christ, because it does not sugarcoat the evil. It invites us to find our consolation in the works of mercy and love that unite us to Christ's victory and so to all of the saints. For, since all of mortal life is a kind of dying, the whole of mortal life, all of its sufferings, can be the occasion of "martyrdom," that is, of "witness." We don't have to wait until death to be a martyr. Faith in Christ permits us to live a life of mercy and love in the face of all the sufferings, small and large, which mortal life entails, and in this way human being is re-created, or re-formed, from the near-nothingness to which it had reduced itself in sin, little by little. Far from celebrating the liberation of the soul from the body, Augustine's imaginative depiction of our final state shows the martyrs with their wounds intact, glorified, but intact, just as are the wounds of Christ. One can generalize: to the extent that any part of mortal life was a faithful "use" of the sufferings it presented, the record of that use, its witness, inscribed on the body will be preserved, be they wrinkles of wisdom or the stretch marks of pregnancy. They will be preserved not as disfigurements, but as glorified, that is, as transparent to the love they "mean" or represent.

So, let's pause to get our bearings. The two ancient strands of reflection on suffering and death we have considered do not really represent an opposition, but an interesting complementarity. Which one is better? My answer is that they are not to be played off one against the other, but both received. Pope John Paul II used to be fond of saying, "Let the Church breathe with both lungs," that is, with the theological insights and genius of both the Eastern and the Western Church. It is way too much to claim that these two ancient paradigms fully represent Eastern and Western theologies when it comes to suffering and death, but it is fair to say, I think, that they persist as characteristic tendencies. We should receive the gift of their complementarity in the church.

Irenaeus's theology, on the face of it more optimistic, provides some guidance for our instinct that suffering is in some way good for human beings, and that, in the words of Aeschylus, it begets wisdom. The structure of human life is such that growth, development, and the struggle that these always entail, are encoded into human nature as a created good. Struggle brings us into contact with our status as both created and good, and with our being as a gift. As we are progressively able to acquire discipline, self-control, and, in the end, love, we progressively understand how good and noble what we call human being is, and even in the midst of continuing struggle, we are more and more conscious of the great gift we have been given. We come to live in gratitude, come more and more to realize our calling as "image and likeness" of God, or, as Irenaeus would say, become "divinized." It is precisely in the suffering of the individual that we meet, inalienably, our ability to struggle and to grow. The miracle that Christ provides is that this dynamic is not cancelled by the fall. We might be inclined to think that Irenaeus was naïve, that he did not really know the extent to which evil can go. Yet we possess eye-witness accounts of the suffering of the martyrs of Lyons. The tortures applied to the Christians in Lyons were the equal or better of any horror in our contemporary repertoire of terror. Irenaeus's doctrine does not arise from naiveté, but rather is a doctrine that true life and true growth, the victory of the martyrs, comes from trust and confidence in the goodness of the Creator: they can harm your body, but they cannot take your soul, and human nature is such that you can encounter it in your pain because that pain, at least, is always and inalienably yours.

However, Irenaeus gets a little fuzzy when it comes to how to regard the things that cause suffering as we know it, in this mortal life. Not sin, of course: Irenaeus is clear that sin is, in fact, the only real evil. But I mean here the evils of mortal life, such as sickness, accidental physical harm, and ignorance. If death is in some way a remedial good, is everything associated with mortality also in some way a remedial good? Is the suffering occasioned by mortality, and the harm inflicted by personal sin, always willed by God as useful occasions of the struggles that cause us to grow? Are we to understand that there is some intrinsic good, some intrinsic usefulness, in the sufferings associated with mortality? Also, does it strain credibility to believe that, looking upon some of the evil perpetrated by free agents, sin is at its origin something analogous to the disobedience of children? Even such events as genocide? Here is where the complementary strength of the Augustinian system kicks in. There is no reason at all to regard any of these events as having any benefit, usefulness or any particle of good within them, and they do not seem, as evil, to reflect the mistakes of childlike creatures, but rather to point back to some primordial malice that is purely gratuitous and evil without remainder. In these events, we are not presented with lessons to be learned. We are seeing, as it were, the distant aftershocks, like the faint, cold X-rays of the Big Bang of evil. There is no need to find the "rationale" for this or that evil event in God's plan: there is none. Though foreseen, they are not part of the plan. Yet it is part and parcel of the victory of God in Christ that good can be drawn even from these evils without making them in any way good. Faith in Christ permits a patient endurance, or an active resistance, which is a virtue and that is, in fact, good.

But where Augustine gets fuzzy is with regard to suffering that does not seem so closely related to evil: athletic training and competition, and all that can be compared to it, including the athleticism of the martyrs, academic and artistic training, etc. Augustine looked back on his own education with loathing because of the disciplinary methods of the teachers, which he regarded (rightly, it would seem) as barbaric and understandable only as a form of evil dependent upon the fall. True learning would be almost effortless, like the way little children learn to speak without any formal training or discipline whatsoever. Perhaps there is an undeveloped hint here, in Book I of the *Confessions*, of a view of a kind of unfallen suffering. Likewise with regard to the labor that God enjoined on Adam and Eve before the fall, in tilling the garden. But all of this, for Augustine, would be accomplished with ease, without the hard labor that was the curse of Adam after the fall. Augustine does not seem to be able to imagine any kind of suffering that is real, but not the result of sin.

It's also important to keep these "paradigms" in mind when assessing spiritualities that we might be inclined to judge negatively if we see them as instances of the wrong paradigm. For instance, it is easy to find a text contoured by Augustine's paradigm of death and the suffering of mortality as "not good but able to be put to a good use," and "hear" it in Irenaeus's paradigm of "death as remedial and suffering as an occasion to grow." *The Little Flowers of St. Francis* (chapter 8) picture Francis telling Brother Leo that perfect joy is found in coming home after a long journey and being rejected, thrown out into the cold and mud as imposters and rogues, and yet bearing it patiently. One could "hear" this narrative, which operates in a basic Augustinian framework, as claiming that perfect joy is found in abusive treatment. Perfect joy is found, rather, in the faith in Christ that enables one to put the evil of such treatment to a good use. The other way around is also unhelpful. The *Way of a Pilgrim*, for example, is a nineteenth century Russian novel[12] about a crippled man who has lost everything, his wife, the use of his arm, his home and property, who learns the Jesus prayer of the heart, and decides to make a pilgrimage to Jerusalem. This is a story very much written in the Irenaean framework. But if it is read with Augustinian eyes, it looks like the author, who admires the literal step by step progress the pilgrim makes, is saying that the sort of thing Augustine calls suffering, unredeemable evil, is good for you in some way. In both cases of crossing the wires, so to speak, you end up with a masochistic spirituality that seems to promote self-destruction as a good, when that is not the intention of either way of thinking under its own steam.

But this kind of wire crossing is not the only way for the two strands of reflection to intertwine. For the strengths of each way of thinking can complement and help to fill out the fuzziness that each also exhibits. I

---

12. In *The Way of a Pilgrim: and The Pilgrim Continues His Way.*

would argue, without being able to demonstrate it here, that one example of the complementary intertwining of the strengths of each strand is in the *Rule* of St. Benedict, drawn as much from Eastern as from Augustinian sources. Benedict has the optimism of Irenaeus and the sense that one can provide, as he says, a "school for God's service,"[13] the monastery as a place where one can learn humility, justice and love. It will involve suffering, and this suffering is a form of training. And yet the *Rule* is equally formed in the Augustinian sense that no suffering of ours is ultimately a good simply as suffering, simply as *ours*, but only as Christ's, that is, as something which faith in Christ permits one to use but which would carry no utility or benefit that was not *tout court* tragic apart from this faith.

Another complementary intertwining of the two strands, and I believe self-consciously so, is in John Paul II's 1984 Apostolic Letter *Salvifici Doloris, On the Christian Meaning of Human Suffering*.[14] I believe it is a kind of a test case, an example of how to fulfill his injunction, already mentioned, to "let the Church breathe with both lungs" instead of playing them off against each other.

> Down through the centuries ... [he writes,] it has been seen that in suffering there is concealed a particular power that draws a person interiorly close to Christ, a special grace. . . . When this body is gravely ill, totally incapacitated, and the person is almost incapable of living and acting, all the more do interior maturity and spiritual greatness become evident, constituting a touching lesson to those who are healthy and normal. (sec. 26)

This is basically a thread from the theological fabric of St. Irenaeus. But we read, just a little later, that,

> Suffering is in itself an experience of evil. But Christ had made suffering the firmest basis of the definitive good, namely the good of eternal salvation. By his suffering on the Cross, Christ reached the very roots of evil, of sin and death. He conquered the author of evil, Satan, and his permanent rebellion against the Creator. To the suffering brother or sister Christ discloses and gradually reveals the horizons of the kingdom of God: the horizons of a world converted to the Creator, or a world free

13. Prologue, p. 45 in *The Rule of St. Benedict*, trans. Anthony C. Meisel and M. L. del Mastro (New York: Doubleday, 1975).

14. See www.vatican.va.

from sin, a world being built on the saving power of love. (sec. 26)

We can recognize in this the interweaving of the Augustinian strand, in which suffering is regarded as an experience, in itself, of evil, not of good. Yet, without turning it into an experience of good in itself, Christ enables it to be put to a good use, as the locus of a gradual discernment, to faith, of the only saving power there is in the world, that of God's self-emptying love. The "glory" hidden in the suffering of Christ, and in others who are not even believers, is not in this text a glory that can be understood independent of the love revealed in Christ's suffering, as though suffering on its own had any absolute value. Christ's suffering is redemptive not as suffering *per se* but as an act of solidarity and love, an "openness to every human suffering," and so an invitation to take up the Cross, not because it is suffering, but because it is Christ's. It is subsumed under the injunction to "Follow *me*!"

> For it is above all a call. It is a vocation . . . Gradually, as the individual takes up his cross, spiritually uniting himself to the cross of Christ, the salvific meaning of suffering is revealed before him. He does not discover this meaning at his own human level, but at the level of the suffering of Christ. (sec. 26)

In a passage like this we see the integration of the two strands of reflection. The idea of suffering as a kind of call or vocation is, on the one hand, related to the idea that suffering is part of what it means to be human, a way of life, and in that sense a good. It is a call to human greatness. That's Irenaeus. And yet the call or vocation is not in the first instance to suffer, but to follow Christ, that is, to be formed, through faith, in his love, to be open and attentive to all human suffering, to that of others, and to one's own both because attentiveness to the suffering of others will require suffering of one's own, and because in one's own suffering one is presented with a kind of internalized memory of the loving solidarity of Christ, awakening us to the full dimensions of the Kingdom of God.

Should we be surprised, in the end, that these two paradigms can in fact converge?

Conclusion

There is probably no greater cliché among historians of theology than that Augustine invented the doctrine of original sin, and so changed the paradigm of Christian thought regarding suffering and death. But our work here has located the natural point of convergence of the two theologies. Augustine's system is obviously Christocentric. But Irenaeus's system, for all its faith in human nature even after the fall, is nevertheless ultimately, and I would insist equally, Christocentric. Like Aeschylus, Irenaeus believes that suffering can bring wisdom, but unlike Aeschylus, it does so only because Christ has "summed up," or "recapitulated," as he puts it, all of human history, re-living every moment of it as it should have been lived by Adam, opting for obedience even under the horrific conditions which disobedience has produced, and so, after the fall, it is Christ who reveals that human nature can still struggle and grow; Christ, in a way, restores the form of human life as the possibility of struggle and growth. Irenaeus emphasizes that this is indeed an original human possibility; Augustine emphasizes that there is no such possibility except in Christ, and the possibility *is* Christ. Unlike Aeschylus where wisdom means humility in resignation to the will of the gods, in both Irenaeus and Augustine wisdom means humility in the acceptance of Christ's call to be formed according to his love, and so to seek out where appropriate, and otherwise to lovingly accept, the suffering, at once our own and others', which this inevitably will require.

BIBLIOGRAPHY

Aeschylus. "Agamemnon." In *The Complete Aeschylus*, vol. 1: *The Oresteia*. Edited by Peter Burian and Alan Shapiro, 44–105. New York: Oxford University Press, 2011.

Anonymous. *The Way of a Pilgrim: and The Pilgrim Continues His Way*. Translated by R. M. French. Reprint. San Francisco: HarperOne, 1991.

Augustine. *City of God*. Translated by Henry Bettenson. London: Penguin Classics, 2003.

Cavadini, John C. "Ambrose and Augustine de bono mortis." In *The Limits of Ancient Christianity*, edited by William Klingshirn and Mark Vessey, 232–49. Ann Arbor: University of Michigan Press, 1999.

Crouzel, Henri. *Origen*. Translated by A. S. Worrall. San Francisco: Harper and Row, 1989.

Hick, John. *Evil and the God of Love*. New York: Harper and Row, 1966.

Musurillo, Herbert. *The Acts of the Christian Martyrs*. Oxford: Clarendon Press, 1971.

Scott, Mark S. M. "Suffering and Soul-Making: Rethinking John Hick's Theodicy." *The Journal of Religion* 90 (2010) 313–34.

Weil, Simone. *Waiting for God*. New York: Harper Perennial Modern Classics, 2009.

Chapter 5

"O the wonder! What is this mystery which has happened to us?"

Death and Dying in the Orthodox Christian Tradition

MARCUS PLESTED

THIS ESSAY IS LARGELY structured around the liturgical materials associated with death and dying in the Orthodox Christian tradition. These materials provide a rich vein of discourse surrounding this inescapable theme of human life and reveal much of acute theological interest thereby conforming to the ancient principle: *lex orandi, lex credendi*. I shall begin with the most common liturgical form: the Orthodox funeral service for a layperson. The service is a theologically dense and sophisticated text partly authored by St. John of Damascus (and I quote principally from that portion in what immediately follows). I should note that it is normal and indeed expected for the coffin to be open in church during a liturgy (with the face of priests being veiled and monastics sown into their cassocks). This is a theological and liturgical culture that shuns any sort of denial of the gravity and reality of death. The funeral service consists not only in prayers for the departed—and these are certainly deemed efficacious—but also some sustained reflections on the nature of death and the experience of the recently departed who, strikingly, speaks on occasion in the first person in the course of the service. It is well worth quoting *in extenso*.

The Idiomels by Monk John, the Damascene[1]

As a flower withers and as a dream passes, so every human being is dissolved. But once again, at the sound of the trumpet, all the dead will arise as by an earthquake to go to meet you, Christ God. Then, Christ our Master, establish in the tents of your Saints the spirit of your servant whom you have taken over from us.

Alas, what an ordeal the soul endures once separated from the body! Alas, what tears then, and there is none to pity her! She turns towards the Angels, her entreaty is without effect; she stretches out her hands to men, she has none to help. Therefore my dear brethren, thinking on the shortness of our life, let us ask of Christ rest for him who has passed over, and for ourselves his great mercy.

Everything human which does not survive death is vanity; wealth does not last, glory does not travel with us; for at death's approach all of them disappear; and so let us cry out to Christ the Immortal one: Give rest to him who has passed from us, in the dwelling of all those who rejoice.

Truly most fearful is the mystery of death, how the soul is forcibly parted from the body, from its frame, and how that most natural bond of union is cut off by the will of God. Therefore we entreat you: Give rest in the tents of your just ones, him/her who has passed over, O Giver of life, Lover of mankind.

Having fashioned man in the beginning in your image and likeness, you placed him in Paradise to govern your creatures; but led astray by the envy of the devil he tasted the food and became a transgressor of your commandments; and so you condemned him, O Lord, to return again to the earth from which he had been taken, and to beg for rest.

---

1. The translation is by Archimandrite Ephrem Lash who died on the Ides of March, 2016. I should like to dedicate this paper to his memory. The translation was hosted at anastasis.org.uk. At time of writing (September 2016) this was still accessible in archive form. Fr Ephrem was, I am told, working on a new translation of the funeral service at the time of his death.

I grieve and lament when I contemplate death, and see the beauty fashioned for us in God's image lying in the graves, without form, without glory, without shape. O the wonder! What is this mystery which has happened to us? How have we been handed over to corruption, and yoked with death? Truly it is at God's command, as it is written, God who grants rest to him who has passed over.

Death is unambiguously a tragedy consequent upon the fall. It is a violent and unnatural sundering of the soul from the body. At the same time it is permitted by command of God to serve as a vehicle for our translation to eternal life. It is a wonder, a mystery—even a sacrament. The final kiss is perhaps the most poignant part of the funeral service—the point at which all those present come up and kiss the body of the departed—usually making a full prostration to the ground before doing so.

What is this parting, O brethren? What the grieving, what the lamentation in this present instant? Come then, kiss him/her who a moment ago was with us; he/she is being entrusted to a grave, covered by a stone, left to dwell in darkness, buried with the dead; all we his/her relatives and friends as we are now being parted, let us pray that the Lord will give him/her rest.

What is our life? Merely a flower, a vapour and morning dew. Come then, let us look closely at the graves; where is the body's beauty? Where its youth? Where are the eyes and the form of the flesh? All have withered like grass, all have vanished; come, let us fall down before Christ with tears.

Great the weeping and lamentation, great the sighing and constraint at the parting of the soul; Hell and destruction, the life of transitory things, the insubstantial shadow, the sleep of error, the untimely fancied toil of earthly life. Let us fly far from every worldly sin that we may inherit the things of heaven.

As we look on one who lies dead let us accept this expression of the final moment; for he/she passes like smoke from the earth, he/she blossomed like a flower, was cut down like grass, is wrapped in a winding sheet, hidden in earth. When we have left him/her out of sight, let us pray to Christ to give him/her rest for ever.

Come, offspring of Adam, let us look at one in our image who has been laid in earth, who has discarded all his/her beauty, been dissolved in a grave by the rottenness of worms, wasted by darkness, hidden in earth. When we have left him/her out of sight, let us pray to Christ to give him/her rest for ever.

When the soul is about to be snatched by force from the body by fearsome Angels, it forgets relatives and friends and its concern is for its stand at the coming trial of vanity and much wearied flesh. Come, let us all beseech the Judge and pray that the Lord pardon all that he/she has done.

Now all the body's organs are idle, that a little while ago were active; all useless, dead, insensible; for eyes are dimmed, feet bound, hands lie still and hearing with them, tongue is locked in silence, is entrusted to a grave; truly everything human is vanity.

Towards the end the ceremony of the final kiss, the departed soul herself speaks:

As you see me lying without voice and without breath, all weep for me, brothers and friends, relatives and acquaintances; for only yesterday I was talking with you, and suddenly the dread hour of death came upon me. But come, all who loved me, and kiss me for the last time; for I shall not walk with you again, nor speak with you anymore; because I am on my way to the Judge, with whom there is no respect of persons; for slave and master stand alike before him, king and soldier, rich and poor, with the same rank; for each will be glorified or shamed in accordance with their own deeds. But I ask and implore you all, pray for me without ceasing to Christ God, that I may not be condemned because of my sins to the place of torment, but that he will establish me in the place of the light of life.

It is difficult to unpick all the theological elements of this immensely rich service. Much of it is, of course, directed at the edification of the living. One may note especially the reverence paid to the body even as it sinks into decay and corruption. This is God's vestigial image still even as it lies in the grave "without form, without glory, without shape." Man is the beauty and the glory and the cosmos but has through the fall become subject to the grave, doomed to rot: "The beauty of the face has rotted and death has withered all the flower of youth." He has become subject to the violent wrenching of the soul from the body—a painful but necessary part of his birth into new life (or, as the case may be, eternal torment). The reverence for the body and the hope of the bodily resurrection preclude cremation. Cremation as an act of wilful violence upon the body created in the image of God is, at most, permitted by concession to the principle of economy.

Without pretending that all of these elements come through to the attendees at a given funeral (and note that the service is often—especially in Greek Churches—celebrated in truncated form)—there is much that will necessarily make an impact even to the casual observer or the non-believer. The powerful presence of the departed in the open coffin, the reverence paid to the body—by incense, prostrations, and the last kiss—can hardly be ignored. Growing up in the Orthodox Church, a child will almost always see several dead bodies being venerated in this way—and this cannot fail to make an impression. At the same time it is evident that the body in the coffin is an empty vessel—life, the soul, having departed from it. This frank encounter with death and the dead even from childhood strikes me as profoundly salutary. And death, as I say, is presented unambiguously a tragedy and one which shows up the vanity of our earthly preoccupations. As the funeral service puts it: "Now the whole wretched festival of life's vanity is being dissolved; for the spirit has left its dwelling, the clay has turned black, the vessel has been broken, without voice, without sensation, without movement." But yet in all this darkness and tragedy there is always the hope of resurrection to eternal glory and a place in the place of the eternal light.

Other liturgical offices round out the Orthodox approach to death and dying, for instance the anointing service corresponding to the Latin rite of extreme unction but offered, in the Orthodox tradition, to anyone suffering sickness ("for the healing of soul and body") and indeed offered to all the faithful in Holy Week in the Greek tradition. Prior to the funeral office there is also an office to be said at the parting of the soul from the body. And after the funeral, one must take account of the memorial services that are such an inescapable feature—even an obsession—in Orthodox life and thought. These are to be celebrated in principle on the third, ninth, and fortieth day after death and then again at each year's mind. In these services further prayers are said for the forgiveness of sins and God—in the declamation "Eternal Memory!"—is entreated to remember the soul of the departed in his Kingdom.

Death of course is not only a theme addressed in the services specifically relating to death. It is a prominent theme in the services of Great

Lent—for instance in the Great Canon of St. Andrew of Crete that is appointed for the first week of Lent. A typical text from this great song of repentance, for example, exhorts us: "Turn back, wretched soul, and lament, before the fairground of life comes to an end, before the Lord shuts the door of the bridechamber." Similarly: "The time of my life is short, filled with trouble and evil. But accept me in repentance and call me back to knowledge. Let me not become the possession and food of the enemy; but do thou, O Saviour, take pity upon me." And finally: "My soul, O my soul, rise up! Why art thou sleeping? The end draws near, and soon shalt thou be troubled. Watch, then, that Christ our God may spare thee, for he is everywhere present and fills all things."

Much, I think, can also be gleaned as to the Orthodox approach to the mystery of death in the various customs surrounding death. It is, for instance, customary not to leave the body of the departed alone but to keep it company throughout the night preceding the funeral—with the Psalter being read over laypeople and the Gospels over departed clergy. The idea of leaving the "loved one" alone in some funeral parlor is quite horrifying for many Orthodox. Equally, any suggestion that a funeral can be some sort of celebration of life is foreign to the very acute and visceral Orthodox sense of the utter catastrophe that is death—the wailing, mourning, and ululation that accompany death in many traditionally Orthodox cultures belies this particular manifestation of the Western incapacity to deal with death. Customs surrounding the translation of bones (especially in Mediterranean and Middle Eastern Contexts) are also deeply revealing as to the Orthodox approach to death. In Greece, for example, bones are typically dug up after three or more years, washed with wine, and reverently installed in an ossuary.

Of course there is a vast deal more that can be said about the Orthodox approach to death and dying. We might think of the vivid and regular references to death in the ascetic and hagiographical literature that forms such a staple part of the reading of the devout Orthodox Christian. Abba Sisoes is a prime instance:

> It was said of Abba Sisoes that when he was at the point of death, while the Fathers were sitting beside him, his face shone like the sun. He said to them, "Look, Abba Anthony is coming." A little later he said, "Look, the choir of prophets is coming." Again his countenance shone with brightness and he said, "Look, the choir of apostles is coming." His countenance increased in brightness and lo, he spoke with someone. Then the old men asked him,

"With whom are you speaking, Father?" He said, "Look, the angels are coming to fetch me, and I am begging them to let me do a little penance." The old men said to him, "You have no need to do penance, Father." But the old man said to them, "Truly, I do not think I have even begun to repent."[2]

Abba Sisoes is also said to have come across the tomb and bones of the Great Alexander, sometime ruler of the greater part of the known world. The inscription to the much-copied icon has the astonished Sisoes exclaim:

The mere sight of you, tomb, dismays me and causes my heart to shed tears, as I contemplate the debt we, all men, owe. How can I possibly stand it? Oh, death! Who can evade you?

The *Sayings of the Desert Fathers* contain many examples of the permeable boundary between the living and the dead in this literature. One striking example has St. Macarius of Egypt strike up a conversation with a skull by the side of the road. The skull turns out to have been a pagan priest in the vicinity now languishing in hell. Naturally curious, Macarius asks what hell is like and receives this reply:

As far as the sky is removed from the earth, so great is the fire beneath us; we are ourselves standing in the midst of the fire, from the feet up to the head. It is not possible to see anyone face to face, but the face of one is fixed to the back of another. Yet when you pray for us, each of us can see the other's face a little. Such is our respite.[3]

Moved to tears. Macarius buries the skull. The Anglican writer Charles Williams seems to me to preserve something of this same sense of the permeable boundary between the living and the dead, for instance in his *All Hallows' Eve*. It is only some distance into this work that one realises that the main characters are, in fact, dead.

There is, similarly, no separation between the Church militant and the Church triumphant for the Orthodox. One of the striking things about an Athonite Church or *katholikon* is the way in which the monks and laymen installed in the seats lining the walls of the church form part of the iconography of the building. The serried ranks of the Church triumphant give way to the figures—standing, sitting, or snoozing—of the

2. *Sayings of the Desert Fathers*, Sisoes 14, translation lightly adapted.
3. *Sayings of the Desert Fathers*, Macarius 18.

Church militant. Whatever the spiritual alertness of the occupants of the stalls, the point is quite clear: we belong even now, in this life, to the communion of the saints, to the Church of the *eschaton*.

This is principle of unity is also evident in the service of preparation preceding the Divine Liturgy (the *proskomidia*). In this service the living and the dead are remembered at the liturgy through the process of removing particles of bread from a loaf set aside for this purpose. Particles representing the living are taken from the top of the loaf and those representing the dead from the bottom of the loaf—but it is the same undivided loaf. There is, it must be allowed, some speculation as to the nature of the soul's journey after death—and here I think of the image of the heavenly tollbooths. But such speculations remain in practice more the province of folklore rather than Church doctrine. Generally speaking, the Orthodox are reticent about the precise nature of the afterlife—we have nothing quite like C. S. Lewis's *The Great Divorce* and even that brilliant work only pretended to sketch the lineaments of the outer threshold of heaven. The Orthodox Church has also traditionally found the very idea of purgatory as an intermediate place or state problematic and has tended to favour a healthy reticence or agnosticism when it comes to the fate of the soul after death.

Much more can of course be said about the Orthodox approach to death and dying but I believe these thoughts, drawn largely from the liturgical tradition, give us a reasonable insight into the Orthodox practice of death. This is a culture in which death is not denied, or shut away, or sidelined, but confronted head-on in all its appalling wonder and hideous mystery. Death is a grim and inescapable reality but we will only defeat it if we confront it—and confront it in full confession and acknowledgment of the ultimate historical fact of the Resurrection. While death looms large in the Orthodox consciousness it is of course swallowed up by the light and joy of the resurrection. This comes over very well in the sermon attributed to St. John Chrysostom and read at the service of Easter night:

> Let no one fear death, for the Saviour's death has set us free. He that was held prisoner of it has annihilated it. By descending into Hell, He made Hell captive. He embittered it when it tasted of His flesh. And Isaiah, foretelling this, did cry: Hell, said he, was embittered, when it encountered Thee in the lower regions (cf. Isaiah 14:9 LXX). It was embittered, for it was abolished. It was embittered, for it was mocked. It was embittered, for it was slain. It was embittered, for it was overthrown. It was embittered, for it

was fettered in chains. It took a body, and met God face to face. It took earth, and encountered Heaven. It took that which was seen, and fell upon the unseen.

O Death, where is your sting? O Hell, where is your victory? (cf. 1 Cor 15:55). Christ is risen, and you are overthrown. Christ is risen, and the demons are fallen. Christ is risen, and the angels rejoice. Christ is risen, and life reigns. Christ is risen, and not one dead remains in the grave. For Christ, being risen from the dead, is become the first fruits of those who have fallen asleep. To Him be glory and dominion unto ages of ages. Amen.[4]

If we are to truly live we must confront death. Death must become, as it were, part of our life. In the Church—to borrow from Heraclitus— we live each other's death and die each other's life. But death is always construed and indeed overcome in the light of the resurrection. This I think is the essential message of the Orthodox tradition in relation to the mystery of death and dying.

BIBLIOGRAPHY

Chrysostom, John. "The Paschal Sermon." Widely available online for example at https://oca.org/fs/sermons/the-paschal-sermon.

The Sayings of the Desert Fathers: The Alphabetical Collection. Translated by Benedicta Ward. Kalamazoo: Cistercian Publications, 1975.

4. See Chrysostom, "The Paschal Sermon." The Sermon is read at the end of Paschal Matins and before the commencement of the Paschal liturgy.

Chapter 6

The Father's Vindication of the Word

Mark A. McIntosh

THE DYING AND RISING of Christ grounds and constitutes the Christian understanding of death and its meaning for our future. In this paper, I want to offer a thought experiment: thinking through the meaning for our dying of Christ's death and resurrection, and doing so through the conceptuality of the divine ideas tradition in the history of Christian theology and spirituality. I believe that this once ubiquitous tradition in fact affords us a rich resource for faith's desire to understand something of how the Father raises Jesus from the dead and why that resurrection is the beginning of our own.

At its fundamental level, the divine ideas tradition holds that in the same eternal act of self-knowing by which the Father eternally begets the Son (to use the creedal language), the Father also knows (and, in the Holy Spirit, wills) all the particular forms by which the creatures-to-be will come to exist in time. On other occasions, I would argue that the relative obscurity of the divine ideas tradition—at least in contemporary Western theology—diminishes our theological awareness of this crucially Trinitarian dimension at the ground of all creatures: namely that all creatures come to share in existence precisely in and through the free and intelligent relational love that is the Trinitarian life of God. Thomas Aquinas had of course felt it important to underscore the importance of this Trinitarian dimension because, he said, it is

> necessary for the right idea of creation . . . The fact of saying that
> God made all things by his Word excludes the error of those

who say that God produced things by necessity. [And] when we
say that in him there is a procession of Love we show that God
produced creatures not because he needed them, nor because
of any extrinsic reason, but on account of the love of his own
goodness.[1]

God creates the universe in freedom, intelligence, and love; this characterization of the inner Trinitarian life of God, i.e., the very fact that
God is the blessed Trinity, is in Thomas's view what governs adequate
speech about the creatures. Theology can and should regard and respect
the loving and lovable gratuity at the heart of all creatures because it is
the echo within them of this loving freedom of their Author. What the
divine ideas tradition serves to do, in an instance such as this, is to help
us contemplate precisely this crucial nexus between the creatures, in all
their particularity and vulnerable cherishability in time, *and* the eternal
activity of knowing and loving by which God is God and in virtue of
which the creatures have their existence.

As further adumbration of this point, one might consider Augustine's deployment of the "artisan's design" trope (also found in the *Ti-
maeus*, Philo, Origen, Anselm, and Aquinas, among others) in order to
consider the nature of creaturely existence. Commenting on John 1:4
("What has come into being through him, in him was life") Augustine
writes:

> A carpenter makes a box. First he has the box in design; for if he
> had it not in design, how could he produce it by workmanship?
> But the box in theory is not the very box as it appears to the eyes.
> . . . Behold, it is made in the work; has it ceased to exist in de-
> sign? The one is made in the work, and the other remains which
> exists in design . . . The actual box is not life, the box in design
> is life; because the soul of the artificer, where all these things are
> before they are brought forth, is living. So, dearly beloved breth-
> ren, because the Wisdom of God, by which all things have been
> made, contains everything according to design before it is made,
> therefore those things which are made through this design itself
> are not. . . life, but whatever has been made is life in Him.[2]

---

1. Thomas Aquinas, *Summa theologica* [*ST*] I, q. 32, a. 1 ad. 3. All references to
the *Summa theologiae*, unless otherwise indicated, will be from the translation of the
Fathers of the English Dominican Province, and will be cited parenthetically in the
text.

2. Augustine, *Homilies on the Gospel according to John*, 12.

Here we can see Augustine working hard to explain the analogical or dependent form of existence enjoyed by the creatures in time as compared with their existence in the mind of their author. Augustine highlights the living quality of the artisan's mind, continually capable in its living creativity of conceiving the archetypes by which the box will come to exist in wood or leather or brass; it is this very creative life of the thinking mind of the maker that grounds the analogous "life" or existence of the particular box in time; and it's important to see that this living quality of the artisan's *idea* of the box is not meant to denigrate the existence of the box in time but, rather, both grounds its existence and, importantly, is thus the means of its renewal and renovation should it fall into ruin, "for that box may rot, and another be fashioned according to that which exists in design."[3] By comparison with the living, creative idea in the mind of the maker, the existence of the box in time is limited and ephemeral. Yet its re-fashioning in time is nonetheless possible precisely in virtue of the living and expressive form of existence of the archetypal idea of the box as the artisan knows it can and should exist in its fullness.

Augustine's great interpreter, Anselm of Canterbury, illustrates this same theme in the *Monologion*. Asking his monks to consider the relative reality of the creatures and the Word in whom and through whom they exist, Anselm cleverly coaxes out into the open the likely misapprehension at work in their thinking. We're used to the way ideas of things we've seen in the world exist in our minds as a kind of imitation of those things, but, he asks, "What about the Word which says everything and through which everything was made?" Surely we don't think the truth of things in the Word by whom they are spoken into existence is only a kind of imitation of a passing, mutable reality, for then the Word would not be "consubstantial with supreme immutability," and that is not true. But neither do we want to say that the Word doesn't contain the truth of things, for then the "Word of the supreme truth" wouldn't be altogether true, "which is absurd." Anselm then leads his students out of the puzzle by suggesting the example of a living human being, and the painting that is his or her likeness:

> The truth of a human being is said to exist in a living human being, whereas in a painted one there is the likeness or image of that truth. In the same way, the truth of existing is understood to be in the Word, whose essence exists so supremely that in a

3. Ibid.

certain sense it alone exists, whereas in the things that by comparison with him in a certain sense do not exist, and yet have
been made something through him and in accordance with
him, there is judged to be an imitation of that supreme essence.[4]
(*Monologion* 31)

Thus Anselm wants us to recognize that our habitual experience—we see
and know things because they are—needs to be reversed in order for analogical reasoning in theology to work: things are only *because* God knows
them; i.e., it is not that the Word, the eternal knowing of God, reflects the
things that are, but rather that they come to be and are reflections in time
only in virtue of the fact that God knows them eternally.

Anselm's position highlights a couple of points that are particularly
helpful to bear in mind. The first is simply that we do, as fallen creatures,
tend nearly incorrigibly (and often without realizing it) to make our own
present experience of existence the norm or measure of existence per se.
Hence Anselm asks us to consider that what we think of as ourselves is
more like a portrait or image painted onto the canvass of time, reflecting the archetype in whose image we exist. The Renaissance theologian
and philosopher Marsilio Ficino captures this tendency of ours very well
when he advises a friend who feels uncertain about his course in life:

> Seek yourself beyond the world . . . You believe yourself to be in
> the abyss of this world simply because you do not discern your-
> self flying above the heavens, but see your shadow, the body, in
> the abyss. It is as if a boy leaning over a well were to imagine
> himself at the bottom, although it is only his shadow he sees
> reflected there, until he turns back to himself.[5]

Mesmerized by our shadow-image in time, we find it hard to recall and
recognize the true and vibrant reality of our identity and calling as that is
always present in the divine knowing and loving of the Trinity.

Or, put another way: "seek the things that are above, where Christ is,
seated at the right hand of God. Set your minds on things that are above,
not on things that are on earth, for you have died, and your life is hidden
with Christ in God" (Col 3:1–3). Throughout the Pauline literature, we
see this common assertion, that the self we have been led by sin into accepting—asserting it against others and suffering self-undoing through
its idolatries—is the self that, in our baptism, has died with Christ. It is a

---

4. Anselm of Canterbury, *Monologion* 31, p. 50.

5. Ficino, *Letters*, vol. 1, Letter 110, p. 165–66.

self shaped by our mortal life, by our biology and our culture and by all the vitiations that sin has inflicted so stuntingly upon this self—the most fundamental of which being our hypnotic belief that it is really and exclusively the whole truth of who we are. The divine ideas tradition helps us to see how and why the world's mendacious grip on our identity, undone in Christ's death, could never have been the authoritative truth of us, which flows exclusively through the life-giving self-sharing of the Trinity.

In the history of Christian mystical thought we note how often these teachers point to what should have been our natural, contemplative instinct as intelligent creatures—namely to refer our present experience of all things (including ourselves) to the expansive, liberating, and authoritative truth of all things in the Word. Perhaps seeking to inspire our emulation of the contemplative habits of the angels, Augustine beautifully describes their wondering gaze during the unfolding of creation, turning from the relatively faint and shadowy realization of creaturely existence in time to the full bright vivacity of the creatures' reality in the Word:

> The holy angels, whose equals we shall be after the resurrection, if to the end we hold to Christ our Way, always behold the face of God and rejoice in His Word, the only-begotten Son, equal to the Father; and in them first of all wisdom was created. They, therefore, without any doubt know all creation, of which they are the creatures first made, and they have this knowledge first in the Word of God Himself, in whom are the eternal reasons of all things made in time, existing in Him through whom all things have been created. And they have this knowledge in creation itself, as they look down upon it and refer it to the praise of Him in whose immutable truth they behold, as in the source of all creation, the reasons by which creatures have been made. There the knowledge they have is like day, and so that blessed company, perfectly united by participation in the same Truth, is the day first created; here among creatures their knowledge is like evening. But immediately morning comes (and this happens on all six days), because the knowledge angels have does not remain fixed in a creature without their immediately referring it to the praise and love of Him in whom they know not the fact, but the reason, of its creation.[6]

In this remarkable passage, time itself seems to be the reflection of this contemplative turning of the angels—from the "vesperal" mortal existence of things to their full vivacity and ever-dawning freshness in the

6. Augustine, *Literal Meaning of Genesis*, IV.24.41, p. 132.

Word. Perhaps in this sense temporal rhythms have at their deep ground this contemplative relinquishment and accession: the offering and renunciation of the transitory mortal expression of all things as the prelude to praise and rejoicing over their full consummation in God.

Did space permit, one might consider whether this relinquishment of one form of reality for the joyful accession to its accomplished fullness might turn out to be a particularly helpful frame for thinking about the meaning of Christian dying. Could the contemplative pattern of relinquishment for the sake of accession to yet greater reality perhaps be seen as the echoing, within daily life, of that pattern which must be the rhythm at the heart of all dying and rising, both Christ's and humanity's? "Very truly I tell you, unless a grain of wheat fall into the earth and dies, it remains just a single grain; but if it dies, it bears much fruit" (John 12:24).

But now I want to turn to the second, more positive side of Anselm's lesson. The negative aspect is our fallen tendency to remain stuck in the mortal version of ourselves that sin teaches us to believe is all there is (threatening thus to vitiate the *genuine* goodness of our mortal material existence by idolizing it instead of revering its authentic beauty as icon). The positive point is that, as we've just seen with Augustine's angels, a glimpse of—and better yet a life-long fidelity to—the Word who bears within himself the full truth of our existence can be liberating and life-giving. As Athanasius had said long before Anselm, if the creaturely portrait has been distorted and ruined, the original sitter would need to return to renew the image with its full, unvanquishable truth.[7] Few Christian teachers have expressed this urgent hope more clearly than Maximus the Confessor, whose costly witness to the full sharing of Christ in our humanity underscores the seriousness of his words. Commenting on Col 1:15–17, Maximus speaks of how the echoes of the *Logos* can be discerned contemplatively, heard as the *logoi* of creation. But then he adds that this is equally and crucially true for human persons, who need to re-discover the truth of the particular echo of the *Logos* that we each are:

> Because he [the *Logos*] held together in himself the *logoi* before they came to be . . . [s]urely then, if someone is moved according to the *Logos*, he will come to be in God, in whom the *logos* of his being pre-exists as his beginning and his cause . . . By drawing on wisdom and reason and by appropriate movement he lays hold of his proper beginning and cause. For there is no end

7. Athanasius, *On the Incarnation*, §14, pp. 41–42.

toward which he can be moved, nor is he moved in any other
way than toward his beginning, that is, he ascends to the *Logos*
by whom he was created and in whom all things will ultimately
be restored.[8]

This fidelity to Christ, worked out through one's mortal life, says Maximus, is in fact the precursor to full ascent and union with him, and in him with the ultimate truth of oneself as that is eternally known and loved by God. The mystical journey of ascesis and contemplation ascends through God's speaking of the truth within the creatures, and thence to God's speaking the truth of the creatures themselves—eternally in God. And at the risk of getting ahead of myself, of course this union with Christ is ultimately only achieved by dying to the old sinful self by sharing in Christ's dying, so that, as Paul says, we might also "be united with him in a resurrection like his" (Rom 6:5).

Now we come to a crucial step in the thought experiment I'm proposing: so far we've considered how, in the divine ideas tradition, God's eternal knowing of the creatures in the Word is the very ground of their existence in time and, in a certain way, the imperishable and perfect truth of what they each have it in them to be—a truth that, necessarily because they *are* creatures, we must arrive at through the adventure of an earthly life. But how is all this connected to the death and resurrection of Christ, and thus to our understanding of Christian dying? They are linked, as of course you'll have guessed by now, by the fact that this creative knowing of the creatures takes place as the eternal activity of the Father's self-knowing in the Son or Word, and as the Son or Word's perfect expression of all that the Father is, and in that eternal event of mutual love and delight whom we call God the Holy Spirit. And these eternal processions have their expression in time in the earthly missions of the Son and the Spirit, that is, in the paschal mystery and Pentecost.

In other words, the eternally perfect expression of the Father in the Word (and of course the imperishable truth of all creatures therein), is manifest in our world as the Incarnation of the Word and his earthly ministry—and this is why Jesus holds such compelling authority among us, for he bears within himself the deep truth of everyone. One could perhaps go on, at another time, to consider how so many of Jesus' actions in the earthly ministry of his mortal life do indeed seem to restore within creatures some fresh spring of that deep, unstinting truth of them

8. Maximus the Confessor, *Cosmic Mystery*, Ambiguum 7, pp. 54–56.

in God's knowledge and purposes for them. Loaves and fishes become miraculously imbued with a primal fullness and abundance; men, women, and children are recovered into the wholeness of their identity and life. By bearing the creatures up into the self-giving generosity of his life, Jesus seems able to release within them the fullness of their meaning, the divine idea of them, that lives imperishably in the Word's eternal expression of the Father—which, I am arguing, is represented in our world as the Incarnation of the Word made flesh.

The Orthodox theologian Olivier Clément expresses well this profound sense in which Christ restores their own agency and truth to the creatures by uniting them through his self-offering with their deep truth in God:

> The incarnate *Logos* frees the speechless tongue of creation.
> . . . Christ has become the direct divine-human subject of the
> cosmic *logoi*. He confers on them their deepest meaning, their
> paschal nature, the power of the resurrection to work in them.
> He reveals their root in the abyss of the three-Personed God.[9]

Clément here points to the paschal dimension within all of Christ's ministry, expressing as it does the self-donation at the heart of his life, consummated in his death, and expressing within our world the inexhaustible self-giving of the Trinity. As Jesus takes the world to himself, he draws it into his paschal mystery, and that of course means that the mortal, biological, and world-constructed "truth" of things will die in Christ's death; it also means that, just as in his earthly ministry Jesus was able to renew within creatures their deep truth in God, so infinitely more profoundly Jesus in his resurrection is able to *re-create* the imperishable truth of the creatures—precisely in and with the Father's raising of Christ into the eternal truth of his generation as the Father's Word.

For Aquinas, the Word's eternal and perfect expression of the Father is the very basis of truth itself. For in the case of God, says Thomas, "his being is not only conformed to his intellect, but it is the very act of his intellect; and his act of understanding is the measure and cause of every other being and every other intellect . . . Whence it follows not only that the truth is in him, but that he is truth itself, and the sovereign and first truth" (*ST* I.16.5). God is truth, in other words, precisely because the eternal event of knowing and delighted recognition, of the eternal begetting of the Word and spiration of the Spirit, is the very life

9. Clément, *Roots of Christian Mysticism*, 216.

of God—and that life is coincident with the eternal event of Truth, its "sovereign" occasion and ground of whatsoever truths there could be. It's crucial for the argument I'm making that we see that Truth is thus, for Thomas, not only or merely a divine attribute, but flows directly from the eternal Trinitarian "event" by which God is God, namely, *the Father's recognition of the Word's perfect imaging of God in the joy of their Spirit.* And this eternal event, I'm suggesting, is made present in our world in and through the resurrection of Jesus, by which the Father vindicates the truth and identity of his beloved Child, overturning the false finality of death as the world's last "word" about Jesus and his mission.

In the world we have made, the mortal expression of the creatures falls into ruin and is distorted by lies and every kind of mistruth; Jesus the Word incarnate, Christians believe, willingly accepts to enter into this condition, falling under the cruel mendacity of those who insisted that he was dangerous and a blasphemer and, ultimately, accursed by God—and all this was apparently confirmed definitively by his subjection to death. That would seem to be the last word and the ultimate truth about him, the final determination of his meaning. The resurrection, I am arguing, is nothing less that the expression within this sinful situation of the Father's eternal recognition of his beloved Child as the Truth itself, the true Word and meaning of God's very existence as self-giving love. And, following Thomas, because this inexhaustible truth is the very life of God, it is of course infinitely stronger than death. The resurrection of Jesus, the True Word of the Father, is also the making present within our world of that imperishable truth of all creatures as they exist within God's knowing and loving of them. As Thomas says at *ST* I.37.2 *ad.* 3:

> As the Father speaks himself and every creature by his begotten
> Word, inasmuch as the Word begotten adequately represents the
> Father and every creature; so he loves himself and every creature
> by the Holy Spirit, inasmuch as the Holy Spirit proceeds as the
> love of the primal goodness whereby the Father loves himself
> and every creature.

Thus, I have argued, the divine ideas tradition offers theology a way by which faith might come to some preliminary understanding regarding the efficacy of Christ's resurrection for the whole creation. Christians believe that dying with Christ, they also live with him. I have suggested in this essay how this being crucified with Christ might indeed be a relinquishment of the good and lovely iconic biological body, and also a surrendering of its state of ensnarement within the toils of the world's mistruths about us all—from idolatry to racism and every kind of xenophobia and bigotry—so that God's imperishable and inexhaustible truth of each beloved creature, as it really is, and as it has been cherished eternally in the Spirit's joy at the Word's perfect imaging, might spring forth as the new creation, of which the risen Christ is the first fruit.

BIBLIOGRAPHY

Anselm of Canterbury. *Monologion and Proslogion, with the Replies of Gaunilo and Anselm*. Translated by Thomas Williams. Indianapolis: Hackett, 1995.

Athanasius. *On the Incarnation*. Translated by a religious of C.S.M.V. Crestwood, NY: St. Vladimir's, 1996.

Augustine. *Homilies on the Gospel according to John*. Translated by John Gibb and James Innes. In *The Nicene and Post-Nicene Father*, First Series, vol. 5, 7–452. Edited by Philip Schaff. Grand Rapids: Eerdmans, 1986.

———. *The Literal Meaning of Genesis*, vol. 1. Translated by John Hammond Taylor. Ancient Christian Writers. New York: Paulist, 1982.

Clément, Olivier. *The Roots of Christian Mysticism*. Translated by Theodore Berkeley. New York: New City, 1995.

Ficino, Marsilio. *The Letters of Marsilio Ficino*, vol. 1. Translated by Members of the Language Department of the School of Economic Science, London. London: Shepheard-Walwyn, 1975.

Maximus the Confessor. *On the Cosmic Mystery of Jesus Christ: Selected Writings from St Maximus the Confessor*. Translated by Paul M. Blowers and Robert Louis Wilken. Crestwood, NY: St. Vladimir's, 2003.

Thomas Aquinas. *Summa theologica*. Translated by the Fathers of the English Dominican Province. 2nd rev. ed. Reprint ed. in 5 vols. Westminster, MD: Christian Classics, 1981.

Chapter 7

Dying for the Last Time
Martin Luther on Christian Death[1]

DAVID LUY

MARTIN LUTHER WRITES OFTEN about the topic of Christian dying. At various points in his career, for instance, Luther composes texts, which supply pastoral counsel to Christians confronted with their own impending death, or the death of someone within their immediate sphere of experience.[2] A well-known example occurs in his "Sermon on Preparing to Die," composed in 1519. In this sermon, Luther recommends a variety of strategies to the dying Christian, each of which is designed to guard against fear, doubt and despair through an intentional and persistent contemplation of Christ, the One who conquers sin and death. From the vantage point of this sermon, the prospect of "preparing to die" may seem to apply for Luther only to a narrowly circumscribed segment of the Christian's life; namely, that penultimate period of time in which death is experienced as imminent.[3] Within such a circumscription, the Christian's

---

1. I am grateful to Ron Rittgers, Alex Pierce and the members of the Deerfield Dialogue Group for helpful feedback on an earlier draft of this essay.

2. See, for instance, Leroux, *Martin Luther As Comforter.* Leroux provides a thorough examination of these writings, calling special attention to Luther's use of rhetorical skill in addressing the topic of death.

3. Even within this sermon, Luther encourages his readership to reflect upon death well in advance of its drawing near. *Luther's Works* [LW] 42.102.

salient concern is a fairly restricted one: Will the existential posture in which she dies be one of faith turned outward or despair turned inward?

There can be no denial of the fact that Luther regards this specific question as a vitally important one, but does it encapsulate the sum of what he thinks it means for the Christian to prepare for death? A broader survey of the theme of dying within Luther's other writings suggests not, for he is often wont to insist upon a much broader frame of reference. "[T]he life of a Christian," Luther states in 1519, "from baptism to the grave, is nothing less than the beginning of a holy death."[4] Within this more expansive framework, the Christian's "preparation for death" consists only derivatively in the remedial application of bedside counsel.[5] The true preparation for death is rather to be located in the purgative rigors, which are natively entailed by the indelible, baptismal shape of the Christian life. In short, to live the Christian life well is essentially what it means, on Luther's understanding, to prepare rightly for death.[6]

It is the intent of this essay to specify the particular sense in which Luther regards this to be so. In what precise way does Christian *living* prepare one for Christian *dying*?[7] Naturally, the answer depends entire-

4. Luther, "The Holy and Blessed Sacrament of Baptism," trans. Dirk G. Lange, in *The Annotated Luther*, vol. 1, *The Roots of Reform*, ed. Timothy J. Wengert (Minneapolis: Fortress, 2015), 209. This edition of translated texts will hereafter be referred to as "TAL I." Luther's sermon on baptism appeared in print in November of 1519 (n.b. the same month and year in which Luther published the aforementioned "Sermon on Preparing to Die").

5. For other instances of this broader claim (i.e., the Christian life is the essential preparation for Christian death), see ibid., 218–19. See also "The Blessed Sacrament of the Holy and True Body of Christ, and the Brotherhoods", in TAL I, 247–48; and *Treatise on Good Works*, in TAL I, 327 and 335.

6. Another oft-cited instance of this theme of "living in view of death" surfaces in Luther's so-called "Invocavit sermons" of 1522, preached soon after his return to Wittenberg from a period of isolation at Wartburg castle. Luther begins the first of these eight sermons with an emphasis upon Christian maturity as a crucial mode of preparation for death. "The summons of death comes to us all, and no one can die for another. Every one must fight his own battle with death by himself, alone. We can shout into another's ears, but every one must himself be prepared for the time of death, for I will not be with you then, nor you with me. Therefore every one must himself know and be armed with the chief things which concern a Christian." LW 51.70.

7. A significant amount of recent literature has sought to highlight the distinctiveness of Luther's view of this posture by contrasting it with the literature of the so-called *ars moriendi* (i.e., a series of sermons, tracts and manuals on the topic of preparing to die, which appear in the from the late 14th to early 16th century). Though the comparison is an instructive and important one, the present essay will restrict itself primarily to the presentation of Luther's own perspective, and will not attempt

ly upon what Luther thinks it means to live as a Christian and to die as a Christian, and these two domains accordingly constitute the structure of the present essay. The first section furnishes a synoptic sketch of Luther's conception of the Christian life. This sketch is intended to provide the framework within which Luther's statements about preparation for death receive their determinate sense.[8] The second section turns its attention to Luther's explicit description of Christian death and dying and demonstrates the profound extent to which that description is simply an extension of what Luther presupposes to be true about the Christian life.

In the end, it will be argued that Luther interprets the Christian life as an ascetic pedagogy unto Godwardness. This pedagogy unfolds in the midst of contrary gravities (e.g., temptation, wayward desire, affliction, earthly comforts), which threaten to dislocate the Christian from a posture of alignment with God, and redirect her onto disordered trajectories. The resultant experiential antagonism serves a purgative function within Luther's understanding of the Christian life. This is so, because instances of existential dissonance constitute occasions in which the anarchic tendencies of the concupiscent flesh may either be mortified or nourished. Death constitutes precisely just this sort of antagonistic moment. In many ways, it is the decisive one. It is the occasion of dissonance *par excellence*; the critical juncture at which the Christian is called to persist

---

to draw any conclusions as to the way in which that perspective represents a *novum* in the history of Christian thought. For a nuanced engagement with Luther's relation to preexisting accounts of Christian dying, see Rittgers, *The Reformation of Suffering*, chapters 1–3; Reinis, *Reforming*; Goez, "Luthers 'Ein Sermon,'" 97–114; Jared Wicks, "Applied Theology," 345–68; Akerboom, "'Only the Image,'" 209–72.

8. The overview focuses extensively, though not exclusively, upon a selection of texts composed in the late 1510s and early 1520s. These texts are emphasized on account of their programmatic contents and especially because of their sustained preoccupation with the Christian life as a preparation for holy dying. Luther is busily at work during this period of time on his "Sermon on Preparing to Die." According to Martin H. Betram in LW 42, 97–98, the sermon had been commissioned by Markus Schart, a "counselor in the court of elector Frederick the Wise," in May of 1519, but was only finished in November of the same year. During the intervening months Luther was also writing a number of brief, programmatic treatises, some of which were distributed together in the form of vernacular, devotional pamphlets. Included here is Luther's treatment of baptism, a short treatise on the Lord's Supper and several other works of comparable scope and length. As Dirk Lange has suggested, the confluence of these various textual histories undoubtedly accounts for Luther's continual reference to death during this period, and the tendency extends into Luther's longer *Treatise on Good Works*, which is composed in the following year. See Lange's prefatory essay to the "Sermon on the Sacrament of Penance" (1519) in TAL I, 181–85.

in alignment with God, even in the face of an overwhelming tide of contrary, empirical deterrents. Framed within this ascetic conception of the Christian life, Luther's account of Christian preparation for death and dying consists finally in an "alignment persistence," which includes two distinct aspects: 1) the exercise of "dialectical perception" (i.e., clinging to divine mercy in the midst of contrary experience); and 2) the exercise of "ascetic attunement" (i.e., mortifying the concupiscent flesh in the midst of contrary pressure).

A Life unto Death

Luther conceives of the Christian life in strongly antagonistic terms. It is a life characterized above all by God-wardness, but whose pathos consists in the persistent experience of contrariety. The Christian's pilgrimage of faith is punctuated at every turn by dissuasive pressures of various kinds. These pressures represent occasions in which the Christian may either persist in a God-ward course or swerve aside under the inordinate influence of disordered proclivity. Embedded within this agonistic depiction are three constituent elements, which cumulatively lend structure to Luther's conception of the Christian life: 1) the posture and trajectory of "God-wardness"; 2) the source(s) of dissuasion; and 3) the process of purgation in which "1" prevails incrementally over "2."[9] These constituent elements supply the framework of intelligibility within which Luther's statements about Christian dying receive their determinate sense.

"God-wardness"

Luther's description of the Christian life presupposes a determinate picture of what it would look like for a human person to live consistently as a rightly ordered subject; that is, as a human being within whom every operation of reason, every determination of will and every impulse of desire is attuned properly in relation to God. This archetypal conception of ideal human agency will be expressed here though the heuristic term of "God-wardness."[10] In its purest and most consistent form (i.e., unspoiled

9. It should be noted that these specific, descriptive terms are not taken from Luther, but are intended to function as heuristic placeholders encapsulating essential aspects of Luther's theological outlook.

10. The term is intended to encompass an idea, which is expressed by Luther in

by any contrary inclination of sin), Luther refers to maximally aligned agency through the traditional concept of original righteousness.[11] In his *Lectures on Genesis* (1535–1546), for instance, Luther describes original righteousness as referring to a comprehensive attunement of the human person unto God, an attunment which determines the operation of reason, thought, speech, inclination and action. In the case of pre-lapsarian Adam, it meant:

> that man was righteous, truthful, and upright not only in body but especially in soul, that he knew God, that he obeyed God with the utmost joy, and that he understood the works of God even without prompting . . . It is part of this original righteousness that Adam loved God and His works with an outstanding and very pure attachment; that he lived among the creatures of God in peace, without fear of death, and without any fear of sickness; and that he had a very obedient body, without evil inclinations and the hideous lust which we now experience.[12]

According to Luther, original righteousness entails a hierarchical ordering of human agency. An orientation of "God-wardness" prevails across the entire spectrum of the soul's capacities. The alignment of the higher faculties trickles down, as it were, and lends structure to the operation of the lower faculties as well. Although Luther does not often deploy the term "original righteousness" as a means for describing the ideal of the Christian life, he envisages precisely this sort of hierarchical attunement as emerging necessarily within the life of a baptized Christian, even if only incrementally so.

The *Treatise on Good Works* (1520) illustrates the importance of this hierarchical paradigm, even though the specific nomenclature of "original righteousness" is absent.[13] The stated intent of the treatise is to

---

a cluster of terms and concepts, which describe the disposition of a rightly ordered human being (e.g., faith, hope, trust, love, dependency, reliance, obedience, etc.). See, for instance, *Treatise on Good Works* in TAL I, 275.

11. The idea is not original to Luther, though he does take exception to the manner in which original righteousness had been understood by a number of his late medieval teachers. See, for instance, his criticism of those who view original righteousness as a *donum superadditum* in LW 1, 164f.

12. This section is taken from lectures, which Luther is likely to have delivered in the summer of 1535. LW 1, 113.

13. The *Treatise on Good Works* is written in the spring of 1520, some 15 years prior to the aforementioned section taken from the *Lectures on Genesis*. It belongs to a series of five other texts, which are generally received within Luther's scholarship as

provide a sketch of Christian holiness, thus invalidating the supposition, proffered by opponents and supporters alike, that Luther's theological program amounts to a sort of laxist libertinism.[14] In attending to this task, Luther turns to the Decalogue, and especially the first commandment, from which he derives a normative anatomy of the Christian life, its source and its operations.[15] A hierarchically ordered conception of spiritual agency is woven into the fabric of Luther's description. The hierarchical ideal is reflected, for him, even in the way that the ten commandments are sequentially arranged.[16]

> The first four commandments do their work on human reason. That is, they take human beings captive, rule them, and make them subjects, so that they do not rule themselves, think for themselves, or think too much of themselves but instead show humility and let themselves be led in order to protect against arrogance. The following commandments [i.e., 5–10] take up human desires and lusting in order to slay them.[17]

---

possessing singular importance as expressions of Luther's emerging, reformation-al program. For a more precise description of the treatise's composition, see Timothy Wengert, "Treatise on Good Works" in TAL I, 257–64.

14. Luther is perceived in this manner throughout his career by friends and foes alike. As Scott Hendrix points out, there were at least some who accepted Luther's theological claims, but misunderstood them as license for a slackened emphasis upon the importance of holy living. As an example, Hendrix cites the response of a "Lutheran preacher in south Germany who summarized what he heard: 'If we do not need to perform good works, all the better. We will gladly take faith alone. And if praying, fasting, holy days, and almsgiving are not required, then we will lie near the stove, warm our feet on its tiles, turn the roasting apples, open our mouths, and let grilled doves fly into them.'" Hendrix, *Martin Luther*, 86. Many of Luther's Roman Catholic opponents interpreted him along similar lines, but differ rather diametrically in their appraisal, condemning what seemed for them to be an egregious minimization of sanctification within the Christian life.

15. Luther insists, in essence, that what he means by "faith" consists essentially in the keeping of the first commandment, and that this "work" is the source, substance, and end of all other good works (*Treatise on Good Works* in TAL I, 275). See also ibid., 267–68.

16. This is not the only organizational scheme, which appears in the treatise. Luther also adopts the traditional distinction between first and second table, which refer to vertical (1–3/4) and horizontal (4/5–10) obligations respectively. The fourth commandment functions as a hinge within this scheme, because it represents the site at which vertical authority intersects horizontal responsibility. See, for instance: ibid., 330–31.

17. Ibid., 351. As Wengert's marginal notation observes, this paragraph reflects Luther's ongoing use of a classical, philosophical distinction between intellect and will

A significant theme throughout the treatise is Luther's insistence that the holiness of a Christian must proceed from an appropriate, dispositional posture of dependency upon God. In most cases, Luther refers to this posture of dependency simply as "faith". Such faith, for him, is precisely what it means, most fundamentally, to *keep* the first commandment. It is also the root posture from which all other commandments draw their basic significance. To the extent that external works are performed in the absence of such a posture, they are, to that same degree, spurious manifestations of lingering pride (i.e., the inverse of dependency), and thus not truly good. In this way, faith constitutes the Christian's principal orientation and is therefore the source and *sine qua non* of genuine holiness.[18]

> And this faith, trust, and confidence, which come from the bottom of the heart, are the true fulfillment of the first commandment. Without them no work of any kind can satisfy its demand. Just as this commandment is the first, highest, and best, from which and to which all the others flow and by which they are evaluated and judged, so also the work that fulfills it (trust and confidence in God's favor at all times) is the first, noblest, and best work from which and to which all the others flow, in which they abide and by which they must be judged and evaluated.[19]

Here again, the concept of hierarchical ordering (i.e., "God-wardness") performs an important role. Luther's point is not to suggest that faith simply *is* the comprehensive substance of what it means rightly to be ordered to God, but rather that it is the essential and principal attunement, without which all else falls necessarily into disorder. At one point, Luther explains the directive function of faith by likening it to the presence of health in the physical body.

(ibid., 351n123). For more on the specific sense in which Luther's scholastic teachers define the concepts of intellect and will, see Grane, *Contra Gabrielem*, 97–113.

18. Luther regards the definition of faith as "mere assent" as hopelessly anemic. "[W]here are those who, when we preach about faith, accuse of us denying that any good work should be taught or done. Is it not true that the first commandment by itself demands more than anybody can do? Even if a single person became a thousand people or all people or every living creature, there would be enough demanded and more than enough, since it [i.e., the first commandment] commands each person at every moment to conduct one's life with faith and confidence in God at all times, putting trust in nothing else, and hence to have no other god than the one true God" (*Treatise on Good Works* in TAL I, 279–80).

19. Ibid., 275.

When some people say that good works are forbidden when we preach faith alone, it is similar to this. Supposed I advised a sick person: "If you were healthy, your body could perform all its functions, but without your health everything you do is nothing," and someone upon hearing this concluded that I had forbidden the sick man's body to perform any of its functions, even though what I meant was that health had to be there first, which could then simulate the actions of all the bodily members. Likewise, in all works, faith must be the master artisan and the captain, or they amount to nothing at all.[20]

The restoration of "God-wardness" in the life of a Christian therefore necessarily presupposes faith, but is not exhausted by its mere presence alone. The remaining commandments of the Decalogue enumerate the derivative entailments of faith, as belonging to the various domains (e.g., vertical and horizontal) and sectors of human agency (e.g., reason, will, and desire). The subordination of these entailments to faith reflects Luther's assumption that they reside "downstream" of a person's principal orientation.

The Source(s) of Contrariety

The *Treatise on Good Works* provides a paradigmatic sketch of what it looks like for Christian agency to function properly. In doing so, it deals extensively in idealistic terms, describing the archetypal Christian life, in which aberrant inclinations do not exercise deterrent pressure.[21] But, of course, Luther simultaneously insists that aberrant inclinations *do* remain in the life of a Christian, and this implies that the sinner's return to God-wardness will necessarily be a contested one. The root of the antagonism resides in concupiscence, the corruption of human nature, which issues from the sin of Adam and Eve. Luther describes concupiscence and its effects in a variety of ways. At its core, he portrays it as a disordered condition of "self-wardness," and thus nearly synonymous with pride.[22]

20. Ibid., 280. The fundamental issue, then, has to do with the basic, orientation-al calibration of human agency. Is it "God-ward" at its root, or not? If not, then even the grandest displays of moral excellence are something of an empty husk, because they are ordered necessarily to something other than God, and are thus basically idolatrous when viewed from a spiritual vantage point.

21. This "idealism" is intentional. See ibid., 281–83.

22. In addition to the considerable influence of Augustine, Luther is also strongly indebted to the theological anthropology expressed in the so-called "German

Concupiscence is therefore ineluctably on a collision course with the first and greatest commandment. Luther describes the root opposition in starkly diametric terms. "Man is by nature unable to want God to be God. Indeed, he himself wants to be God, and does not want God to be God."[23] The relation between the love of God (i.e., "God-wardness") and the sinner's disordered love of self (i.e., concupiscence) is zero-sum.[24]

Concupiscent "self-wardness" is not merely a posture of one's reason, however (e.g., a refusal of full assent to God's law), but includes a heterogeneous array of inclinations contrary to the will of God. In the same way that the attunement of Adam's pre-lapsarian agency trickled down, as it were, from the higher to lesser faculties, so also has the contamination of original sin spread like leprosy across reason, will, desire and impulse.[25] Luther describes the extent of the pervasive corruption in his lectures on Genesis 3 (1535). We must recognize, Luther insists, that:

> we are born from unclean seed and that from the very nature
> of the seed we acquire ignorance of God, smugness, unbelief,
> hatred against God, disobedience, impatience, and similar
> grave faults. These are so deeply implanted in our flesh, and this
> poison has been so widely spread through flesh, body, mind,
> muscles, and blood, through the bones and the very marrow, in
> the will, in the intellect, and in reason, that they not only cannot
> be fully removed but are not even recognized as sin.[26]

The same material judgment pervades Luther's *Treatise on Good Works* from 1520. For every commandment, there is contrary inclination, which opposes it. The Christian therefore encounters resistance from within at

Theology," a mystical text that Luther originally attributed (incorrectly) to Johann Tauler. Luther published an edition of this text in 1516, famously proclaiming in the preface that "no book except the Bible and St. Augustine has come to my attention from which I have learned more about God, Christ, man, and all things." LW 31, 75.

23. LW 31.10. This is the 17th thesis of Luther's "Disputation against Scholastic Theology" (1517), which primarily criticizes late medieval scholastic theologians, who suggested that human beings were able, outside of grace, to keep the law, albeit in an imperfect manner, in order congruently to merit the grace of God. For more on this particular disputation, see Grane, *Contra Gabrielem*.

24. Luther reinforces this point in a series of texts from the mid to late 1510s. See, for instance, his comments on Romans 4:7 (1516/7) in LW 25.262.

25. For an instance of Luther comparing original sin to "leprosy," and paralleling that disordered condition with original righteousness, see his *Lectures on Genesis* in LW 1.60–73.

26. Ibid., 166.

every layer of her agency. She finds herself inclined to varying degrees of doubt or lack of trust at the level of her reason; and inclined to disobedience at the level of will and desire.[27]

Purgation

It necessarily follows from these contrary realities that the Christian life must consist, to a large extent, in struggle.[28] "[T]he life of the godly in this flesh," Luther summarizes, "is a never-ending conflict of the spirit with the flesh."[29] Although the guilt entailed by concupiscence has been removed, its disordered set of inclinations largely remain. The life of the Christian is therefore one of incremental purgation. Luther provides an overview of this fact in his "Explanations of the Ninety-Five Theses of 1518."

> For in every man, no matter how holy he may be, there are the remains of the old man, and of sin, and the vestige of the former Adam remains, just as the children of Israel in their day were not able to erase entirely the influence of the Jebusites, the Canaanites, and the rest of the heathen. Moreover, this old man consists of error, concupiscence, wrath, fear, apprehension, despair, evil conscience, horror of death, etc. Those are characteristics of the old, carnal man. They diminish, however, in the new man, but they are not extinguished until he himself is extinguished by death, just as the Apostle says, "Though our outer nature is wasting away, our inner nature is being renewed every day" [2 Cor 4:16] . . . [This] process of removal has begun, and as a person increases in spiritual health these evils are removed. This spiritual health is nothing more than faith in or love in Christ.[30]

27. So, for instance, though summoned by the second commandment to praise God, the Christian finds herself deeply driven to pride. "Everyone, no matter how insignificant, wants to count for something and not be the least of all, so deep is the corruption of human nature in its conceit and false trust in itself, contrary to the first and the second commandments." Similar junctures of resistance accompany each of the commandments, whether they apply to the higher functioning of reason (as in worship and speech) or to the comparatively more banal realities of raw, material inclination (see *Treatise on Good Works* in TAL I, 290).

28. See, for instance, "The Holy and Blessed Sacrament of Baptism" (1519) in TAL I, 216 and Luther's lecture on Psalm 90 (1534) in LW 13.89–90.

29. *Lecture on Genesis* in LW 1, 270. See also LW 2.120.

30. This paragraph is excerpted from Luther's "Explanations of the Ninety-Five Theses" (1518) in LW 31.124. Notice that one of the important aspects of the "old

In a treatise composed in the following year, Luther interprets this process of purgation as flowing essentially from baptism, which signifies that "the old creature and the sinful birth of the flesh and blood are to be wholly drowned by the grace of God."[31]

The antipodal relation between Luther's agency-ideal (sub-section 1) and its diametric opposite (sub-section 2) practically necessitates this purgative understanding. To the extent that the lingering disorder of sin's corruption clings to the Christian's agency, the process of sanctification can only take the form of a maximally invasive pedagogy of self-abnegation.[32] This is precisely the view, which emerges in Luther's understanding of repentance, as it comes into focus in the mid to late 1510s. Luther's direct interaction with several sources from German mysticism seem to have played an important role in this aspect of the reformer's theological development.[33] Luther is especially drawn to the radical account of repentance, which predominates within these sources.[34] He embraces, for instance, the sharply contrasted depiction of the Christian life as espoused by Johann Tauler, who defines true repentance as "a total, true turning away from all that is not pure God . . . and a true, total turning to God with all that one is."[35]

---

man," which is being gradually extinguished, is the "horror of death."

31. "The Holy and Blessed Sacrament of Baptism" (1519), in TAL I, 207. For a helpful treatment of Luther's theology of baptism, see Trigg, *Baptism*. Also helpful for this particular theme is Leppin, "Development," 151–69.

32. In this context, self = concupiscent self. Luther affirms, for instance, that there is nothing intrinsically wrong with the will by nature. See thesis 8 of the "Disputation against Scholastic Theology" in LW 31.9.

33. The nature of the association between Luther and mysticism is a contested one. The scholarship of early to mid-20th century Luther interpreters tended rather dramatically to downplay any material influence on Luther's thought. Recent studies have criticized this tendency, however, suggesting that it reveals far more about the anti-mystical prejudices of modern Protestantism than it does about Luther's thought. For a careful documentation of the influence in modern research, see Hamm, *Early Luther*, 109–229; Iserloh, "Luther's Christ-mysticism," 37–58; Leppin, "'Omnem vitam," 7–25; Leppin, "Luther and John Tauler," 339–45; Leppin, "Luther's Transformation," 25–29.

34. See, for instance, Leppin, "*Omnem vitam*," 15–17. Even as late as Luther's *Lectures on Genesis*, Luther continues to refer to precisely this sort of radical self-abnegation, even to the point of monastic notions of a "resignation unto Hell" or a "suspension of grace." See, for instance, LW 2.103f.

35. Copied from Leppin, "Luther's Transformation," 26. In the same way, Luther celebrates the anonymous, mystical treatise entitled the *Theologia Deutsch*, observing that it describes in specific terms the manner in which the old Adam dies and the new Adam comes to life. Ibid., 19.

The Christian life is thus construed by Luther as an extended process of purgative re-alignment, which begins at baptism, and extends until death.[36] Indeed, it is precisely in and through this process that Luther insists a Christian is prepared to die.

> This struggle against the flesh, moreover, is the work of the Holy Spirit, who is given in and through baptism. "From [the hour of baptism] God begins to make you a new person. God pours into you grace and the Holy Spirit, who begins to kill nature and sin *and to prepare you for death* and the resurrection at the Last Day.[37]

Luther consistently insists that this process of purgation takes place primarily in and through experiences of affliction.[38] This is so, because although the tides of contrary dissuasion receive their root potency from an internal condition (i.e., concupiscence), the provocation of experiential dissonance is typically *external* in origin. The experience of suffering is an illustrative case in point. For Luther, suffering functions rather like a winnowing fork, exaggerating the contrast between the mixed trajectories and inclinations, which coexist within a Christian's agency. In cases of extreme trial, the disjunction necessitates choice. Will the Christian persist in obedience even after the corroboratory incentive to self-advantage fades away? Will she give way to doubt under the weight of discordant experience, or cling to the goodness of God in a posture of resilient faith?[39]

36. For a treatment of Luther's understanding of the Christian life as a time of purgation, see Hamm, *Early Luther*, 95.

37. Emphasis added. "The Holy and Blessed Sacrament of Baptism" (1519) in TAL I, 212. Luther depicts this same fundamental process from a variety of vantage points in the late 1510s and early 1520s. In the case of this particular quotation, he adopts a proleptic stance, surveying the path of purgation from the perspective of its constitutive inception. And yet, he also describes the same process from the perspective of it telos looking backwards (e.g., his *Treatise on Good Works* from 1520), as well as from the stance of critical junctures or oases of nourishment and strengthening along the way, as in the case of "'The Blessed Sacrament of the Holy and True Body of Christ, and the Brotherhoods" (1519).

38. Though Luther sees an important place for affliction in the sanctification of the believer, he rejects the prominent, late medieval notion that the Christian's suffering is a form of satisfaction for the *poena* of sin. For more on this contrast, see Rittgers, *The Reformation of Suffering*, 27–32, 104–10.

39. The divinely appointed purpose of contrariety is therefore diagnostic in a twofold sense: 1) It disambiguates the antipodal contrast between two, gravitational systems of spiritual agency (i.e., "self-wardness" vs. "God-wardness"); and 2) It reveals

The experience of affliction is purgative, in other words, because it creates a context in which clinging to God compels the mortification of disordered inclination.[40]

> If God is to work and live in [individuals], all these vices and corruption must be strangled and stamped out so that a rest and ceasing of all our works, words, thoughts, and lives may take place—so that from now on, as Paul says in Gal 2[:20], "not we, but Christ lives in us," acts and speaks. This does not happen in the midst of sweet and pleasant days; instead, here one must inflict pain on human nature and suffer such pain. Now comes the conflict between spirit and flesh, with the spirit resisting anger, lust, and pride while the flesh prefers lasciviousness, honor, and security.[41]

As these teleological orbits drift apart in opposite directions, the Christian must choose to which axis she will hold fast.[42] To the extent that she clings to God, she necessarily resists and subdues the contrary pressures of dissuasion, which would have her do otherwise. All of this happens by divine design, so that the corruptions of sin might be slain, and replaced by proper order at every layer of agency.

> In order to put to death our works and the [old] Adam, God hangs around our necks many unpleasant burdens that make us angry, much suffering that tries our patience, and finally death

whether the apparent "God-wardness" of an individual's life-trajectory is genuine or counterfeit.

40. For example, Luther underscores the significant difference between trusting God in times of plenty (where motives may easily be mixed) and praising God in times of trial or want. See *Treatise on Good Works* in TAL I, 272–74.

41. Ibid., 322.

42. Luther acknowledges that the slaying of disordered inclination can and should take place through particular disciplines (e.g. vigils and fasting), which the Christian undertakes herself. And yet, the deepest re-a,lignment of agency takes place through trials and afflictions, which are not of one's own choosing. See, for instance, "The Holy and Blessed Sacrament of Baptism" in TAL I, 212–13. "God . . . trains and tests you all your life long with many good works and with all kinds of suffering. Thereby God accomplishes what you have desired in baptism, namely, that you want to become free from sin, die, and rise again at the Last Day, and so fulfill your baptism. Therefore, we read and see how bitterly God let the saints be tortured and suffer so much, in order that, at the point of being slain, they fulfilled the sacrament of baptism, died, and were made new. For when this does not happen and we do not suffer or are exercised, then one's evil nature overwhelms a person, makes baptism useless, falls into sin, and remains the same old creature as before." Cf. Luther's description of the "cross" in his "Explanations of the Ninety-Five Theses" in LW 31, 89.

and the world's contempt. By doing these things, God is simply trying to expunge our anger, impatience, and turmoil and replace them with his work, that is, with his peace.[43]

Thus, although human beings are naturally inclined to view suffering as loathsome, Luther insists that affliction is salutary for the Christian insofar as God uses it for the mortification of her flesh and the sanctification of her life.[44] In this sense, the Christian life is an ascetic pedagogy unto "God-wardness."[45]

A Death unto Life

This cursory sketch of the Christian life furnishes an important framework within which to situate Luther's conception of "preparing to die." For, at the end of this pedagogy—at its summit—there is death, that particular occasion of "vector crisis" in which the teleological orientation of

43. *Treatise on Good Works* in TAL I, 327. It is interesting that Luther appears here to take up the patristic motif of holiness consisting as in a sort of sanctified *apatheia*, in which the chaotic discord of the concupiscent flesh is brought into peaceful order. Luther discusses various "intensity levels" of affliction, the worst of which is that particular sort of spiritual affliction, in which the favor of God drifts beyond the reach of immediate perception. See, for instance, his "The Blessed Sacrament of the Holy and True Body of Christ" in TAL I, 235–36; and *The Treatise on Good Works* in TAL I, 272–73. For a visceral presentation of spiritual affliction (sometimes referred to by Luther as "Anfechtung"), see Luther's "Explanations of the Ninety-Five Theses" in LW 31.128f.

44. LW 6.152. "The story is told of a peasant who, when he heard this consolation from his pastor, that the afflictions and troubles by which God afflicts us are signs of His love, replied: 'Ah, how I would like Him to love others and not me!' This was a foolish and impious reply. We should not feel and speak like this, nor should God's works in us be interpreted in this way. But we should know that mortification is very salutary. By it we are instructed for life and salvation, not for destruction, as Paul testifies when he says (Rom 12:2): 'That you may prove' (not only that you may learn by words but that you may also learn by experience) 'what is the will of God, what is good and acceptable and perfect.' For this is God's will, our mortification and sanctification (cf. 1 Thess 4:3). But we cannot be sanctified unless the flesh and the body of sin is mortified, which in this life with all its force is driven into sins of every kind, adulteries, lusts, thefts, etc. God therefore judges, chastises, and scourges until we learn what is the good and acceptable and perfect will of God so that we sing with David (Ps 119:71): 'It is good for me that Thou didst humble me, that I might learn Thy statutes.' I would gladly be exempted; my flesh shrinks from temptation, but I know that this is the excellent will of God."

45. For a more thorough discussion of the role of suffering in Luther's view of the Christian life, see Rittgers, *The Reformation of Suffering*, chapters 4 and 5.

a God-ward life is tested to the sharpest, empirical degree imaginable.[46] The life of purgation is the decisive preparation for death, because Luther regards the resistance of contrary inclination as a spiritual form of dying. It is a practiced mode of losing one's life in order to gain it.[47] The continual reiteration of self-abnegation has the effect of accustoming "[the flesh] to death" and teaching the Christian to "die with gladness."[48] Through purgation, a resilient God-wardness takes root in the life of the Christian, which resolutely holds its course even in the face of radical dissuasion. This resilience of Christian agency assumes two distinct forms, each of which prepares a person for death.

Dialectical Perception

The first kind of resilience applies to perception, for affliction engenders a resilient way of "seeing," which eschews the sensual in exchange for the promissory. In the midst of severe trial, an empirical search for assurance of divine favor necessarily yields empty returns. Intense suffering eclipses the benevolence of divine providence with an opaque cloud. The resulting experience of abandonment intensifies exponentially during seasons in which the Christian's conscious awareness of God's grace may utterly be withdrawn.[49] The strength of one's own spiritual probity fails likewise to bestow assurance, for an honest and strict self-assessment will necessarily reveal, even in the holiest of Christians, a remaining deficit, which separates "is" from "ought."[50] In these ways, the experience of

46. I insert the adjective "empirical" here, because Luther regards the intensive aspect of suffering (i.e., the experience of God's wrath or abandonment) as a test far more radical than the prospect of physical death, which he describes as child's play by comparison. See, for instance, Slenczka, "'Allein durch den Glauben,'" 302.

47. Cf. Matt 10:39.

48. "The Holy and Blessed Sacrament of Baptism," in TAL I, 218.

49. See, for instance, Luther's interpretation of the Noah narrative in his *Lectures on Genesis* in LW 2.103f.

50. Luther asserts this conclusion quite forcefully in his *Lectures on Romans*, steeping his conclusions extensively in the writings of St. Augustine. For example: "Hence, blessed Augustine says in his 29th Epistle, to blessed Jerome: 'Love is the power by which a person loves what he ought to love. In some people this is stronger and in others weaker, and in still others there is none at all; but it is never in its fullest degree, so that it could not be further increased, in any man as long as he lives. But as long as it can be increased, what is less than it ought to be comes from sin. Because of this defect 'there is not a righteous man on earth who does good and never sins' (Cf. 1 Kings 8:46). And because of this defect 'no man living is righteous before God (Ps 143:2). Because of this defect 'if we say we have no sin, we deceive ourselves, and the truth is not in us' (1 John 1:8). Also because of this defect, no matter how much we progress, we are forced to say: 'Forgive us our debts' (Matt 6:12), even though in Baptism all our

intense affliction deprives the Christian of all evidence, which might corroborate the reliability of divine mercy. In the absence of these existential props, the prospect of utter despair heavily looms.

The specter of death sharpens the contrast between promise and empirical appearance. In the coldness of a corpse, the independent operation of the senses fails to detect signs of divine favor. The critical issue, then, concerns the way in which a person "sees" death and affliction. In a pair of funeral sermons that Luther preached in the summer of 1532, Luther insists that a Christian's mode of perceiving death is significantly different than the non-Christian's.

> Since you have been baptized in His name, as well as into His nature and kingdom, death and resurrection, you must remember that your whole attitude toward those things of which the world is terrified should be different, and that you should have eyes, ears, senses, and thoughts which are different from those you had before from Adam, when you were frightened and sorrowful, as those who had no hope.[51]

The one who "sees" the death of a human being according to sense experience alone must necessarily misunderstand its true nature. Such a person is liable to conclude that humans "die like a beast" and exist no more.[52]

As a result of this skewed perception, Luther sees pagan, philosophical treatments of death as insufficiently calibrated to the full weight of what death represents. Such treatments minimize the sting of death by disregarding it either as natural or trivial. Luther confronts these insufficient remedies in an extended lecture on Psalm 90, delivered in 1534.

> I ask you to consider how foolishly the wisest men have discoursed on death, the gravest and most horrible punishment of sin, which, like a flood, has engulfed the whole human race and is accompanied by the most fearful afflictions. Some wise men suggest that one must disregard death, as did the poet who said: "Neither fear, nor long for, the last day." Others, who believe this to be too difficult, try to persuade people that they should mitigate the evil of death by indulging to their heart's content in

---

sins of word, deed, and thought have been forgiven.'" LW 25.276.

51. LW 51.245.

52. Luther explores this way of "seeing death" according to the flesh in his *Lectures on Genesis*. See LW 1.333.

the pleasures of this life . . . No, in order to overcome death and
sin one must employ different means and different remedies.[53]

Luther regards the human, empirical sensorium as specifically blind and
deaf to the efficient and final causality of death. It sees only the physical
reality, and thus equates death merely with the cessation of biological
functioning.

The Christian knows, however, that this physical aspect is mere
"child's play" in comparison with the true fearsomeness of death, which
resides in the fact that its efficient cause is divine wrath.[54] For this reason,
the death of a human being is far worse than simply the silence of biological non-existence.

> Although horses, cows, and all animals die, they do not die be-
> cause God is angry at them. On the contrary, for them death is,
> as it were, a sort of temporal casualty, ordained indeed by God
> but not regarded by Him as punishment. Animals die because
> for some other reason it seemed good to God that they should
> die. But the death of human beings is a genuine disaster. Man's
> death is in itself truly an infinite and eternal wrath. The reason
> is that man is a being created for this purpose: to live forever in
> obedience to the Word and to be like God. He was not created
> for death. In his case death was ordained as a punishment of
> sin; for God said to Adam: "In the day that you eat of this tree,
> you shall die" (Gen 2:17).The death of human beings is, there-
> fore, not like the death of animals. These die because of a law of
> nature. Nor is man's death an event which occurs accidentally
> or has merely an aspect of temporality. On the contrary, man's
> death, if I may so speak, was threatened by God and is caused
> by an incensed and estranged God. If Adam had not eaten of the
> forbidden tree, he would have remained immortal. But because
> he sinned through disobedience, he succumbs to death like the
> animals which are subject to him. Originally death was not part
> of his nature. He dies because he provoked God's wrath. Death
> is, in his case, the inevitable and deserved consequence of his sin
> and disobedience. Therefore it comes to man as shocking news
> to hear that he, who had been created as a good and perfect
> being for life and who was to have his dwelling place in God, is
> now destined for death.[55]

53. LW 13.76. See also ibid., 81f.
54. Ibid., 77, 82, 96. See also Slenczka, "Allein durch den Glauben," 302–3.
55. This is excerpted from Luther's lecture on Psalm 90 (1534) in LW 13.94.

The pagans adopt trivial interpretations of death because they are able neither to perceive nor withstand the full weight of what death represents. They are like the man who turns his face away from an atrocity he cannot change. In this way, it is characteristic of human nature to rationalize death, and render it palatable in some manner.[56] For Luther, this is to be expected, because the infinite intensity of death is unbearable to human nature outside of grace. The undiluted perception of it "begets despair and blasphemy."[57] And yet, trivial interpretations of death are no less hazardous for being understandable. To the extent that a human being fails to understand her plight, she will, to the same degree, fail utterly to grasp its appropriate remedy.

The Christian disavows all such equivocations. Her perception of death presses beyond the physical appearance of an inanimate biological organism to the spiritual reality of an image-bearer condemned to die by the very wrath of God. In so doing, a sensitivity to the quickening sting of death opens up, which teeters on the very precipice of despair.[58] From this debased posture, the human subject sighs desperately after the grace God. Perceived from the perspective of death's nadir, all other remedies appear frivolous by comparison.[59] As in the case of ordinary affliction (but now heightened to an exponential degree), the Christian must renounce the illusion of self-sufficiency, resist the frightful indications of empirical sense, and entrust herself entirely to the mercy of God.

In this way, the terrors of death's efficient causality open up into the consolations of its final causality, which is also imperceptible to carnal sense. For God imposes death not so that human beings might be consigned to eternal condemnation, but so that they might cling to Christ, the One in whom there is victory over death and the promise of resurrection.[60] The result, then, is a sharply dialectical perception of death, a simultaneous maximization of despair and hope. On the one hand, only the Christian beholds the terrors of death in their pure and undiluted form. These terrors consist in grave offense to natural sense (i.e., a corpse, which rots in the earth), but more acutely in the recognition of divine wrath. Renouncing frivolous comforts, in the midst of life, she

56. Ibid., 107–8.
57. *Lectures on Genesis* in LW 1.178.
58. LW 13.116–18.
59. Ibid., 101.
60. For an explication of the final causality of death, see ibid., 77, 98 and 130f.

sees death.[61] On the other hand, the Christian peers through this double abyss and simultaneously "sees" death from the perspective of promised resurrection. In the midst of death, she sees life.[62]

From the vantage point of empirical perception, this second way of "seeing" is absurd, for it cuts against every available indication of sense experience. And yet, the maximal dialectic that emerges here represents precisely the way in which *God* sees death.[63] In acclimating to this divine mode of perception, the Christian learns, in effect, to see corpses differently, as Luther explains at the funeral of his elector in 1532:

> Therefore, even though it is hard, we must learn to look at the death of Christ, through which our death is destroyed, and even though it seems otherwise to our eyes, the Holy Spirit nevertheless mingles this sour vinegar with honey and sugar, that our faith may soar up to God and learn to see the dead, not lying in the grave and coffin, but in Christ. When you see him there, then the dead body is no longer in the coffin. Even though the carcass be foul and stinking it makes no difference; turn your eyes and nose and all five senses away and remember what St. Paul says in the fifteenth chapter of 1 Corinthians [1 Cor 15:42–50]: One buries the body in all dishonor; this is true, but don't look at that, for it will rise again in all glory. It is buried and sown as something perishable and it will rise up imperishable. It is sown in weakness and will rise in power. It is sown a natural body and will rise a spiritual body, etc. Thus he is constantly taming our hearts, because he cannot turn our eyes, away from that which the eyes see to that which God is saying and to Christ, so that we may have no doubt that he will bring us with Christ. So anyone who can believe this will have good comfort in his own death and the death of other people.[64]

This is precisely the sort of dialectical perception that is exercised elsewhere in the Christian life as one clings to the promise of mercy and

61. LW 1.196.

62. LW 13.83.

63. Ibid., 105.

64. LW 51.235–36. "Hence, one must look upon a Christian death with different eyes, not the way a cow stares at a new gate, and smells it in a different way, not as a cow sniffs grass, by learning to speak and think of it as the Scriptures do and not considering deceased Christians to be dead and buried people. To the five senses that is the way it appears. As far as they can lead us, it brings only woe. Therefore go beyond them and listen to what St. Paul says here, that they are sleeping in Christ and God will bring them with Christ [as he brought with him the Savior, the devourer of death, the destroyer of the devil]." Ibid., 239–40.

final vindication, even in the absence of corroboratory experience.[65] Luther often points to the heroic faith of Abraham in this respect, especially in view of the command in Genesis 22 for Abraham to slay Isaac, the child of the promise. Luther's presentation of the episode in his *Lectures on Genesis* emphasizes the sharply dialectical nature of Abraham's trust in God.

> The thoughts of his heart were these: "My son Isaac, whom I am killing, is the father of the promise, and this proposition is absolutely true. Consequently, my son will live forever and will be the heir. Therefore even if he has to die now, he will not nevertheless die in reality but will rise again." Accordingly, faith reconciles opposites and is not an idle quality, as the sophists say; but it has the power to kill death, to condemn hell, to be sin for sin, and a devil for the devil to such an extent that death is not death, even if everybody's reason should bear witness that death is present. Of this Abraham is very sure. He thinks: "I am reducing my son to ashes. Nevertheless, he is not dying. Indeed, those ashes will be the heir."[66]

And yet, it must be noticed here that the fundamental determinant of Christian "seeing" is christological, rather than nakedly dialectical in the strong sense of sheer contradiction. The dialectic of contrariety, in other words, is only penultimate. The Christian life does not consist in the static juxtaposition of antithetical judgments, but has its axis in christological mediation. In Christ, death gives way to life, guilt gives way to pardon, and corruption gives way to incorruption.[67] The Christian accordingly learns to see death only in and through Christ's wounds.[68]

> Just as Christ also, though he lay in the grave, yet in a moment he was both dead and alive and rose again like a lightning flash from heaven. So he will raise us too in an instant, in the twinkling of an eye, out of the grave, the dust, the water, and we shall stand in full view, utterly pure and clean as the bright sun."[69]

65. See, for instance, Luther's presentation of Abraham in the *Lectures on Genesis*, who accepts the promises of God beyond the indications of fleshly perception. For instance, LW 2.261.

66. LW 4.117.

67. For more on the importance of the *Christus Victor* motif within Luther's theology, see Rieske-Braun, *Duellum mirabile*; and Luy, *Dominus Mortis*, chapter 4.

68. Iserloh, "Luther's Christ-mysticism," 46. This emphasis upon theological perception mediated through the sufferings of Christ is apparently indebted to the influence of Johann von Staupitz. See Leppin, *Martin Luther vom Mönch zum Feind*, 26, 30f.

69. LW 51.250. In this respect, the dialectical aspect of Christian experience is the

A lifetime spent in the exercise of this christologically-mediated, dialectical perception prepares one to die well; that is, in a posture of faith and sheer dependency upon the mercy of God.[70] A synopsis of this resilient perception appears in a treatise on the Lord's Supper, written in 1519:

> For death takes away all the things that are seen and separates us from human beings and transient things. To face death, we must have the help of the invisible and eternal, and these are indicated to us in the sacrament and sign, to which we cling by faith until we finally also attain to them openly with the senses. Thus the sacrament is for us a ford, a bridge, a door, a ship and personal transport, by which and in which we pass from this world into eternal life. Therefore everything depends on faith, because the one who does not believe is like the person who is supposed to cross the sea, but who is so timid as not to trust the ship; and so such a one must remain and never become holy out of unwillingness to embark and cross over. This is caused by sensuality and unexercised faith that shrinks from the passage across the Jordan of death—and the devil too has a gruesome hand in it . . . As we then believe, the waters below us depart; that is, the things that are seen and temporary do nothing but flee from us. The waters above us, however, well up high; that is, the horrible torments and images of death from another world terrify us as if they would overwhelm us. If, however, we pay no attention to them and walk over with a firm faith, then we shall enter with dry feet, unharmed into eternal life.[71]

Ascetic Attunement

It is not merely the Christian's perception, which accrues resilience through purgation, however. Affliction and trial serve also to mortify the flesh, and to inscribe a God-ward trajectory onto the inclinations of will

---

simply the outworking of the "wondrous exchange," which saturates Luther's soteriological vision. For more on this theme, see Iserloh, "Luther's Christ-mysticism," 44–51; Allgaier, Der "froehliche Wechsel"; and especially Rieske-Braun, Duellum mirabile.

70. Such a person is equipped with the necessary means for countering the demonic incitement to despair, which presents the efficient causality of death in the absence of its christologically-determined, final causality. To the extent that a Christian fails to see her condition "in Christ," she will succumb to despair. See, for instance, Luther's treatment of Psalm 90 in LW 13.110f.

71. "The Blessed Sacrament of the Holy and True Body of Christ, and the Brotherhoods" (1519) in TAL I, 247–48.

and desire. This process represents a second form of "spiritual dying," because like the first, it involves an abnegation of inclinations experienced
by the Christian as "natural." This means that persistence in obedience
always involves restraint of the flesh, with its disordered passions. In the
short-term, such obedience provokes experiential dissonance, for the
Christian is simultaneously inclined in several directions. In the end,
however, the slaying of sinful inclination bestows peace and rest, which
allows the Christian to endure practically anything without swerving
from her God-ward course.[72]

The emphasis here differs from the previous section. Spiritual dying
involves more than simply clinging to the promise in the midst of trial.
It also entails persistence of obedience in the midst of contrary pressure.
The patriarch Joseph serves as a paradigmatic exemplar of such obedience for Luther. Despite the fact that Joseph has every empirical reason to
doubt the faithfulness of God (i.e., he is sold into slavery, falsely accused
of malfeasance, cast into prison, etc.), he nevertheless resists the overwhelming temptations to sin, which confront him along the way (e.g.,
the enticement to adultery) and choses rather to obey the law of God. The
result of all this is an accrued resilience of obedience. By the work of the
Holy Spirit "the Word planted in his heart is kept impressed and rooted
in such a way that it becomes an immovable rock against the devil on the
right [the allurements of pleasure] and on the left [external affliction]."[73]
Such resilience prepares one for death, because it engenders repose over
time even under provocation. To the extent that the inclinations of concupiscence have been slain, they are unable to incite turmoil in times of
distress. In this way, obedience is the path to a peaceful death.[74]

72. Thus, Luther explains this ascetic attunement of agency in his *Treatise on Good
Works.* "God sends us suffering and turmoil in order to teach us patience and peace.
God permits us to die in order to make us alive until each person is so peaceful and
quiet that it does not matter whether things go well or poorly, whether one lives or dies,
is honored or dishonored. At that point, God alone dwells there and human works are
no more . . . Here there is no human control, delight, or sorrow at all. Instead, God
alone leads each human being, and nothing is present but divine delight, joy, and peace
along with all the other works and virtues." *Treatise on Good Works* in TAL I, 327.

73. LW 7.56. For the bracketed explanations, see ibid., 75.

74. Luther emphasizes this point in the first of two funeral sermons preached on
the occasion of the death of his elector. In the first sermon especially, Luther insists
that the Elector's *true* death had already taken place two years earlier, when he obediently confessed his faith even at profound risk to life and limb. Thus, Luther enjoins
his hearers to practice a similar obedience, so that they may also prepare to die well.
"Therefore humble yourself and improve your life, that you, like him, may be among
those who suffer and die with Christ. I hope that there are many of you who have died

An interesting example of this idea appears in a few ancillary re-marks about Christian parenting, which Luther inserts into his exposi-tion of the fourth commandment in the *Treatise on Good Works*. Luther notes that godly parenting will always be difficult, because it's orientation unto "God-wardness" will necessarily grate against the "selfish will of . . . children."[75] Truly Christian parents will not flee from conflict, how-ever, but will seek rather to redirect their children's proclivities through instruction. The result could usefully be described as a sort of "ascetic parenting" in which godly mothers and fathers impose life-giving disci-plines of various kinds, such as "prayer, fasting, keeping vigils, working, worshipping, hearing God's word, and observing the Sabbath" in an at-tempt to mortify the flesh. This pedagogy of obedience, moreover, is a means through which parents prepare their children eventually to die. Luther continues: "In this way [children] will learn to disdain temporal things, endure misfortune with equanimity, face death without fear, not holding this life too dear."[76]

The connection between the mortification of desire and preparation for death also appears periodically in Luther's treatise on baptism from 1519, where he recommends similar disciplines throughout the Chris-tian life.

> Fasting and all such exercises should be aimed at holding down and overcoming the sinful nature, the old Adam, and accustom-ing it to do without all that is pleasing for this life, thus prepar-ing it more and more each day for death so that the work and purpose of baptism may be fulfilled.[77]

In each of these texts, Luther portrays a preparation for death, which consists in the resilient attunement of a Christian's agency, which is able to confront death peacefully and even with gladness, because the cha-otic passions of the flesh have long since been subdued and reordered through purgation.[78]

---

and suffered as my ruler did at Augsburg, for then you too will attain to such a gentle death that it will come as softly and easily as sleep" (LW 51, 243). See also ibid., 236.

75. *Treatise on Good Works* in TAL I, 332.

76. Ibid., 335.

77. "The Holy and Blessed Sacrament of Baptism" (1519) in TAL I, 219.

78. In this respect, Christ is regarded not principally as the Christian's mediator, but rather as her example. On the distinction between Christ as "sacramentum" and Christ as "exemplum" in Luther's writings, see Iserloh, "Luther's Christ-mysticism," 52–57. See also Jantzen, "Luther and the Mystics," 49. Luther often argues that our persistent

What emerges from these two forms of resilience, is a view of Christian dying that is deeply intertwined with the intrinsic fabric of Christian living. The cumulative picture is summarized in the following table:

	Dialectical Perception	Ascetic Attunement
Teleology	God-ward disposition (faith, trust, hope, love, etc)	God-ward agency (volition, inclination, desire, action, etc.)
Dissuasive contrary	The sense of god-forsakenness (e.g., suspension of grace)	The tug of wayward inclination
Faculty affiliation	Reason	Will (i.e., as an expansive category including the lesser inclinations sourcing raw desire)
Relation to concupiscence	The entailment of guilt and liability to condemnation	The persistent operation of dissuasive counter-pressure
Divine aid	The "grace" of pardon	The "gift" of strength
Purgative pedagogy	The forging of faith in the absence of empirical corroboration	The forging of obedience in the absence of immediate self-advantage
Sacramental affiliation	The promise of baptism (i.e., remission) Lord's supper as promissory testament	The "significance" of baptism (i.e., mortification of the Old Adam by the Holy Spirit) Lord's Supper as strengthening nourishment
Cumulative effect	Heroic trust (e.g., Abraham on the mountain)	Heroic virtue and obedience (e.g., Joseph's extraordinary patience and chastity)
Christ-Relation	Christ as "sacramentum"	Christ as "exemplum"
At the moment of death	Christologically-mediated, dialectical perception	Peace (i.e., apatheia of passions); gladness; bravery; etc.

---

fear of death is a symptom of the disorder of concupiscence. See, for instance, the concluding sections of the "Heidelberg Disputation" in TAL I, 118–19. Thus, this fear decreases steadily as the Christian grows and progresses through the purgative work of the Holy Spirit.

Conclusion

Luther portrays Christian dying as the emblematic instantiation of Christian living. The Christian's preparation for death is not a discrete exercise, but consists essentially in navigating the purgative rigors, which are natively entailed by the indelible, baptismal shape of the Christian life. In the end, the process in and through which a Christian is prepared to die involves the cultivation of resilience in the face of contrariety. This resilience takes the form of dialectical perception, in which the Christian clings to the mercy of God, and ascetic attunement, in which the Christian persists in obedience. This twofold resilience identifies the fullest sense in which Luther intends his programmatic assertion: "[T]he life of a Christian, from baptism to the grave is nothing less than the beginning of a holy death."[79]

BIBLIOGRAPHY

Akerboom, Dick. "'Only the Image of Christ in Us': Continuity and Discontinuity between the Late Medieval ars moriendi and Luther's Sermon von der Bereitung zum Sterben." In *Spirituality Renewed: Studies on Significant Representatives of the Modern Devotion*, edited by Hein Bommestijn et al., 209–72. Leuven: Peeters, 2003.

Allgaier, Walter. *Der "froehliche Wechsel" bei Martin Luther; eine Untersuchung zu Christologie und Soteriologie bei Luther unter besonderer Beruecksichtigung der Schriften bis 1521*. PhD diss., University of Erlangen-Nürnberg, 1966.

Goez, Werner "Luthers 'Ein Sermon von der Bereitung zum Sterben' und die spätmittelalterliche ars moriendi." *LuJ* 48 (1981) 97–114.

Grane, Leif. *Contra Gabrielem: Luthers Auseinandersetzung mit Gabriel Biel in der Disputatio contra scholasticam theologiam 1517*. København: Gyldendal, 1962.

Hamm, Berndt. *The Early Luther: Stages in a Reformation Reorientation*. Lutheran Quarterly Books. Grand Rapids: Eerdmans, 2014.

Hendrix, Scott. *Martin Luther: Visionary Reformer*. New Haven: Yale University Press, 2015.

Iserloh, Erwin. "Luther's Christ-mysticism." In *Catholic Scholars Dialogue with Luther*, edited by Jared Wicks, 37–58. Chicago: Loyola University Press, 1970.

Jantzen, Grace M. "Luther and the Mystics." *King's Theological Review* 8 (1985) 43–50.

Leppin, Volker. "The Development of the Notions of Baptism and Rebirth in Martin Luther's Early Works." *Theology & Life* 30 (2007) 151–69.

———. "Luther and John Tauler: Some Observations about the Mystical Impact on Reformation Theology." *Theology & Life* 36 (2013) 339–45.

———. "Luther's Transformation of Late Medieval Mysticism." *Lutheran Forum* 44 (2010) 25–29.

79. "The Holy and Blessed Sacrament of Baptism" (1519) in TAL I, 209.

————. *Martin Luther vom Mönch zum Feind des Papstes*. Darmstadt: Lambert Schneider Verlag, 2014.

————. "'*Omnem vitam fidelium penitentiam esse voluit*', Zur Aufnahme mystischer Tradition in Luthers erster Ablaßthese." In *Archiv für Reformationsgeschichte* 93 (2002) 7–25.

Leroux, Neil R. *Martin Luther As Comforter: Writings on Death*. Leiden: Brill, 2007.

Luther, Martin. "The Blessed Sacrament of the Holy and True Body of Christ, and the Brotherhoods." Translated by Dirk G. Lange. In *The Annotated Luther*, vol. 1: *The Roots of Reform*. Edited by Timothy J. Wengert, 225–56. Minneapolis: Fortress, 2015.

————. "The Holy and Blessed Sacrament of Baptism." Translated by Dirk G. Lange. In *The Annotated Luther*, vol. 1: *The Roots of Reform*. Edited by Timothy J. Wengert, 203–24. Minneapolis: Fortress, 2015.

————. "Treatise on Good Works." Translated by Timothy J. Wengert. In *The Annotated Luther*, vol. 1: *The Roots of Reform*. Edited by Timothy J. Wengert, 257–368. Minneapolis: Fortress, 2015.

Luy, David. *Dominus Mortis: Martin Luther on the Incorruptibility of God in Christ*. Minneapolis: Fortress, 2014.

Reinis, Austra. *Reforming the Art of Dying: The Ars Moriendi in the German Reformation (1519–1528)*. Aldershot, UK: Ashgate, 2007.

Rieske-Braun, Uwe. *Duellum mirabile: Studien zum Kampfmotiv in Martin Luthers Theologie*. Forschungen zur Kirchen- und Dogmengeschichte 73. Göttingen: Vandenhoeck & Ruprecht, 1999.

Rittgers, Ronald K. *The Reformation of Suffering: Pastoral Theology and Lay Piety in Late Medieval and Early Modern Germany*. Oxford: Oxford University Press, 2012.

Slenczka, Notger. "'Allein durch den Glauben': Antwort auf die Fragen eines mittelalterlichen Mönchs oder Angebot zum Umgang mit einem Problem jades Menschen?" In *Luther und das monastische Erbe*, edited by Christoph Bultmann et al., 291–315. Tübingen: Mohr Siebeck, 2007.

Trigg, Jonathan D. *Baptism in the Theology of Martin Luther*. Leiden: Brill, 1994.

Wicks, Jared. "Applied Theology at the Deathbed: Luther and the Late-Medieval Tradition of the *Ars Moriendi*." *Gregorianum* 79 (1998) 345–68.

Chapter 8

The Training for Dying and Death

A New Reading of Bulgakov's Sophiology

PAUL L. GAVRILYUK

The one aim of those who practice philosophy in the proper manner
is to train for dying and death. (Plato, *Phaedo* 64a3–4)

SERGIUS BULGAKOV'S VAST THEOLOGICAL system is commonly presented under the general heading of "sophiology" or the teaching about
Sophia, the Wisdom of God. For the Russian theologian, sophiological
teaching provided a framework for addressing the central problem of
God's relation to the world by extending the Chalcedonian dogma about
Christ's two natures into the general principle of Godmanhood. Without
rejecting this widely accepted reading of Bulgakov, this paper proposes
that the central inspiration of Bulgakov's system was a set of revelatory
experiences that he had while confronting mortality in various forms.
I show how the encounter with mortality and dying shaped Bulgakov's
worldview from his early childhood experiences to his struggle with
throat cancer towards the end of his life. My contention is that Bulgakov's
central theological intuition—that all things are "in God"—stems from
his earth-shattering experiences of witnessing the deaths of those close
to him that were accompanied by an equally powerful sense of the reality
of eternal life and resurrection.

In order to make my case, I look at the sources that are often ne-
glected in the discussions of Bulgakov's theology: his *Autobiographical
Notes, Spiritual Diary*, and the essay "The Sophiology of Death."[1] Having
established the importance of the *memento mori* theme in Bulgakov's
spirituality, I consider its implications for his theological system. I reach
a conclusion that eternity revealed through death is an existential axle of
Bulgakov's sophiology.

I. Confrontation with Loss, Mortality, and Death in Bulgakov's Lived Experience

Sergius Bulgakov (1871–1944) grew up in the family of a Russian priest,
who was attached to a cemetery chapel in the provincial town of Livny
and whose livelihood depended upon officiating at funeral services. As
a boy, Sergius would find himself regularly participating in a solemn
Easter procession, singing "Christ is risen" outside the cemetery chapel
amidst the old graves.[2] The encounters with death and dying, sanctified
by the solemnity of the Orthodox services for the departed, were a part
of young Bulgakov's everyday existence. Years later Bulgakov would write
about the house of his childhood: "I do not recall any weddings; but I
do recall numerous funerals."[3] In this house, one by one, most members
of his large extended family expired, beginning with his grandfather. As
Bulgakov reminisced years later:

> With his departure, death for the first time entered into my
> young mind (I was 12). I was, on the one hand, mystically shak-
> en, and on the other hand, defended myself with animal self-
> love. Funerals in Livny were done right: it was some sort of an

1. These works were written during different periods of Bulgakov's life. The first
part of *Autobiographical Notes*, entitled "My Motherland," was written in the beginning of 1938 during Bulgakov's trip to Athens; the surviving entries of the *Spiritual
Diary* date to 1924–1926; finally, the first part of "The Sophiology of Death" was
written in 1939, sometime after Bulgakov underwent two surgeries to treat his throat
cancer in May of the same year, while the second part comes from a diary of 1926.
The editions used here are as follows: *Avtobiograficheskoe*, in *S.N. Bulgakov: Pro et
Contra*, vol. 1 (St. Petersburg: RKhGI, 2003), 63–111; *Dnevnik dukhovnyi* (Moscow:
Obshchedostupnyi Pravoslavnyi Universitet osnovannyi Aleksandrom Menem, 2008);
"Sofiologiia smerti," *Vestnik Russkogo khristianskogo dvizheniia* 127 (1978): [I:]18–41;
128 (1978), [II:]13–32.

2. Bulgakov, *Avtobiograficheskoe*, 69.

3. Ibid., 65.

Egypt. And first of all, there was no fear of death. The relatives, first of all women, arrived to dress the departed, to pray for him, and to help with the household chores with a joyous, solemn feeling. Then came the funeral in the church with the carrying of the coffin around town accompanied by the ringing of the bells, the giving of the body back to the earth, the veneration of the tomb, and prayer-filled memory. They bury well in Livny. If it is possible to speak of the sophianicity of a funeral, then it could be said that the burial was sophianic, bearing a mark of eternity, a triumph of life, and a union with nature. "Dust thou art and unto dust shalt thou return." [Gen 3:19, KJV][4]

While these words reflect Bulgakov's much later interpretation of his childhood encounter with the reality of death, it is plausible that even as a child he could experience as vague calls of the heart those things that would with time grow into deeply rooted convictions: the absence of the fear of death, the awareness of the presence of God, the triumph of eternity over time, and a sense of passing into another world in order to reach a greater state of union with the cosmos.

After the death of his grandfather, "the angel of death unceasingly stood in front of our house,"[5] remarked Bulgakov, reflecting on the deaths of five of his siblings, two dying in infancy, one in early childhood, one in adolescence, and one in young adulthood. Perhaps the most profound impact was that of the death of his younger brother Mikhail of consumption:

Even now, after 40 years, my eyes are filled with tears, when I recall his holy, beautiful death. Before he departed this world, he was sent like an angel to pour the treasure of his death into my soul. This was at night. It was evident that his agony had begun. All stood up, surrounded him, and my father began to read the service for those about to die (everybody felt that this was quite natural). "Is this a service for those about to die?"— asked Mikhail and began to say farewell to everybody, kissing everyone for the last time. He kissed me so . . . He particularly wanted me to be near him, when I was so full of myself, only of myself . . . He left peacefully and the mystery of death was filled with light. His hands, as the hands of those dying of consumption, were white. The sun was breaking out, my brother Lelia and I went into the garden, and my heart was filled with heavenly music, with a celebration that is made possible by tender,

4. Ibid., 72–3.
5. Ibid., 75.

quiet, faithful death, which opens up the heavens and angels . . .
Yes, death was our educator in this household, so full of death.[6]

Not all deaths in Bulgakov's family caused him to humbly acquiesce to
the inevitable. Bulgakov's recollection of the death of his infant brother
Kos'ma was quite chilling: "I remember the night with the dead body of
my infant brother at home and my mother's howling cries at night . . .
This event has crept into my heart as a call and dread and awe-inspiring
memory of eternity."[7] Bulgakov noted that he had a similar experience on
the occasion of his grandfather's death in his household. "Awe-inspiring
memory of eternity" remained an existential constant of his subsequent
confrontations with human mortality, animating and shaping his theological thought.

The loss of his five-year-old brother Nikolai was a deeply wounding
and fearful experience, filling Bulgakov's household with grief and lament. Years later, in 1909, Bulgakov would have to endure the agony and
death of his own three-year-old son, Ivan, similar to his parents' suffering
through the deaths of Nikolai and other children. For Bulgakov, Ivan's
death was not only a bleeding wound, a scar upon his family that would
never heal completely, but also a profound epiphany of love. He describes
the revelatory character of confronting Ivan's death in *The Unfading Light*
(1918), a book that is generally regarded as marking a theological turn in
his thinking:

> My holy one, before the holy shrine of your relics, near your
> pure body, my white one, my light-filled boy, I have learned
> *how* God speaks, I understood the meaning of the words "God
> said!" And my heart was granted a new, previously unknown
> clairvoyance as the heavenly joy came upon it and together with
> the darkness of Godforsakenness, God came to reign in it. My
> heart opened itself to the pain and torment of other people and
> their previously foreign and closed hearts opened up to me with
> their pain and grief. For a single moment of my life I came to
> understand what it meant to love with the love of Christ, rather
> than with the love that was human, selfish, and seeking its own.
> It is as if the veil that separated me from others fell off and all the
> darkness, bitterness, hurt, anger, and suffering of their hearts
> was revealed to me. Unspeakably elated, ecstatic, self-forgetting,
> I spoke then—you remember this, my white one!—I spoke: *God*

6. Ibid., 74.
7. Ibid., 75.

said to me, and, hearing you, with equal simplicity added, *you spoke to me too.* And God spoke to me then and you spoke to me! Presently I again see only in darkness and cold and, hence, can speak of these things only from memory, but I have learned the meaning of the words *God said.* [. . .]

Listening to the Epistle Reading [in the church] about the resurrection and about the general sudden transformation . . . I came to understand for the first time that it would happen *for certain* and *how* it would happen.[8]

As Bulgakov was praying at the deathbed of his son, something new and profound had happened. We might recall that, according to his own admission, he defended himself emotionally from the death of his grandfather with "animal self-love" and that he persevered in being "full of himself" when his dying brother Mikhail reached out to him in the last embrace of love. But in the death of Bulgakov's son, it was as if the "the veil that separated him from others fell off" and he was given an epiphany of complete, all-consuming love for others, love that enabled him to enter experientially into the grief and pain of others like never before. In the encounter with his son's death, Bulgakov was also given to understand and experientially enter into the reality behind Paul's words in 1 Cor 15:51–53: "Listen, I will tell you a mystery! We will not all die, but we will all be changed, in a moment, in the twinkling of an eye, at the last trumpet. For the trumpet will sound, and the dead will be raised imperishable, and we will be changed. For this perishable body must put on imperishability, and this mortal body must put on immortality." The death of his son had lifted the veil of his self-love and given him a new, more profound taste of transfigured humanity. In light of these deeply formative and ego-shattering experiences, Bulgakov could write: "One's Motherland is only where there is death. This is why the last word about the Motherland is about death."[9]

The epiphany received in 1909 would continue shedding its light upon Bulgakov's priestly ministry, especially his care for the dying and his sense of the participation of the saints in the Eucharistic communion. I would also suggest that this epiphany gave him peace and spiritual strength in the times of extreme adversity and accounted for the eschatological thrust of his sophiology.

8. Bulgakov, *Svet Nevechernii*, 18.

9. Bulgakov, *Aftobiograficheskoe*, 77.

Following a calling common to the six generations of his ancestors, Bulgakov became a priest in June 1918, less than a year after the Bolshevik coup d'état in Russia. The price that Bulgakov immediately paid for his ordination was the loss of a university post in Moscow for his perceived opposition to the atheist regime. During the time of the Civil War, he found himself serving at a provincial parish in Crimea, not dissimilar to his father's parish in Livny. Here Fr. Sergius would witness with great anguish how some of his parishioners would starve to death and felt guilty for remaining alive, although gradually deprived of basic means of existence. But the Soviet authorities could not rest until they squashed all opposition to their power. In 1922, Bulgakov was arrested and had to watch his fellow-prisoners being shot by the drunken officers of the Red Army. In early 1923, the regime expelled Bulgakov on one of the "Philosophy Steamers" along with other prominent religious thinkers and philosophers of his time. Bulgakov put the matter astringently: "As she was herself rotting in a casket, Russia expelled me as useless, having branded me with the mark of a slave."[10] The experience of expulsion and deracination was both traumatic and stimulating. Not unlike Bulgakov's encounter with death and bereavement, which was at once heartbreaking and transforming, the experience of dying to his own country was a blow and a providential opportunity. Among many burdens of émigré life—the loss of most of his Russian-speaking audience, the challenges of leading St. Sergius Orthodox Theological Institute against much strife and opposition, financial instability, and finally the advent of fascism and World War II—none was as emotionally draining as the permanent separation from his older son, Fyodor (1902–1991), who was left behind the Iron Curtain in 1923, never to be seen by his parents again. Bulgakov often agonized over the fate of his son, especially when for long stretches of time he would not receive any letters from him. After World War II, Fyodor was able to travel abroad for the first time in order to visit his parents' graves at Sainte-Geneviève-des-Bois near Paris.

Bulgakov's *Spiritual Diary*, which he kept from 1924 to 1926 during his first years in Paris, is a unique testament to his life with God. The main thrust of the diary is vertical, rather than horizontal. Bulgakov is primarily addressing God and his soul, as he stands *coram Deo*. He is brutally honest with himself, functioning as his own harshest judge, sometimes to the point of being quite self-effacing. He registers

---

10. Bulgakov, "Iz dnevnika," 351.

his human interactions, but rarely reveals many particulars. The diary is a testament to Bulgakov's profoundly christocentric and Mariological piety. While sophiological motifs appear, Sophia is never made an object of prayer or private adoration, as in Vladimir Solovyov. Whatever one might claim about Bulgakov's theological "modernism," his spiritual life was profoundly grounded in his childhood experiences of death and dying, as well as his attendance at the Orthodox services, especially those of the feast days of Easter and the Dormition of the Theotokos (an Orthodox equivalent of the Assumption of the Blessed Virgin, celebrated on August 15). The diary contains Bulgakov's own Akathistos (hymn of praise) to Mary, in which he speaks of her as "bringing consolation at the hour of death"[11] and "making death a joyous feast by her light."[12] Bulgakov is strikingly traditional and conventional, almost pre-modern, in his piety, especially if one considers the prominence of the *memento mori* theme in his diary. In fact, his observation that "life must be a constant dying for the Lord"[13] could serve as the diary's epigraph. The prevailing tone of the diary reminds one of the spiritual sobriety and clarity of St. John of Kronshtadt's *My Life in Christ*. Bulgakov speaks of the love of God, of prayer, of humble acceptance of suffering, and of being mindful of God, and of his own failures with remarkable honesty and simplicity. The theosophic motifs, associated with the period when he was influenced by Pavel Florensky, are conspicuously absent from the diary, as are sophiological speculations.

Bulgakov reflects on mortality in the context of dying and parting with the dead in several diary entries. For example, in the entry dated October 7(20), 1924, he writes:

> We are created for eternity, it is not here below that we are called to live—this becomes evident when the most precious person departs for the other world but the lover remains here, in this world. How does one save love from powerlessness, how does one save the soul from despair? [One can do so] only by God and in God, only through prayer. The wings of prayer will carry us into another world, they will give us an invisible connection with the beloved, they will carry us closer and closer to him

11. Bulgakov, *Dnevnik dukhovnyi*, 48.
12. Ibid., 49.
13. Ibid., 89.

until the hour of our own call and until the light of our eyes goes out too.[14]

In his capacity of father confessor and parish priest, Bulgakov attended to the needs of those approaching the hour of death, following in the steps of his own father. At times he speaks of this ministry with poetic lyricism. Here, for example, is the beginning of his diary entry dated January 23 (February 5), 1925:

> I witnessed a striking and touching picture of a young maiden's departure to God. The Lord brought me to her deathbed not long before her end. Christ visited her and communed her of His Body and Blood by my sinful hand. Then her soul took flight to the Bridegroom as a bird flying into the blue abyss of the sky. And heaven appeared in that room of sorrow, the Lord was close, granting the miracle of divine mercy. She lay quietly, clearly and plainly, having known everything that we do not know here below. And around her everything was prayerful and solemn.[15]

Tending to the needs of the dying meant that for Bulgakov *memento mori* was not a solitary exercise, as it was often the case for the ascetics of the past, but an experience of entering compassionately into the sorrow of another person's encounter with death: "I was at the deathbed of a young girl dying of consumption and my soul was burning as I was overwhelmed by pity at the sight of this flower cut off from life."[16] For Bulgakov this compassion was hard-earned, for it was the death of his own son Ivan that lifted up the veil of his self-love and broke down the boundaries separating his self from those of others. Death was more than a revelation of human brokenness; it was also a revelation of love, joy, and eternity. In Bulgakov's own words:

> For the first time in my life I have learned by experience that death is the greatest joy, which *awaits* each human being, because the Theotokos and her love, the angels, the saints, the relatives and the loved ones, and the Lord await him. This encounter is full of awe and trepidation, but it is also full of boundless joy. The desire "to depart and be with the Lord" [Phil 1:23]—these

14. Ibid., 53–54.
15. Ibid., 124.
16. Ibid., 10.

words of the apostle have become a living truth for the first time.[17]

Death is more than parting with this life, it is entering into the joy of the Lord, into the communion of the saints. In this context, Bulgakov speaks of love that is "strong as death" (Song 8:6) and, boldly asserts that "love is death and death is love," intending to convey the point that the revelation of true love becomes possible at the threshold of death.

In Bulgakov's own life, two experiences that left him hovering on the brink of death were profoundly transformative. The first occurred during his first serious illness in January 1926, when for several days, if not weeks, he burned with high fever. He described his experience in the second part of his essay "The Sophiology of Death," published posthumously. While he was feverish, Bulgakov "lost the consciousness of being in a limited place in space and time," "the consciousness of having a body that rests on a bed," and "lost awareness of the boundaries of the self, which became 'we,' a plurality into which my 'I' entered as an indefinite point."[18] At the same time, "my spiritual 'I' achieved a greater sharpness and consciousness. It was an unadorned judge of my life. I was seized by fear and trembling. It was as if my soul underwent the trials of hell in which the burning wounds of my soul were being opened up. At that time the Lord spared me and protected me from the visions of the demonic. But fever coupled with the spiritual pangs created a fiery furnace . . . This experience taught me the meaning of burning in the furnace of blazing fire without burning down" [Dan 3:23–27]. The transformation brought about by this hellish experience was most extraordinary:

> Suddenly—after this burning—cool and consolation penetrated the fiery furnace of my heart. How can I relate this miracle of God's mercy, of forgiveness? With all my being I felt its boundless joy and lightness. My guardian angel, who was with me ceaselessly, put this into my heart. I suddenly felt that nothing separated me from the Lord for I had been redeemed by the Lord . . . Even during confession I felt that I already had forgiveness. I had a feeling that my sins had been burned away, that they were no more.
>
> But this mystery of forgiveness was revealed to me only in conjunction with the mystery of death, for I felt at the same time that my life had ended and that I was dying. But where

17. Ibid., 39.
18. Bulgakov, "Sofiologiia smerti," II: 13.

was the fear of death? Only the joy of death was there, the joy
of the Lord. Heavenly joy, which cannot be expressed in human
language, filled all my being.[19]

Bulgakov goes on to say that during his illness he had periods of being
terrified of death primarily because he despaired of leaving his family
without his care. But this feeling was a passing weakness, which was
soon replaced by the sense of entering into the communion of the saints
and of the breaking of the boundary between the living and the dead.
This experience was accompanied by an equally potent feeling of being
reunited with his deceased son, Ivan, and of "the presence of God reign-
ing over everything. I have learned forever that only God and his mercy
exist, that we must live only for God, love only God, and seek only the
kingdom of God, and that everything that blocks God is a delusion."[20]
The sense of the abiding presence of God coupled with liberation from
the fear of death is present with great consistency in Bulgakov's earlier accounts of his encounters with death and dying. The novel element in the
experience of 1926 is that of profound assurance of forgiveness. While
such experience is sanctioned by the Orthodox Church in the sacrament
of confession, the matter of assurance is not generally emphasized, as it
is in Pietism, Methodism, and other Christian movements. Elsewhere,
Bulgakov speaks more concretely of being relieved from his fascination
with the particularly dubious forms of theosophy and from the Gnostic
elements in his sophiology.[21] Whatever the particulars of this experience,
the effect was purgative and profoundly freeing. The experience only re-
inforced the conviction with which Bulgakov continued to theologize *sub
specie aeternitatis*.

One may also find in these experiences the wellspring of Bulgakov's
remarkable tranquility in the face of the Sophia Affair, which cast a long
shadow of ecclesiastical condemnation upon his theological system and
threatened to subject to *damnatio memoriae* his life's work. In 1935, as
the theological opposition to sophiology began to mount in the Orthodox Church, Bulgakov demonstrated extraordinary intellectual tenacity
in upholding his views and developing his system with an even greater
speculative depth rather than maintaining silence in order not to provoke

19. Ibid., II: 14.

20. Ibid., II: 15.

21. Bulgakov, Letter to G. Florovsky, 8 (21) February 1926, GFP PUL, Box 12, f.
11.

his numerous detractors. It could be said that Bulgakov showed more tolerance towards his theological enemies than some of his close friends, who rose rather passionately to his defense. In his memoirs he attributes this attitude to his aversion to fighting and cowardice, while one might be more disposed to ascribe Bulgakov's reaction to the nobility of his spirit and gentleness.

In 1939, Bulgakov was diagnosed with throat cancer and endured a second encounter with death during his surgery. It was the experience of living through the operation and its aftermath that occasioned the writing of the first part of "The Sophiology of Death" in the same year. In this essay, Bulgakov's description of his near-death experience reaches a new level of sincerity and immediacy. He does not gloss over the parts of the experience that do not fit into the canons of conventional piety. His description is more direct, sober, and free from rosy sentimentality. He paints on the canvas of his soul with the assurance of a man who has glimpsed eternity and who no longer has anything to hide either from others or from himself. It is in this essay that Bulgakov offers his most nuanced theological analysis of dying.

He had a series of two surgeries during which his throat was cut up without general anesthetic. Since he was conscious throughout the surgery, he could see the implements with which the cancerous growth was being removed from his body. The main physiological state that he described was that of suffocation in which he was no longer capable of praying. Bulgakov was hovering on the brink of death and was exhausted by the sufferings of his body to the point of being unable to experience what he had previously experienced on several occasions, namely, the joy of death as entering into the light-filled life with God. Instead, this experience was a new revelation of co-suffering and co-dying with the crucified Christ:

> Christ died our human death in order to accept through it the death of the Godman. This is why our dying, as co-dying with Him, is a revelation about Christ's death, although not a revelation about His glory. I have come to know the meaning of the apostle's words "always carrying in the body the death of Jesus, so that the life of Jesus may also be made visible in our bodies. For while we live, we are always being given up to death for Jesus' sake, so that the life of Jesus may be made visible in our mortal flesh. So death is at work in us, but life in you" (2 Cor 4: 10–12). And also, "the whole creation has been groaning in labor pains

until now; and not only the creation, but we ourselves, who have the first fruits of the Spirit, groan inwardly while we wait for adoption, the redemption of our bodies" (Rom 8: 22–23).

Pondering the matter further, Bulgakov noted that

> Dying was not resolved in a death, but remained a revelation about the way of death, which, after Christ, awaits each man, whether he wishes it or not. Mortality is contained in the fallen human nature that was assumed by Christ in his mortal human being. Each illness is an awareness of mortality, its revelation, which nobody can avoid. Its measure is determined by the strength of illness, by how close it brings us to death. Objectively I was at a hair's length from death during the first part of my illness, subjectively I was nearly completely enveloped by mortality and came to know it for this reason. I came to know my mortality as the Lord's cruciform dying in his Godforsakenness even to death, from "why have You forsaken me" to "into Your hands I commend my spirit." Dying does not contain a revelation about the death itself, such revelation is given only to those who have tasted death and thereby have left this world without return. Behind the threshold of death there follows a revelation of life after death as the beginning of new existence; the experience on this side of death has nothing to tell us about this reality. Dying knows nothing of the revelation of the life after death and of the resurrection.[22]

It is remarkable that Bulgakov's last recorded and analyzed experience of confronting his mortality was a revelation of his co-dying with Christ, rather than the revelation of entering into the communion of the saints and the life with God. While the two revelatory experiences were closely related and followed one upon the other, Bulgakov sought to differentiate them as clearly as possible, for this very differentiation was not solely a matter of theoretical speculation, but the content of a divine disclosure. In the same essay he admitted that even in dying it was possible, by the grace of God, to receive a foretaste of the joy of the resurrection, as he himself had done during his purgative illness of 1926, and as he had received on other occasions when he witnessed the deaths of those dear to him. But in the revelatory experience of 1939 it was the sorrow of Godforsakenness, rather than the joyous foretaste of the resurrection, that was disclosed to him.

22. Bulgakov, "Sofiologiia smerti," I: 41.

Throughout his life, Bulgakov remembered and carefully recorded his encounters with death and dying. In his childhood experiences, the predominant motif was the acceptance of the reality of death within the framework of Orthodox beliefs and practices, which his family took for granted. His grandfather's death left Bulgakov "mystically shaken," yet the experience itself was solemn and filled with a sense of God's abiding presence and even beauty. Of the siblings that he lost while he was still a child, his most vivid memory was that of the death of his younger brother, Mikhail. Strikingly, Bulgakov speaks of this experience without any lingering bitterness or rebellion; the dominant feeling is that of humbly accepting human fragility and mortality. There is also a lingering regret that this death did not break his self-centeredness. Only years later, when his own son Ivan died, did Bulgakov experience a shattering of his selfish defenses and experienced this particular loss as a revelation of compassionate love, indeed a divine call to selfless love. In his priestly ministry, Bulgakov often attended to the needs of the dying. Again, the dominant hue of these experiences is the sorrowful joy of sending a soul to God, purified and released of its burden. The experiences of 1926 and 1939 distinguish themselves from the rest as Bulgakov's confrontations with his own mortality, rather than that of others. The experience of 1926 brought about the assurance of having his sins purged in the burning fiery furnace of suffering. With this assurance also came a profound sense of Christ's victory over the power of death and the joy of the resurrection. The experience of 1939 enabled Bulgakov to enter into the mystery of co-dying with Christ.

II. The Revelatory Character of Death in Bulgakov's Sophiology

Such a profound and frequent confrontation with mortality had a deep impact on Bulgakov as a churchman and as a thinker. It would be naïve to claim that the causal connection was unidirectional, that the experiences influenced theology and not vice versa. It would be safe to assume instead that he came to interpret his experiences in light of his theological assumptions and that his theological views were in turn shaped and deepened by his experiences. One undisputable example of Bulgakov interpreting the phenomenological content of his *childhood* experience in light of his later theological views is his discussion of the "sophianic" character of death in his *Autobiographic Notes*. Obviously, as a twelve-year-old child he could not possibly think of the solemn acceptance of death received within the context of the Orthodox funeral service in terms of his later teaching about Sophia, the Wisdom of God. It is also significant that during the period when he lived through the deaths of his grandfather and his five brothers he turned away from the faith of his parents, rebelled against traditional Christianity by embracing nihilism and materialism in a Marxist form. But his fifteen-year-long rebellion, lasting approximately from 1888 to 1904,[23] does not surface in his much later recollections (1938) of how he reacted to the deaths of his relatives. Was the trauma of so many deaths in the family also a factor in his temporary loss of his childhood faith? One would search in vain for any such connection in Bulgakov's writings. His existential crisis seems to have been caused by a failed system of state-sponsored theological education rather than by the anguish of losses.

What was, then, the relationship between Bulgakov's sophiology and his experiences of death? Did such experiences factor at all into his theological thinking? What existential impulses gave birth to his thought? A commonly accepted answer to the last question is that the main driving force of his sophiological teaching was his lifelong effort to resolve the metaphysical problems surrounding cosmology, especially the problem of an intermediary between God and creation. His solution was to extend the Chalcedonian dogma of Christ's two natures into a general metaphysical principle of Godmanhood, or divine-human unity, along the lines earlier proposed by Vladimir Solovyov. This is a plausible interpretation of the central impulse behind sophiology, corroborated by ample evidence from Bulgakov's writings. Nevertheless, I would propose more controversially that the central intuition of sophiology—that all things find their eternal ground in God and that God is present in all things—also has a crucial *existential* dimension conveyed by the experiences of death and dying.

This claim becomes more plausible if we examine *how* the earth-shattering experience of his son's death is introduced in *The Unfading Light*. In the beginning of the book, Bulgakov sets out to show, in a quasi-Kantian fashion, what makes religion possible. For Bulgakov, the main factor is experiential: people reporting an encounter with the divine. While claims of religious experiences could be challenged on various

23. Bulgakov, *Avtobiograficheskoe*, 78.

skeptical grounds, in the final analysis the skepticism does not do justice to the world-orienting value of such experiences. As one example, Bulgakov mentions his confrontation with the reality of his son's death as a moment when his selfish ego was shattered and his heart was flooded with compassion for all who were suffering and wounded. More importantly, he received these truths not upon reflection, but as a prophetic word, as God speaking directly into his heart. In his later writings Bulgakov consistently placed a very high cognitive premium on private revelations received while facing death and dying. While he had a rich and complex mystical life, and no less complicated spiritual evolution, Bulgakov never trifled with the concept of prophetic speech and did not appeal to direct divine speaking on other occasions. Clearly, the experience of Ivan's death was a cognitive breakthrough that directed and animated his thought, even if the final shape of his speculative system appeared as a result of much deliberation.

A different way of casting the same point would be to say that Bulgakov regarded the sense of the abiding presence of God in all of creation, eternity underlying time, to be the final truth of human existence and that any construal of the world that ignored that truth was a profound distortion. He expresses this point rather forcefully in his *Spiritual Diary*: "Only God exists!," which is to say that the foundation of reality is eternal life with God rather than mortality and contingency. While the sense of the presence of God could be in principle available everywhere—and Bulgakov's enduring interest in "nature mysticism" could be viewed as an important aspect of the "sophianicity of the world" theme—its most concentrated revelation is granted in the experience of passing from this world, in which God's existence is often dubious, into another world, in which it is an evident and overwhelming reality. Death itself (as distinct from dying) was for Bulgakov a revelation of love and joy precisely because death marked an entrance into the communion of the saints and, more importantly, into the communion with God. For these reasons, I would submit that the world-orienting experience underlying sophiology was that of the encounter with death. Like the knight in Ingmar Bergman's film *The Seventh Seal*, Bulgakov met death at the dawn of his life and continued to have transformative encounters with death and dying throughout his life.

In his theological investigations Bulgakov explored the dual nature of death at great length. Death was at once an end of earthly life and the beginning of the new life. As an end of this life, death had the effect of severing vital human bonds and for that reason brought sorrow, misery, and hopelessness; as a beginning of the new life, death could be joyous, peaceful, and liberating. Bulgakov's lifelong acquaintance with death supplied the experiential knowledge of both states. It was this tasted knowledge that fueled Bulgakov's theological investigations into the nature of death.

"The Sophiology of Death" was Bulgakov's second and most definitive exploration of the nature of death, written *after* his cancer surgery of 1939. In the 1930s, sometime before the experience of 1939, Bulgakov also explored a similar set of issues in the seventh chapter of his book, *The Bride of the Lamb*, which had been completely finished by 1939, but could be published only posthumously, in 1945, because of the troubles with Bulgakov's health and World War II.[24] The book is the last volume of his major trilogy on Godmanhood, the previous two volumes dealing with Christology (*The Lamb of God*) and pneumatology (*The Comforter*). *The Bride of the Lamb* covers the doctrine of creation, ecclesiology, and eschatology, to which the seventh chapter "On Death and the State after Death" provides an introduction.

In the introductory chapter, Bulgakov raises two central questions: What is death? and What does it mean for Christ to die? He answers the first question within the framework of the threefold division of human nature into spirit, soul, and body. Bulgakov writes that "death is a release of the soul from the bonds of the body and is a great consecration, a revelation of the spiritual world," adding that "this revelation of the spiritual world in death is a great joy and unspeakable celebration for those who were separated from it in this life but craved it, and an inexpressible terror, hardship, and turmoil for those who did not want this spiritual world, did not know it, and rejected it."[25] Bulgakov's numerous experiences of death and dying underlie this succinct statement of a revelatory dimension of death.

Bulgakov notes that death is a result of the original sin. Because of the original sin, human life is surrounded with decay and dying from the very beginning. Yet, life is not sunken in death, does not emerge from death, as the materialists hold; on the contrary, death is a passing state of life, it has to be understood as a passing from one form of life here below

---

24. Bulgakov, *Nevesta Agntsa*, 374–402.
25. Ibid., 383, 384.

into another form, in the kingdom above. Death is a threshold between two lives.

Bulgakov questions the presupposition of traditional Christian eschatology that there could be no spiritual change in the life after death. He argues that the spirit cannot remain inactive and that the spirits of the dead remain receptive both to God and to the prayer of the living.[26] According to Bulgakov, the souls of the dead are capable of spiritual growth, which takes the form not only of joy and delight, but also of judgment, as the soul comes to recognize its shortcomings and failures in its earthly life. In his reflections, Bulgakov attempts to maintain a dual character of otherworldly experience, a change that presupposes a reevaluation of one's previous life and a deepening of one's orientation towards God and divine things. He emphasizes that the strongest bond that will continue to exist in the life of the age to come is that of prayer and love.[27] For this bond to be effectual, it has to have some bearing upon the fate of the souls in the intermediate state. Bulgakov leaves open the possibility of a profound spiritual transformation in the life of the age to come without overdetermining the precise form that such a transformation might take.

The second central question that he raises is how to understand the death of Christ. What does it mean for the Godman to die? Does such a death entail a separation of the Logos from his human nature? In *The Bride of the Lamb*, Bulgakov answers negatively, for such a separation would have implied dis-incarnation (*razvoploshchenie*), which is impossible, since the unity of Christ's divine and human natures is inseparable and endures even in death. In "The Sophiology of Death," he gives a more profound and extended answer: "The death of Christ is included in the general divine kenosis as His voluntary self-abasement and self-emptying."[28] For the sake of human salvation, "God accepts death freely and sacrificially."[29] "The revelation of the Godman for us is inevitably also a revelation of His *death* in us and we have to comprehend His measureless sacrificial love for us in His co-dying with us. This is only possible through our co-dying with Him."[30] Here Bulgakov speaks through the prism of his experience of co-dying with Christ in 1939. It is noteworthy

26. See my article "Universal Salvation," 110–32.

27. Bulgakov, *Nevesta Agntsa*, 389.

28. Bulgakov, "Sofiologiia smerti," I: 18.

29. Ibid., I: 20.

30. Ibid., I: 20.

that the theme of Christ's co-dying with those who die is absent from *The Bride of the Lamb*, which was finished before his battle with throat cancer.

According to Bulgakov, the kenosis of the Son of God renders not only the human nature but also the divine nature of Christ accessible to death, although in different respects. The divine Logos accepts human death into himself in order to conquer death, for mortality can only be overcome by God. This overcoming is achieved through the act of self-sacrificial and self-emptying love, rather than through an omnipotent act of creation.[31] God empties himself in the life of Christ by rendering the union of his nature with the lowly human nature possible. For Bulgakov kenosis consists in God's acceptance of all conditions and deprivations of human mortality, including fatigue, hunger, thirst, cold, and so on. Following an influential trope in patristic theology, Bulgakov insists that it is possible to speak of the death of the Godman. Death does not mean annihilation. Death means the acceptance of human mortality into the life of God, God's co-dying with man. The death of each individual human being is included in the death of Christ because his human nature is at once individual and universal, and includes all humanity. In the death of Christ, God temporarily withholds the power of the resurrection from human nature, while remaining God. Bulgakov insists that such withholding also happens in the case of the death of all human beings, since God could spare them from death by his power. It is in this specific sense that each human death is co-dying with Christ.

The kenosis of the crucified Christ also has a trinitarian dimension, of the Father co-suffering with the Son in sending the Son to death (Bulgakov does not seemed to be concerned about the Patripassian connotations of this claim), of the Son's obedience to the salvific will of the Father, and of the Holy Spirit's kenotic withdrawal from the Son. God takes human dying into his divine nature in order to draw human nature into the life of resurrection, into eternity.

Bulgakov's reflections on divine kenosis are not always clear or consistent. He is aware of the range of speculative alternatives available in German and British kenoticism. His project is to include the valid insights of the nineteenth- and twentieth-century theologians without overturning the classical trinitarian doctrine and the Chalcedonian Christology. Whether he succeeds in the latter undertaking is somewhat questionable. What cannot be doubted, however, is that in "The Sophiology of

31. Ibid., II: 19.

Death," Bulgakov's own experience of co-dying with Christ comes to bear upon his theology. Bulgakov's theology achieves a seamless fusion of lived mystical experience and speculative theology, which constitutes a distinguishing mark of any authentic Orthodox theology. While one might question various individual elements of Bulgakov's thinking—and he never intended his thinking to become church dogma—one cannot doubt his genuineness. The revelatory experiences of death constitute an experiential kernel of his sophiology. Philosophical theology was for Bulgakov the Christian Platonist what philosophy was for Plato: "a training for dying and death."[32]

Bulgakov died in 1944, about four years after completing "The Sophiology of Death." His final agony, which brought about his death, was not something he had an opportunity or need to analyze. As he passed into the realm beyond all words, those witnessing his last moments reported different things. One witness noticed the signs of profound spiritual struggle on his face, a struggle that remained to the end. Another witness, a nun present at his deathbed, saw an expression of unutterable joy on his face and exclaimed: "Fr. Sergius is approaching the throne of God and is being surrounded by the light of His Glory!"[33]

BIBLIOGRAPHY

Bulgakov, Sergius. *Avtobiograficheskoe.* In *S.N. Bulgakov: Pro et Contra*, vol. 1, 63–111. St. Petersburg: RKhGI, 2003.
———. *Dnevnik dukhovnyi.* Moscow: Obshchedostupnyi Pravoslavnyi Universitet osnovannyi Aleksandrom Menem, 2008.
———. "Iz dnevnika." In *Tikhie dumy.* Moscow: Respublika, 1996.
———. *Nevesta Agntsa.* Moscow: Obshchedostupnyi Pravoslavnyi Universitet osnovannyi Aleksandrom Menem, 2005.
———. "Sofiologiia smerti," *Vestnik Russkogo khristianskogo dvizheniia* 127 (1978) [I:]18–41; 128 (1978), [II:]13–32.
———. *Svet Nevechernii.* Moscow: Respublika, 1994.
Gavrilyuk, Paul. "Universal Salvation in the Eschatology of Sergius Bulgakov." *The Journal of Theological Studies* 57 (2006) 110–32.
Nun Elena. "Professor protoierei Sergii Bulgakov." *Bogoslovskie trudy* 27 (1986) 101–78.

32. Plato, *Phaedo* 64a4, cf. 67e.
33. Nun Elena, "Professor protoierei Sergii Bulgakov," 101–178.

Chapter 9

In the Realm of Apocalypse

Heidegger and the Impossibility of Christian Death

Cyril O'Regan

When it comes to Christian death we could and perhaps should begin and end with the pattern of Christ's ordering of existence towards death as revealed in the Gospels and speak boldly to the hope that is within us. And throughout the essay I will recur to this pattern and the theological reflection it both prompts and guides. Yet I will do so only indirectly and discuss it only in the context of the critical conversation between Catholic theology and Martin Heidegger's apocalyptic figuration of death. This conversation was in one sense extraordinarily congenial in that Heidegger's mindfulness regarding human finitude made him an asset in the Church's fight against the amnesia of death and its promotion of a dramatic view of human existence as a trial in which and for which there were eternal and immutable consequences, and at the core of which was the eternal enjoyment or loss of enjoyment of and participation in the triune God. In another sense, however, the conversation was not congenial, nor could it be for Catholic thinkers such as Erich Przywara, Edith Stein, and Hans Urs von Balthasar, who were worried about what they sensed were Heidegger's nihilistic commitments, which were not always apparent given his willingness—albeit selective—to call upon Christian symbols and texts and turn them against the common enemy of enlightenment and bourgeois modernity. In his master-work, *Being and Time* (1927),[1] Heidegger had all but absolutized death, such that it proscribed thinking of God as the term of human desire and activity. The boundary of finitude or being-towards-death (*Sein zum Tode*) is "nothing" or "the nothing."[2] Heidegger gives modernity and the Catholic Church the "gift of death."[3] Yet the gift is two-faced at best and terrible at worst in that it forecloses specifically theological as well as phenomenological-philosophical options. While major 20th-century Catholic thinkers were energized by Heidegger's thanatology, they also saw through its exaggerations, its elevated heroism that does not rhyme with the Gospel or the precepts of courage, acceptance, humility, faith, and hope that were long the Catholic staple. They judge as simply dogmatic the claim that the "end," which comes from the future and cannot be anticipated, necessarily wears the face of "nothing" and not God. Although Heidegger could plausibly plead that his existential phenomenology is only "methodologically atheistic,"[4] the legislation as to what will count as evidence or not seems sufficiently pointed to conclude that God, who might have been the polestar for a life that careens towards death, is not only put in brackets, but is in fact dismissed with prejudice. The dismissal of God, or even his very possibility, from being an intention of experience, in turn makes impossible traditional eschatology, which concerns judgment, heaven and hell, as well as death. For a number of the major Catholic readers of Heidegger, the ironic outcome of what might be called his eschatological escalation is making theological reflection on the eschata obsolete.

1. Heidegger, *Being and Time*.

2. For Heidegger's discussion of "being-towards-death," see *Being and Time*, Division 2. 1, 279–311; for "nothing," see 279, 308, also 186–89.

3. This locution is borrowed from a book by Jacques Derrida who critiques Heidegger's view of death by means of Levinas. See Derrida, *The Gift of Death*. If Levinas is a major presence throughout the text as offering a particular view on death focused on the other, Levinas is also used critically against Heidegger's view of the "mineness" (*Jemeinigkeit*) of death. See The *Gift of Death*, 35–52, esp. 41–47.

4. "Methodogical atheism" operates at an implicit level in *Being and Time* and is more or less an implicate of the commitment to phenomenology as a method that brackets beliefs, convictions, and presuppositions. Although in *Being and Time* Heidegger subverts Husserlian-style phenomenology by making an ontological turn, he is largely faithful to it in bracketing appeals to God. See *Being and Time* #7, 49–55. The concept functions more explicitly in Heidegger's essay from the same period, "Phänomenologie und Theologie" (1927/28). For a good English translation, see "Phenomenology and Theology," in *The Piety of Thinking*, 5–21. This essay functions significantly in Hemming, *Heidegger's Atheism*, 64–66.

Although my reflection here is at a slant to a positive account of Christian death that would call upon the wisdom of scripture and the entire Catholic tradition and the entire armory of precept, ritual, and sacrament, at the very least it brings the ineluctable scaffolding of a Catholic view of death in particular and a Catholic eschatology in general into view by exploring how far and how long Catholic theology can travel the thanatological road with Heidegger as a companion. The essay is made up of three parts or sections. In the first I try to make sense of why Heidegger's eschatologically exacerbated thanatology could appeal to Catholic thinkers, and answer that though there are many reasons— many of which were quite contingent—the main one was that Heidegger was regarded as an ally in the overcoming of the amnesia of death, even if there was no evidence of hospitability to the specific ways in which Catholic mindfulness was practiced. In the second section I speak to emergent 20th-century Catholic critiques of Heidegger's banning of God as the point of reference of human temporality and finitude. In this section, the horizon of investigation is largely phenomenological, with the specific concern being whether Heidegger's focus on death should necessarily involve a love affair with "nothing." While I want to underscore that all three major Catholic thinkers of whom I speak have interesting things to say here, I would like especially to underscore the contribution of Edith Stein. In the third section, I deal with Heidegger's exclusion of eschatological data. In one sense such exclusion is a corollary of the dismissal of God, understood to be the ground of all beings and thus from Heidegger's point of view the item in the authoritarian regime of metaphysics. In another sense, however, the exclusion suggests not only a bias against doctrines, which function, according to the early Heidegger, at a remove from experience and sometimes contrary to it, but also against revelation as the font and motor of doctrine. Despite Heidegger's early appeal to the biblical text,[5] the Bible has no authority as such. A traditional eschatology such as that offered by Augustine in *The City of God* cannot be thought in the descriptive-prescriptive philosophical horizon of *Being and Time*. It cannot be thought for two closely related reasons: (a) because of the propositional (apophantic) claims it makes, which, on

5. I am speaking in particular of Heidegger's Lectures on Paul and in particular 1 & 2 Thessalonians in 1920–1921. See *Phenomenology of Religious Life*, 47–111. See also Kisiel, *Genesis*, 173–89; also, van Buren, *Young Heidegger*, 155–68, also 174–202.

Heidegger's account, trespass against experience; (b) because of the con-
solatory role eschatology plays in suggesting that death is passage rather
than absolute.

The Necessity of Heidegger:
Remembering the Forgetting of Death

The necessity of Heidegger for Catholic thought on death—and the attitude one takes to it in advance—is that he recovers its seriousness in
the face of a double eclipse: the eclipse consequent on embourgeoisi-
ment in modernity which distances itself from the reality of death and
effects changes in memorial practices, while at the same time pronounc-
ing as morbid any expression of interest in death; and the gaping hole
in the meaning of life that arises from the taking in of mass death in
the trenches in WWI.[6] Heidegger does not so much respond to the at-
tenuation of focus on the limit of life in the apocalypse of death by providing a genealogy of its erasure such as that provided by sociologists
like Philippe Aries,[7] but responds to it in the way his preferred Russian
authors, Dostoyevsky and Tolstoy,[8] did, that is, by exposing the furious
denial of death, which in effect dooms life to the mode of the et cetera,
thus in effect opening a new line of credit for nihilism. And, as has been
well-documented,[9] Heidegger responds to the meaninglessness of the
trenches not by inveighing against death as such but by denouncing its
exteriority. For him the problem is not the unveiling of finitude, nor even
the mind-numbing nature of war, but whether an individual can really
grasp that the event of death, or the event that is death, is not an event
in our biography but its limit that can come to function as the guiding
thread of one's life.

6. There is a good deal of literature on the effect of WWI on the ideology of heroic
death in German thought and also vice versa. One of the more focused is Lesurdo,
Heidegger, 11–70.

7. See Aries, *Hour of Our Death*; Aries, *Attitudes to Death*.

8. For Heidegger on Dostoyevsky and Tolstoy, see van Buren, *Young Heidegger*,
153.

9. Heidegger was greatly influenced by Ernest Jünger and Friedrich Georg
Jünger who thought of WWI as an opportunity to transcend the modern age defined
by technology. Heidegger kept faith with the Jüngers to the very end of his life. The
best single account of the relationship is provided by Zimmerman, *Confrontation with
Modernity*, 46–93.

Heidegger is well aware that there are Christian resources available to him when thinking of the fundamental orientation of human being and those "moods" at which reality is more likely to be exposed. Before *Being and Time* he permits Augustine, the Carmelite mystics, Luther, and Kierkegaard, and also the biblical text—or at least the New Testament— to be in play,[10] even if he appears to have set aside much of Christian thought—especially Catholicism—as moralizing in its doctrinal, homiletic, devotional and liturgical apparatus for reminding human beings of death and its significance. From Heidegger's perspective Catholic Christianity is itself an agent in the forgetting of death and thus can play no role in bringing into view its disruptive quality and its existential seriousness. Even as Heidegger begins to self-consciously define his interests as philosophical rather than theological—and follows Kant in insisting both on their separation and that philosophy can provide criteria of distinction—he continues to enlist religious discourse that might have something to say regarding death and finitude and, more broadly, reality, gauged as unanticipatable event or as a form of apocalypse. Much of the religious or theological discourse Heidegger provisionally takes on board will in due course either be jettisoned or etherized by becoming merely a "formal indication" of what can be phenomenologically exposited and only thereby validated. The first major thinker jettisoned is Augustine. In his 1921 lectures on Augustine the vehicle for overcoming the foundational Catholic thinker is the now familiar one of construing Augustine as being in the last instance a Platonist.[11] In line both with the liberal Protestant Adolf von Harnack and Protestant recoveries of original apocalyptic Christianity in the early decades of the twentieth century,[12] in his famous 1921 Lectures on the Bishop of Hippo Heidegger

10. Kisiel, *Genesis*, 69–115; van Buren, *Young Heidegger*, 113–29.

11. Heidegger, *Phenomenology of Religious Life*, 115–237. In these lectures Heidegger does his best to distinguish Augustine from Platonism and Neoplatonism and assess how much of his teachings can be redeemed for an existential phenomenology. At the same time Augustine's "objective" discourse of God and the soul make things difficult. Six years later Heidegger has given up entirely on the prospects of phenomenological redemption of even Augustine's more existential vocabulary. For this point, see O'Regan, "Answering Back," 134–84, esp. 136–44.

12. For the recovery of apocalyptic theology in the late nineteenth and early twentieth century and their appropriation by Heidegger before *Being and Time*, see Wolfe, *Heidegger's Eschatology*. Wolfe makes a compelling case about the importance of the work of Franz Overbeck who in the latter quarter of the nineteenth century argued for the apocalyptic origins of Christianity (even if its recovery was not quite what he was recommending).

judges that Augustine's thought fundamentally distorts the basic inspiration of Christianity which is naked openness to a transformation event for which there are no sufficient conditions. Again in line with trenchant philosophical critiques of Platonism in the nineteenth century, presumptively in Kierkegaard and transparently in Nietzsche and his early twentieth century epigones,[13] Heidegger judges that Augustine also makes for bad philosophy. In these pre-*Being and Time* lectures, as will turn out to be his common practice later when dealing with canonic Western thinkers, Heidegger concentrates on a few thematic elements that he regards as truly illustrative of Augustine's thought, and focuses on a select band of texts that he regards as pivotal.

In his 1921 lectures Heidegger looks at Augustine's reflections on *curare* and *concupiscentia*, and *curiositas* and will reflect deeply on Book 10 of the *Confessions* together with supporting passages of an anthropological sort to be found in a variety of other texts.[14] God does not make an appearance in Heidegger's reflections, establishing the precedent for the prohibition of the appearing of God in *Being and Time* (1927). The logic here, as it is later when Heidegger names the original sin of the metaphysical tradition to be "ontotheology"[15]—the mistake of identifying Being with the highest being—is that to speak of God when considering the appearance of Being is to provide a comfort to the self that is as costly as it is cozy: it takes away death's seriousness and the opportunity death provides of focusing the self in the venture of finitude. The phenomenological promise of Augustine's thought is betrayed at its very origin and infected not only by the consoling thought of God, who is either taken for granted or as a metaphysical necessity, but also by Neoplatonic metaphysics, which provides consolations of its own in its irrefragable commitment to an immutable ground to a mutable reality and the immortality of the soul.[16] Heidegger's objection to Platonism and Neoplatonism is both pointed and general. It is pointed in that it takes exception to the guarantee of immortality, which is both aboriginal and eschatological, on the grounds that it trivializes the finitude of the self and derogates its embodiment. And it is general in the way that Nietzsche's critique of Platonism and Neoplatonism is general: it implies a rejection

13. Van Buren, *Young Heidegger*, 166–76.

14. Heidegger, *Phenomenology of Religious Life*, 151–68.

15. See "The Ontotheological Constitution of Metaphysics," 33–67.

16. Heidegger makes a determined attempt to distinguish himself from Adolf von Harnack in this respect. See *Phenomenology of Religious Life*, 117–18.

of the classic view of philosophy as the practice of death, the ideologi-
cal implication of which is comedic: nothing is serious in an individual
biography except the ascesis required to focus on the immortality of self
that the passions and embodiment of the self tend to disguise.[17]

I have already hinted at another debt that Heidegger pays off, that is,
his early debt to the New Testament, which makes complete sense of his
emerging relation to Bultmann at Marburg.[18] Here again Heidegger is selective both thematically and textually. He focuses on the decision for self
that arises when faced with that event that cannot be extrapolated from
past and present, that in a sense is pure future. From the New Testament
Heidegger selects First and Second Thessalonians as a guide,[19] and either
takes for granted that they are typical of the Pauline corpus or finds it
irrelevant. In the last instance, what truly matters for him is that this text
serve as a formal indication of what is universal or universalizable. This
demands a different discourse, a discourse of interpretive translation, in
fact precisely the kind of discourse exhibited later in *Being and Time*. Or
in other words, First and Second Thessalonians point to a key ingredi-
ent of a fundamental ontology licensed not by faith or doctrine but by
an existential phenomenology. What is crucial in these scriptural texts
as they announce heightened vigilance regarding what is coming is the
phenomenon of coming itself and not so much what is coming. Coming
is changing utterly what is. There are a number of potential vehicles, for
example, Christ or the apostle Paul, apotheosis or destruction, or death.
In his commentary, Heidegger is taking advantage of the recovery of the
apocalyptic dimensions of Christianity, while apparently feeling himself
bound under no obligation toward its central figure. There is a deafening
silence on Christ: Christ is not ruled out as a possible form of coming,

17. It is evident that from the very foundation of philosophy in Plato philosophy
is not simply a theoretical enterprise but it is connected with particular forms of life.
In the *Phaedo* and other texts Plato suggests that philosophy is nothing less than the
daily practice of death in that it enacts the separation between body and soul in its
mastery of the passions that comes to full realization in death itself defined by such a
separation. Of course, this definition of philosophy and interiorization of death can be
prosecuted without Plato's dualism, as the Stoics and Spinoza both show.

18. Hans-Georg Gadamer is especially good on the close relation between Heidegger and Bultmann during the early to late 1920s. See Gadamer, "The Marburg
Theology," 29–44. For what is still, arguably, the best account of the importance of
the relation between Heidegger and Bultmann from the theological point of view, see
MacQuarrie, *Existential Theology*.

19. For Heidegger's reflections on First and Second Thessalonians, see *Phenomenology of Religious Life*, 61–82, also 97–111. See also Kisiel, *Genesis*, 179–89.

but Heidegger gives us no reason to suppose that Christ is the preferred form. While Heidegger's negotiation with the Christian tradition regarding death in *Being and Time* occurs under the auspices of an engagement with Kierkegaard and especially his reflection on angst as a prehension of the horizon of finitude focused in death,[20] there remains a trace of the reflection-generalization of apocalyptic in that being-towards-death is precisely an orientation towards an absolute future that cannot be integrated into an individual's biography. Death, as the impossibility of the self, has a paradoxical quality: precisely as a coming that has not arrived death is a condition of the integrity of a self that otherwise would be dissipated in the "everyday";[21] as a coming, however, it betokens the scattering of the self that appears to be irredeemable. After *Being and Time* the word for the event is *Ereignis*,[22] which once again is general and allows of a variety of forms as well as instances: it can be an experience of disclosure that focuses an individual or establishes a community; it can be destruction (kakophany), or it can imply the providing of epoch-making founders or leaders (*Fuhrers*). It should be noted that in his post-*Kehre* work, unlike Hölderlin whom Heidegger routinely comments on, Jesus of Nazareth will never be one of these founding figures adduced. In the main neither is Paul. Nonetheless, in Heidegger's continuing recurring to apocalyptic motifs such as *Ereignis*, Paul manages to persist as a trace in the way Christ does not. In any event, recognizable forms of Christianity, Protestant as well as Catholic, continue to be either left behind or sublated in Heidegger's later work. This encourages the suspicion that if ever Heidegger felt inclined to ascribe genius to Christianity, he would take the path of Nietzsche and ultimately ascribe this genius to Paul, the inventor of Christianity, rather than Christ, who Paul (and the Gospels) take to render God in a dynamic life through death towards resurrection.

In *Being and Time* Heidegger advances the paradoxical view that in order for the self or *Dasein* to be rendered coherent it must face death as its absolute future that makes it fundamentally incoherent. Authenticity,

20. Heidegger, *Being and Time*, 229–35, 492n4.

21. For a treatment of "everydayness" (*Alltäglichkeit*) in its pathological form, see *Being and Time*, 163–68 (They), 211–17 (Idle Chatter), 302, 395–96 (Belief in the Afterlife).

22. *Ereignis* is a term that occurs from time to time in *Being and Time*, but is not deployed in a technical sense. It is so later. The *locus classicus* is in Heidegger's *Beiträge* from the 1930s, which was, however, only published posthumously. For an English translation, see Heidegger, *Contributions to Philosophy*.

he argues, through facing death as "my ownmost possibility,"²³ is precisely facing death not in the abstract, but in my own case. It is only by
being orientated to my own annihilation or nihilation that my biography
is rendered meaningful. It is important to understand that in Heidegger's
masterwork the language of mortality is never used. Even as this early
stage of Heidegger's brilliant career when the denunciatory rhetoric
against metaphysics has not reached its apogee, metaphysics has already
been banished: mortality belongs with immortality, mutability and immutability to a metaphysical regime left behind in existential phenomenology. Albeit at a less obvious level, involved also are proscriptions
against particular Christian ways of talking about dying, for example, the
moralistic recognition of the inevitability of death, which has the invidi-
ous effect of introducing a false teleology. Against the view of death considered as an exposition of an inevitability, Heidegger insists that death's
liminality is genuinely apocalyptic and thus intrinsically dis-teleological.
One could say that at the deepest level the issue for Heidegger concerns
the *vector* of death. Whereas typically the vector in Christianity—and
especially Catholic Christianity—is inside-out, the vector authorized in
and by phenomenology—with some assistance in and through a hermeneutic of a thinker like Kierkegaard—is outside-in. It is not an accident
that in the reception of Heidegger's thanatology this focus on vector was
appropriated, then magnified and generalized as the "outside" that vio-
lates the self constructed by the routines that stay the unimaginable and
unthinkable.²⁴ From Heidegger's perspective, there is a spurious philosophical depth to thinking of each day of life as the piece-rate acquisition
of total death, as if death were given at birth as a parasite and continued
to grow at the expense of the life host who is defeated not so much in time
but by time. A corollary of the apocalyptic characterization of death and
our orientation to it is that one has to suspend the religious wisdom that
adopts and adapts philosophical wisdom and serves as a catchall for all
the manifestations of death: fulfillment of long life, death at birth, death
variously quick or slow, death with or without suffering, death as abrupt
accident or the result of disease.

23. For death as precisely "my death," see *Being and Time*, 290–311.

24. Maurice Blanchot is the thinker who generalized the apocalyptic side of death
as being beyond the economy of memory and anticipation and made it integral to the
semiotics of the text which could not command meaning. He is as foundational for
Derrida's commitment to semiosis as de Saussure.

The change of vector and its implied derogation of the consolations delivered by philosophy and Christianity has the following paradoxical effect: in suggesting that authenticity is predicated on facing up to the apocalypse of death, Heidegger thereby implies that selfhood as such is predicated on response to the "nothing" which precisely cannot be experienced. It is only in facing the possibility of one's own impossibility that gives the self density and, in a real sense, constructs it.[25] The irony should not be lost: Heidegger gets rid of the teleology in the self only to reintroduce it under the mantle now of constitutive dissatisfaction rather than satisfaction. Although the importance of Nietzsche for Heidegger is not yet at its peak—this will have to wait until the late 1930s—clearly something like Nietzsche's heroic model of self-hood is in play. What binds and elevates a life is the bowing before death and the acceptance of the finitude and temporality of the self.[26] Seeing into nothingness as the impossible possibility of myself is the mark of that authenticity which proceeds without positing or even postulating the existence of God, immortality, universal reason, or being remembered. Precisely its heroic response to the apocalypse of death, the coming that abolishes experience, suggests that the apocalyptic form in play is that of Nietzsche rather than Kierkegaard. What Heidegger picks up from Kierkegaard (who, if he is only a Christian thinker—thus something of a contradiction in terms—at least is a Protestant Christian thinker) are those notes of dismantling of the quotidian self and opening of the self towards a future that itself cannot become an object of memory. In Being and Time Heidegger will remove, however, any suggestions that the unanticipatable future could be a redemption of time, which is intimated by Kierkegaard throughout his oeuvre, but most notably in Philosophical Fragments and Concluding Unscientific Postscript. Here Heidegger is entirely consistent with his earlier rejection of the Augustine of the Confessions (Bk. 10) for whom time is redeemed by the touch of God who is eternity itself.[27]

25. For Augustine the density or "weight" (pondus) of the being of human existence is a concern. Unlike Plotinus, in Augustine weight or weightlessness is a function of our fundamental orientations or our loves. Much of his work makes the claim that the "weight" and ontological value of our existence derives from our love of God.

26. There is a serviceable translation of Heidegger's 1939 lectures on the concept of eternal recurrence in Nietzsche, see Nietzsche, vol. 3, esp. 159–83, 209–15.

27. Ricoeur, Time and Narrative, 5–30.

Binding the Strongman:
Catholic Appropriation and Resistance to Heidegger

Heidegger's later modification of the heroic position after his so-called "Turn" (*Kehre*) and his recommendation of the posture of humble opening to whatever inbreaks the self, whether death or the sacred as the surplus of life,[28] complicates the Heideggerian picture and changes the ratio of potential assimilation by Catholic reflection on death and dying. The obstacle presented by the heroic—ultimately Nietzschean—cast of the apocalypse of death and its response of being-towards-death to Catholic reception are fairly obvious pretty soon after the appearance of *Being and Time*. For Balthasar,[29] the writer of *Apokalypse der deutschen Seele* (1937–1939), heroism was a vitiating feature of Heidegger's analytic of the self in *Being in Time*, and one which had to be rejected for what it is: the heroism ultimately belongs to an entirely different regime of response to reality than Christianity, while being at the same time possibly a simulacrum of an authentically Christian attitude towards death. In the same text Balthasar makes it clear that this heroic alternative finds any number of cultural expressions in literature and art as well as philosophy in the modern period. With respect to the discovery of death as the horizon of the self he names Rilke as an immediate precursor of Heidegger.[30] Balthasar does so based on the striking similarities between Rilke and Heidegger in the demand that the apocalypse of death be kept foremost in mind and that the very venture of the self be predicated on a single-minded relation to death as the phenomenon that is uncontainable or the phenomenon of the uncontainable. Balthasar is a sufficiently good reader of poetry to understand that not all dimensions of Rilke's handling of death are heroic. Even more specifically he grasps that Rilke's figure of the poet as the authentic human is one subject to a kind of leakage from the inside, which hints at the presence of the kind of nihilism that Nietzsche decried in Schopenhauer and subsequently in Wagner and

28. The so-called *Kehre* or "Turn" has, arguably, been an interpretive concept in Heidegger commentary since WWII. It made its way into North American commentary through the pioneering work of William J. Richardson. See Richardson, *Heidegger*. Needless to say, this interpretive concept has been challenged. The most powerful challenge is that of Laurence Paul Hemming. See Hemming, *Heidegger's Atheism*.

29. Hans Urs von Balthasar, *Apokalypse der deutschen Seele*.

30. In *Apokalypse 3*, 193–315. Balthasar's treatment of Rilke is contiguous with his treatment of Heidegger and is more focused on one's relation to death being constitutive of authentic existence which is fully realized in the poet.

which Heidegger's apocalyptic manifesto on death is anxious to avoid. In *Apokalypse* Balthasar's main Heidegger texts are *Being and Time* and the *Kantbuch* (1929), and his meditations on these two major "eschatological" thinkers proceed without Balthasar having access to Heidegger's reflection on poetry in which if Hölderlin is the poetic figure of figures, Rilke's work also becomes an object of elucidation.[31] In his later works, largely in and through Hölderlin's poetry with a plausible assist from the Christian mystical tradition of Meister Eckhart[32]—whose Christianity and Neoplatonism have both been discharged—Heidegger will place the emphasis elsewhere: on human fragility and receptivity, on waiting, on acceptance of the gift of the impossible.

We will attend to this major shift shortly, but perhaps we can draw out Balthasar's reaction to what he deems to be apocalyptic excess in the early Heidegger. It does not seem to be the case that in Balthasar's distancing of himself from Heidegger's heroic model that he is denying the courage it takes to be mindful of death and facing it in oneself and others when the need arises. For Balthasar courage before death is a virtue worthy of acclamation since it cuts against—yet does not quite conquer—our very natural fear of ceasing to exist. He seems to understand that we are creatures who desire to continue in being, or put otherwise that our *conatus essendi* is illiminable. Regarding Heidegger's existential phenomenology we can say that, for Balthasar, Heidegger is and is not talking about courage as it has been parsed in the philosophical and Christian tradition: he remains in contact with these traditions to the degree to which the emphasis falls on the demand to leave behind our diversions and distractions and come to face the horizon of our finitude—both traditions are replete with such demands. Heidegger has also stepped outside, since courage in Heidegger is no longer unreflective and we might say

31. As is well-known, Heidegger was a reader of Rilke even before WWI, and Hölderlin in his teens. In his turn to language after *Being and Time*, Rilke is often used to illustrate Hölderlin, and Hölderlin is used to correct the subjectivity orientation of Rilke. Perhaps the single best essay Heidegger ever wrote on Rilke is "*Wozu Dichte*" (1946). For an English translation, see "What Are Poets For," 89–142.

32. The most obvious expression of Heidegger's allegiance to Meister Eckhart is a short text that goes under the name of *Gelassenheit*, perhaps the identifying Eckhartian symbol. The German text was published in 1959. The two best scholars on this aspect on the relation are John D. Caputo and Reiner Schürmann. For Caputo, see his still valuable *Mystical Element*. For Schürmann, see his *Meister Eckhart*. Meister Eckhart is a long-time companion of Heidegger. Eckhart is read with other mystics throughout during the years 1917–1919. See Kisiel, *Genesis*, 108–12.

"right-sized." For being-towards-death is not a response to a phenom-enon among other phenomena that put one at stake in the muddle of life, as is the case, for example, in Aristotle and Aquinas. Rather courage is the reflective positing of oneself in the orienting of oneself towards the phenomenon of phenomena, precisely because it is not a phenomenon that I will experience. For Balthasar, this is courage inherently without modesty, whose modality is essentially histrionic. When Balthasar writes *Apokalypse* the French existentialist reception of Heidegger's analytic of *Dasein* has not yet occurred. When it does occur in the 1940s and 1950s the histrionic modality of courage finds expression in Sartre's *bon mot* to the effect that "man is a useless passion." As Sartre constructs himself as being Heideggerian—whether justified or not[33]—he can be understood also to bring out the hysterical direction of the courage of *Dasein*, that is, the way in which human being rises above her interpersonal and social imbrication and the emotions and feelings that confuse, all of which are part of the weave of human life. In contrast, Camus reproduces Hei-degger's hyperbole of courage in the figure of Sisyphus while also reduc-ing it to scale. Pointing to a mythical Greek figure is *ipso facto* to elevate a particular approach to the world as the authentic stance. At the same time there is a counter-tendency to deflate: faced with our finitude we do not stand above anyone, but simply discover our insistence in living, the buried *conatus essendi* that is common to all. This turns out to be sufficient in a world in which hope that admits of validation is not a pos-sibility, but also in which there is a natural block against suicide and its sometimes mock heroics. From a Christian point of view, Camus can only herald the nature of real hope: his hope is the hope exemplified in Greek tragedy, that is, hope precisely as the hope against hope.

Of course, when Balthasar lodges his objection concerning the hy-perbolic form of courage, he did not fail to take note that Heidegger's apocalyptic twist made hope at once necessary and impossible. Balthasar recognizes in *Apokalypse*—even if he is much clearer later on—that Hei-degger has removed the prospects for the theological virtues, and espe-cially hope. Faith as faith in God, or value, or reason is not allowed in *Being and Time*. Nor, it is clear, is faith as trust allowed either; certainly not trust in God or human fellowship. Being-with (*Mit-Sein*) others is a feature of the contingency of our being, our "throwness" (*Geforfenheit*)

---

33. Heidegger seems to deny that validity of a French existentialist interpreta-tion of *Dasein* in his *Brief über Humanismus*. Frank A. Capuzi provides a more than competent translation in *Martin Heidegger: Pathmarks*, 239–78.

or fallenness (*Verfallenheit*):[34] loving others beyond measure, however, is not constitutive of our human vocation. Above all, hope, even as, or precisely as, the hope against hope that neither oneself nor one's loved ones are lost despite death and its abrupt ending of the story I am and others are, cannot be entertained in Heidegger's existential phenomenology. Anything that we could plausibly pick out and be able to offer as a description and that would function as a guarantee that, appearances to the contrary, not all is lost would be the wrong thing. And Heidegger will not allow us to plead: perhaps we have no hope on our own, but perhaps we have been given hope through hearing the Word of God, or we have hope in the Christ who unimaginably has purchased us from death. For Heidegger, these are truth claims that cannot be redeemed and on the face of it their function is more nearly therapeutic than philosophical in the rigorously epistemological sense of philosophy to which Heidegger subscribes. In fact, for Heidegger, genuine philosophy is methodologically atheistic. Balthasar pays no attention in *Apokalypse* to the way in which in other works from the same period—more than likely because he does not know of them—Heidegger goes beyond Christianity or theology having a role in the philosophical domain. Heidegger insists that Christianity appear before the bar of philosophy and refuses it all prerogatives when it comes to make claims about Christ and his unsurpassable significance. This Heidegger, before the appearance of *Being and Time*, is brazenly stipulative regarding the Bible itself, which in terms of Christianity is alone left standing after doctrines and practices have been dismissed with prejudice. If the Bible has value, it is precisely because it indicates an ecstatic disposition that reaches out to the event that cannot be grasped or even anticipated.

Of course, it is not only the posture of *Dasein* in Heidegger's classic text that can be found wanting from a Christian point of view. Even the revised mode of Heidegger's prescriptions of authentic human response to finitude, time, and death, which emphasizes humility and receptivity, can be perceived to deviate from the Christian tradition, and their relative likeness to traditional Christian renderings of and responses to human finitude and death admit of being diagnosed to be misleading doubles. Whether Hölderlin, whom Heidegger enlists and whom Rilke repeats, is Christian or has genuine Christian elements, ultimately does not matter. What is of real moment is whether the "later" Heidegger or

---

34. *Being and Time*, para. 38, 219–24.

Rilke to whom he is linked on the issue of death and human authenticity still operates within a paradigm of authenticity which, if it has Greek roots, is not denied German instantiation. Romano Guardini's analysis of the *Duino Elegies*,[35] and their rendering of human mindfulness with its non-aggressive profile, suggest that even at their most accommodating—where one might say that the essential figure is more nearly that of Diotima than Dionysius or Prometheus—one is dealing with a simulacrum of Christ. Guardini makes a fundamental objection to the later Heidegger as well as Rilke by suggesting that mindfulness regarding one's own death is at best preliminary to giving oneself entirely away in love for others. Two things are at work in the refusal of Rilke, which is at the same time a refusal of Heidegger. On the one hand, a philosophy of the person, turned neither to stone nor divinity by facing death, but in full appreciation of the gift of life given in the horizon of death, thinks of the self in terms both of relation and gift. For Guardini, relationality is foundational of the very identity of the self. This identity in turn is most intensively realized in love, wherein the self gives itself away even unto death. On the other hand, all human life necessarily refers to the figure of Christ in the Gospels. The one who comports himself towards death as towards his Father in fear and trembling is the one who is willing to spill his blood for all of us who do not deserve the gift of this death. In *The Gift of Death*, Derrida—availing of the Jewish philosopher not only of alterity but of vicarious substitution, Emmanuel Levinas—makes this criticism of Heidegger on behalf of an open-eyed philosophy that cannot help but be a form of ethics. It should be noted, however, that the critique of Heidegger was made in Catholic thought not only in advance of Derrida, but in advance of Levinas's mature thought.

Possibly more interesting, and interestingly both earlier than Balthasar's interrogation of Heidegger's eschatological or apocalyptic escalation in his analytic of *Dasein* and Guardini's critique of Heidegger's solipsist preference, are the questioning of Heidegger's existential phenomenology conducted by both Erich Przywara and Edith Stein. The criticisms are there from the appearance of *Being and Time*. In an essay in 1928 that attempts an adjudication of the remit of Heidegger's fundamental ontology in Catholic thought, Przywara sounds something of

35. Guardini, *Rilke's Duino Elegies*. Guardini reads Rilke's great set of poems as a genuine theological resource, but also warns against the narcissism of Rilke's view of love, death and their interconnection. His analysis is especially prescient given the basic line of argument of Derrida against Heidegger in *The Gift of Death*.

an alarm. While appreciative of Heidegger's emphasis on existence and temporality—and considering it to be an advance over Husserl's essentialism—Przywara is worried by *Being and Time*'s relentless finitism. This finitism is everywhere in Heidegger's magisterial text, but is particularly betrayed in the notion of the "throwness" and "fallenness" of human being, who is strictly abyssal. Przywara abjures Heidegger's insistence on "nothing" functioning as the horizon of finite being and thinks of it as a reification calculated to foreclose a Christian option that would have God as the horizon of tensed human finitude and the unimaginable term of its self-transcendence. Przywara repeats essentially the same objection to Heidegger's finitism and his elevating of nothingness in *Analogia Entis*,[36] but this time in the context of a richer metaphysical alternative that Catholic thought can call upon. Heidegger simply rules out beforehand the possibility that the horizon of human being's self-transcendence is God. For Przywara, despite Kierkegaard's reflections on angst, it is by no means self-evident why even phenomenologically nothingness should have the last word. Why could it not be the case that God as the superabundance of being is the ultimate horizon and death is his gracious touch promising to extend our biography beyond its breaking? Moreover, does it have to be the case that with God rather than death as the ultimate horizon of our finitude that human life is less dynamic, less a venture and adventure, than is the case in Heidegger? So while, undoubtedly, the presence of God as horizon or the possibility of God being such a horizon has the implication for Przywara that human being is neither alien nor alone, our being borne up by God is not the same as standing on a secure foundation. The gift of death, which is the gift of eternal life, is sheer gratuity.

Przywara's argument against Heidegger both in his early review essay and in *Analogia Entis* is general. The crucial point is whether we are living towards nothing or God, towards dissolution or absolution. One could say that in this respect death is the incognito capable of wearing either the mask of nothing and God. What matters is the decision made as to which: the ethos of self-transcendence will look different in either

36. See Przywara, *Analogia Entis: Metaphysics: Original Structure and Universal Rhythm*, trans. John. R. Betz and David Bentley Hart (Grand Rapids: Eerdmans, 2014). This translates *Analogia Entis: Metaphysik, Ur-Struktur und All-Rythmus* (Einsiedeln, Switzerland: Johannes Verlag, 1962). This is a compilation made up from Przywara's original 1932 text plus thirteen essays. See from *Analogia Entis* as such, 213, 217–18, 224, 226, 229. It should be noted that the classical figure who is providing the measure of judgment is more nearly Augustine than Aquinas, although Aquinas's metaphysics of *esse* is also in play. For other essays, see *Analogia Entis*, 349–51.

case. This is a case of fundamental option. Although Rahner is often cast as a thinker whose theology is determined by Heidegger's analysis of the finitude of the self, his own use of Heidegger in *Spirit in the World* (1937) suggests that at the level of philosophy and/or philosophy of religion that Rahner has turned against Heidegger. In his account the pre-thematic apprehension of the horizon of human self-transcendence Rahner is almost cavalier in identifying this horizon with self-subsistent being, which is also Aquinas's definition of God. It is quite evident that he is refusing to allow the Heidegger of *Being and Time* or the *Kantbuch* (1929) to set the terms for what Catholic theology can admit as proper theological locutions. While for Rahner God is not an object of experience, thus neither percept nor concept, God can be allowed into discourse as the horizon of all finite experience. Heidegger's "nothing" is sidelined, as is the heroic modulation of Heidegger's depiction of human self-transcendence. In his short essay on Heidegger and Catholic theology in 1940,[37] Rahner is more explicit. In fact, he says something Przywara had said a dozen years earlier and had repeated in *Analogia Entis*: the affirmation of nothing as the horizon of human existence cannot itself be justified by an existential phenomenology. Rahner also shows himself prepared to draw the conclusion that Heidegger's existential phenomenology is marked by nihilism. Rahner does not remark on the irony that while Heidegger's main aim is to overcome the operational nihilism of everyday life by encouraging people to take a leap beyond enchaining custom and the repressive "they," his reflections on angst and "resoluteness" (*Entschlossenheit*) in fact inscribe a heroic and far more decadent form of it. And, of course, although at this stage Rahner's theological speciality is fundamental rather than dogmatic theology, like Przywara, he thinks of fundamental theology as open to its completion by dogmatic theology as the guardian of the Word spoken in history and achieving its consummate expression in Jesus of Nazareth. Rahner does not ask either Heidegger or the Heideggerians for permission to ignore the proscription of moving from a phenomenological philosophy to the givens of faith. If in the end, in relation to his teacher Martin Heidegger, Rahner is at best a heretical Heideggerian, obviously there were other Catholic thinkers who thought of Heidegger's "destruction" (*Destruktion*) of Catholic truth to be liberating and his opening up of the Nothing before and the abyss beneath to be

37. For an English translation of this essay, see Karl Rahner, "Concept of Existential Philosophy," 126–37.

a tonic. Here Bernard Welte is neither the only, nor the more important Catholic voice.[38]

Balthasar, who genuinely admires Heidegger, thinks highly of phenomenology, and is convinced that Heidegger is the greatest phenomenologist,[39] is hardly an unqualified admirer. In *Wahrheit* (1947), which in due course is recycled as *Theo-Logic 1*,[40] Balthasar deems Heidegger to have made an extraordinary contribution to the theory of truth, the importance of the question, and the dynamic orientation of the finite self towards a horizon that cannot be encompassed. By the same token, however, he is made anxious by Heidegger's peremptory dismissal of the transcendentals of Truth, Goodness, and Beauty, and questions Heidegger's finitism.[41] Balthasar queries whether Heidegger is philosophically entitled to his finitism, and wonders—here rehearsing a point made earlier in *Apokalypse*—whether the tradition-shy Heidegger is not after all working out of a particular tradition of assumption, thus failing to ask the radical question of the identity of the horizon. As an exercise in fundamental theology or philosophy of religion, *Wahrheit* is a book dealing with truth and especially about whether truth disclosed in time is trustworthy. Unlike Heidegger, Balthasar believes that truth and erring are not synonymous; though the disclosure of truth to finite human beings is also necessarily finite, this neither means (a) that a finite disclosure cannot intimate an infinite truth, or (b) that the finite expressions of truth are not trustworthy as supported by self-subsistent truth. The register here is basically that of Przywara's *Analogia Entis*. It is important also to say, however, that it is very important to Balthasar that the imbrication of truth and goodness in particular gets emphasized. There are a number of reasons. One is to avoid Heidegger's characterization of Truth as sheer neutrality and essentially careless. Heidegger's major

38. See Welte, *Denken in Begegnung mit den Denkern*, II,; also Sheehan, *Karl Rahner*; O'Leary, *Questioning Back*.

39. Balthasar, *Apokalypse* 3, 275.

40. Balthasar, *Wahrheit der Welt* (1947) is recycled as *Theo-Logik*, Bd. 1 (1985). See Balthasar, *Theo-Logic*, vol. 1: *Truth of the World*. This represents an engagement between Aquinas's and Heidegger's notion of truth as well as the dynamism of the embodied and worlded self in its orientation towards it.

41. While *Theo-Logic*, vol. 1 represents Balthasar's deepest engagement with Heidegger by far, it is fundamentally critical and essentially rebuts not only Heidegger's view of truth as finite but also his exclusion of goodness from the horizon of finite reality. One of his main arguments concerns the ontological reliability of Being at its deepest and ultimately most personal level.

antecedents here are Heraclitus and Nietzsche, both of whom insisted on the playfulness of disclosure. Disclosure is uncanny and cannot be regulated by reason or morality. This is Balthasar's interpretation of Heidegger's *es gibt* in 1947.This will also be his interpretation in *Glory of the Lord*, vol. 5 (1965).[42] Thinking of Truth as Logos, which for Balthasar means precisely not thinking of Truth as Logos in the Heraclitean and Nietzschean manner preferred by Heidegger, means that Truth has an intelligible structure even if it resists being reduced to instrumental reason. In *Wahrheit* Balthasar also believes that the community of Truth and Goodness sanctioned in the classical philosophical tradition and ratified in Christianity during the long conversation between philosophy and theology makes two essential contributions: (a) first, it reinforces the view of reality being solicitous rather than capricious; and (b) second, it suggests that our response to the communication of reality is neither once and for all nor in the mode of a spectator. We are talking rather of responsiveness that takes time, and shapes it, and which also has the form of a pledge. As is well-known, what is hinted at in *Wahrheit* becomes thematic in *Theo-Drama*. Of course, the genre of *Theo-Drama* is not that of fundamental but dogmatic theology in which Christ is the central actor in the drama of salvation history and in which the perichoretic Trinity is the englobing horizon of all of reality.[43] It would not be an exaggeration to say that for Balthasar the entire dance of the Trinity is love, even as he makes Augustinian-Thomistic distinctions between the Son as Logos and the Spirit as gift.[44] In an important sense *Theo-Drama* does not have the power to answer Heidegger in the way it answers Hegel,[45] since Heidegger has refused a theological voice in a way that Hegel has not. Even allowing for this, however, we can see a way in which Heidegger's nihilism

42. Balthasar, *The Glory of the Lord*, vol. 5: *The Realm of Metaphysics in the Modern Age*, 429–50, 613–56.

43. Balthasar on the Trinity is a huge topic and, unlike other major Catholic theologians, does not take the form of a treatise but is everywhere present in his work, his historical no less than his systematic work. It is fair to speak, however, of privileged sites. See *Theo-Drama*, vol. 5: *The Last Act* (German original 1983); *Theo-Logic*, vol. 2: *The Truth of God* (German original 1985); *Theo-Logic*, vol. 3: *The Spirit of Truth* (German original 1987).

44. The most thorough account of Trinitarian distinctions is provided by volumes 2 & 3 of *Theo-Logic*.

45. I have treated the Balthasar-Hegel relation in considerable detail in *The Anatomy of Misremembering*, vol. 1: *Hegel*.

seems to be out-bidden in Christ's descent into Sheol.[46] Just as important as Balthasar's picturesque account of a passive rather than active Christ, and the dependence of this account on 2 Peter, is the physiognomy of the lost: inexpressive, inarticulate, and evacuated of the insistence of being. Among the dead—among those who move towards zero—Christ makes all the difference: the possible nothing will not be, because love engenders, because love in Christ is negentropy.

I would like to conclude the second and most substantial part of this essay by speaking to Edith Stein's rejection of Heidegger's philosophy in general and his thanatology in particular. Eric Przywara and Edith Stein were interlocutors, so it comes as no surprise that they tend to echo each other when it comes to reservations about Heidegger. Yet, it is almost impossible to provide the genetic code of whom influenced whom. When Stein in her illuminating appendix on Heidegger to *Finite and Infinite Being* (1936) criticizes Heidegger's nihilism and his correlative ruling God out of court as the unimaginable reference point of human existence,[47] it is possible—maybe even probable—that her thought had been affected by her long conversations with the author of *Analogia Entis*. It is probably also true to say that when Przywara wrote *Analogia Entis* he had heard Stein, read her review of *Being and Time* (1928), and understood—if not necessarily assented—to why she held the view that the form of phenomenology with which Catholic thought could deal was that of Husserl rather than Heidegger. For Stein, the tendency in Husserl towards essentialism was moderated in his later work. For her also, Husserl's phenomenology encourages the kind of work on intersubjectivity that both she and Max Scheler understood to be central to Husserl's program and which was in her view set aside by Heidegger in *Being and Time*. And finally, and most importantly, given her conversion from Judaism to Catholicism and her vocation as a Catholic intellectual, she was of the opinion that Husserl's neutrality with regard to religion in general and

46. Stein, *Finite and Eternal Being*. This is the translation of *Endliches und Ewiges Sein*. The text, however, was written in 1936 and published only after WWII. Stein takes her distance from Heidegger early on in the text (54–59). Against Heidegger, Stein insists that her dissatisfaction with *Dasein* is fueled by ontological fullness rather than nothingness.

47. Unfortunately the Appendix on Heidegger is to be found only in the German edition. Stein's 1928 review of *Being and Time*, that is, "Martin *Heideggers Existentialphilosophie*" is preserved as an appendix in *Welt und Person*. In that essay Stein complains loudly of Heidegger's absolutization of death, which is underscored in his having "nothing" as the horizon of human thinking and action.

Christianity in particular was real in the way that Heidegger's was not. The avowal of methodological atheism has a different meaning in both phenomenologists; on her view Heidegger proscribes and prescribes in ways she finds foreign to Husserl. As already indicated, very much in line with Przywara, Stein sees the main proscriptions to be God and eternity, and the main prescription to be "nothing" as the horizon of an incurably temporal ecstatic being. But she also figures Heidegger to have stepped outside the precincts of the capacious non-reductive reason of the classical tradition with which—whatever their differences—Husserl's phenomenology was in sync. Again Stein's judgment is in agreement with what is implied by Przywara in *Analogia Entis* and *The Crisis of European Sciences and Transcendental Phenomenology* (1936), which came out the same year as *Finite and Eternal Being*. Still, it is only fair to underscore the entirely different weight of this judgment for Stein, who worked with Heidegger as an assistant to Husserl.

The presence in *Finite and Infinite Being* of a reflection on Heidegger cuts against both the view that Stein had entirely abandoned phenomenological investigation for metaphysics and the view that in her review of *Being and Time* in 1928 she had essentially bid adieu to Heidegger. It would be tempting to think that Stein's entry into the cloistered life, which was as much the product of her reflections on Carmelite spirituality as the context for exploration, ended all association with phenomenology and all reflection on Heidegger, the errant or heterodox phenomenologist. There is much to suggest that neither is the case. The very title of Stein's second masterpiece, *Science of the Cross*,[48] strongly suggests that the conversation between Catholic thought and phenomenology continues to be in operation. It is not only the case that "science" is in the title of what is perhaps Husserl's most famous essay, "Philosophy as a Rigorous Science,"[49] but also that the meaning of "science" seems to be essentially the same. For both, the "science" of which they speak is not defined by the assumptions and practices of the natural or human sciences; nor does it correspond to something like Kant's architectonic of reason whereby we entertain the ideal of comprehending all phenomena, if only eventually. Rather "science" is the discipline of the painstaking and meticulous describing of a phenomenon from all relevant points of view and tracing the lines of relation with other phenomena. This remains true whether

48. Stein, *Science of the Cross*.

49. I am speaking of Husserl's famous 1911 essay *"Philosophie als strenge Wissenschaft."*

we are talking of non-religious or religious phenomena. Adequate exposition is an act of fidelity to the phenomenon and a pledge to continue to
respond to it. For Stein, what requires exposition is the Cross. And it is at
this point that one can see the continuing conversation with Heidegger,
even after the fiasco of his Rectorship at Freiburg (1934/1935). Practicing
theology in the mode of exegesis, in this case the exegesis of Saint John of
the Cross's *Living Flame of Love*, Stein suggests that our prime way to the
cross is through the images of darkness that more nearly speak to God's
absence than presence and more nearly of hopelessness than hope. In
"the dark night" (*La Noche oscura*) the searcher or lover undergoes the
mystic death, which involves the surrendering of our lust for satisfaction
and warrant and also the end of the process of idolatry in which God's
main function is to satisfy our need for security and consolation. In the
mystic death we do not so much find God as God finds us. As Stein reads
John of the Cross, she makes sure of two things: (a) that the mystic death
is an imitation of Christ's death on the Cross in which he is, nonetheless,
found by the Father; and (b) that the mystic death remains tied to the real
base of death in which we go in fear and trembling into the yonder. With
regard to the former we read:

> No human heart has ever entered as dark a night as did the
> God-man in Gethsemane and on Golgotha. No searching hu-
> man spirit can penetrate the unfathomable mystery of the dying
> God-man's abandonment by God. But Jesus gives to some cho-
> sen souls some taste of this extreme bitterness. They are his most
> faithful friends from who he exacts the final test of their love.
> If they do not shrink back from it but allow themselves to be
> drawn willingly into the dark night, it will become their leader.
> . . . This great experience of the Cross: extreme abandonment,
> and precisely in this abandonment, union with the Crucified . . .
> Cross and night are the way to heavenly light: that is the joyful
> message of the Cross.[50]

Here Stein takes account of all Heidegger's Nietzsche-laced objections
to Christian faith as a machinery of security and consolation. As she
reads the pitch and pith of Christian faith through an interpretation of
the poetry of Saint John of the Cross, she finds the Christian answer.
Not surprisingly, it is the very Christ, excluded from consideration even
in the early Heidegger who is experimenting with non-doctrinal forms
of Christianity including the Carmelites, who now is allowed to answer

50. Stein, *Science of the Cross*, 30–31.

back. Christ is the one who goes without security and consolation into the dark, who goes naked and unaccommodated into his very real death. It is in his very abandonment that he finds the Father or rather the Father finds him. Which is to say that Love finds him and raises him above the nothing which is the referent of his fear.

Stein also wants us to see that the mystic death has also our own death—or the perfection of our death—in view. Christ's death is not only the paradigm of a mystic death but of our real death, which we relate to in fear and a hope beyond hope. To speak to one is to speak to the other. Beyond our waiting and our patience is the waiting and patience of God who reaches us in the darkness of an end that has to be endured, just as beyond nothing is the everything and beyond death is ever brimming and generating life. The mystical theology of the Cross is Stein's final answer to Heidegger's nihilism. In terms of an answer to Heidegger, the metaphysics of Aquinas proved penultimate. Moreover, the mystical theology of *The Science of the Cross* is overtly existential in the way that the Aquinas of *Finite and Infinite Being* is not, although Stein is convinced that she has managed successfully to solder together phenomenology and Thomist metaphysics, which Heidegger could only reject.[51] Appearances to the contrary, however, in her commentary on the poems of Saint John of the Cross, Stein is not talking to a Christian spiritual elite, or at least not solely talking to such an elite. She can, and indeed should, be read as talking—at least by extension—to all Christians mindful of their own death or the death of a loved one. To face death is to become naked and to have set aside all pre-packaged securities and consolation. It is to go into the dark not in the mode of the hero who would conquer death in and by his resoluteness, but to face the impossible possibility of death with a humble courage not inconsistent with the "affliction" of which Simone Weil—Stein's contemporary—speaks. Stein is writing of and encouraging a spiritual practice which she hopes she too will be able to enact when the time comes. The time does come, and comes before she has finished her commentary on John of the Cross, which is left open as she is snatched from her convent in Holland and is transferred to Auschwitz where she dies in the Gas Chambers. Auschwitz is her own practicum and this practice is also an answer to Heidegger, ingloriously compromised by his behavior towards Husserl, his rhetoric against Jews, and his collaboration with the Third Reich. In particular, it is the answer that

51. The kind of synthesis between Heidegger and Catholic thought (especially Thomistic thought) found its best expression in Siewerth, *Schicksal der Metaphysik*.

gets pledged in another disposition entirely to the inflationary vanity of resoluteness and being-towards-death. One is ruined and walks towards life's nadir in the hope that death is the mask or screen for exuberant eternal life. Moreover, while death is ineluctably mine—in this Heidegger was right—it is also the shared human condition in the nightmare time that was a shared condition for Jews and for Christians. For Stein, whose earlier work on empathy expanded on Husserl's burgeoning reflections on intersubjectivity,[52] we are truly given to ourselves in our feeling for others. As it is in life, so it is on the razor's edge of death. The edge is also the edge of witness. And here too the Cross is the key.

Eschatological Exacerbation and Eschatological Contraction: Heidegger and Augustine

In the last section we looked at a number of mid 20th-century Catholic theologians who, though attracted to Heidegger's overcoming of the denial of death, expressed reservations concerning the role "nothing" played as the horizon of finitude. Like the protagonist who lets go of customary consolation in one of Iris Murdoch's more ambitious novels, *Bruno's Dream*,[53] for these Catholic thinkers, the limit is not so unambiguous. Even allowing for experiential reduction, death gives itself equivocally as nothing or God or God or nothing. But there is experiential reduction and experiential reduction; there is reduction as leading Christian beliefs and doctrines back to experience to the extent to which this is possible. This is the sense of reduction as *reducere*. There is also reduction as displacement-replacement: what experience cannot authorize has to be set aside, and even those cases where a concept or image can be connected to an experience, once the experience comes into view it essentially displaces the image or concept of which it was correlative. In the 1920s, and especially in *Being and Time*, Heidegger tended to talk as if he were engaged in the former. Yet in almost every case that mattered he illustrated the latter. This leads to the following paradox: Heidegger's refiguring of philosophy in the direction of an unanticipatable future that energizes,

52. A devotee of Husserl and an admirer of the sort of phenomenology practiced by Max Scheler, Stein's first major book was on the topic of empathy. For an English translation, see *Problem of Empathy*.

53. See Murdoch, *Bruno's Dream*. The protagonist, Bruno, is very old and is dying at home attended by a nurse and attempting to come to the terms with the event that he cannot command and undoes him.

rather than being controlled by, human temporality, together with his view that the only viable form of Christianity is a radically eschatological form, essentially represents a refusal of Christian eschatology. The Christian who would be philosophically instructed is not justified in talking about three of the four eschata. One can talk about neither heaven or hell, nor judgment. One can talk about death, but one has to avoid talking about it as the separation of soul and body. Such language is the language of an objectivistic metaphysics which, according to Heidegger in *Being and Time*, has no place in an existential phenomenology which provides access to the question of questions, that is, the very meaning of Being. One might also note that while divine judgment is an inadmissible feature of a phenomenology with ontological aspirations, one can also see that judgment has been displaced from God to the self, which rises to choose itself to the degree to which it becomes oriented to its own demise or its own structural impossibility. In Heidegger, *Dasein* is crisis, and is defined by the decision taken regarding a disclosure that is utmost and yet cannot be experienced; an apocalypse none greater than which can be thought, which removes the conditions of seeing.

To get traction on the phenomenon of eschatological escalation in the Heidegger of *Being and Time*, which leads to the impossibility of a classical Christian eschatology, involves a return to the Heidegger of the early 1920s who tested Christian thinkers and the biblical text. As noted in section 1, in his inquiry into what is phenomenologically living and dead in Augustine, Heidegger ultimately came to the conclusion that Augustine beggared fundamental questions by having answers in place from the outset, whether the answers were taken from Neoplatonic philosophy or from the Christian world of assumption. Augustinian convictions about eternity and immutability and convictions about the reality of a personal God compromised a thought that was extraordinarily promising in its earmarking of the questionability of the self and its constitutive capacity for inquiry as search. A corollary of Heidegger's critique of Augustine is the putting out of action of Augustinian eschatology which is the backbone of the Western doctrinal tradition, assumed even as it was nuanced by medieval thinkers such Aquinas and Bonaventure, imaginatively expanded by Dante, and enshrined in the Catechism of the Catholic Church.[54] Arguably, Heidegger's engagement with First and Second Thessalonians also leads to eschatological truncation. On the

54. See *The Catechism of the Catholic Church* #1020–1066.

one hand, Heidegger's interpretation of this Pauline text suggests that existential philosophy can do business with the biblical text in the way it cannot do either with metaphysics or doctrinal forms of theology. This extension from a part to the whole of the biblical text seems to be justified in light of Heidegger's famous 1928 lecture on "Phenomenology and Theology" and ratified decades later in Heidegger's lecture in Zurich in 1954 to Lutheran pastors on the biblical word.[55] Nonetheless, Heidegger's reflections on First and Second Thessalonians do not suggest that Paul as a whole can be enlisted in the critical side of Heidegger's eschatological project, which demands the deconstruction of our cultural and philosophical habits and the laying aside of our certitudes. While there are references to other texts in the Pauline canon, Paul is trimmed: what is central to Paul is our heightened expectation of what is coming. This is a Paul without Christ as the realization of history and a new dispensation; Paul without Christ as the New Adam and thus the redemption of Gentile and Jew; Paul without the resurrected Christ who is guarantee of our own resurrection. What is the case with respect to Paul can be extended to the New Testament as a whole and from there to Hebrew Scripture. Anything in Scripture that involves a belief in a divine figure and post-mortem existence is forbidden a hearing. These are over-claims that can neither be phenomenologically nor existentially redeemed. Here Heidegger is quintessentially Kantian. The turn to the Bible is the reflex that accompanies the dismissal of doctrine; but then the Bible is submitted to protocols—in Heidegger's case existential protocols, in Kant's case ethical protocols—which means that huge swathes of the biblical text will never receive a hearing, and those parts that do can only say as much as the protocols allow them to say.[56] Just as with Kant, and following him Fichte and Hegel, revelation is effectively abjured because it appears to be simply a brute fact (*Positivität*).

However much, then, Heidegger jousts with monumental philosophical precursors such as Kant and Hegel, on most important matters relating to Christianity he repeats them, even if not as much as he repeats

---

55. The Zurich lecture was given to old Bultmannians and revolved around the question whether Being and God are identical. He denies that they are. For a good discussion of Heidegger's lecture, which essentially repeats what he wrote in his 1928 piece on "Phenomenology and Theology," see Hemming, *Heidegger's Atheism*, 184–90.

56. For Kant, see *Religion within the Boundaries of Reason Alone*. For a convenient translation by George di Giovanni, see *Religion and Rational Theology*, 41–215. See also, Cyril O'Regan, "Kant: Boundaries, Blind-Spots, and Supplements," 87–126.

Nietzsche. The consequences for classical Christian eschatology are nothing short of disastrous. This is easy to see by taking the most cursory of
glances at *The City of God*, the foundational eschatological text of Western
Christianity. Augustine's eschatology is not a philosophical construct and
does not evolve—as his critics might want to believe—from Christian
adoption/adaptation of Platonic eschatology with its belief in immortality
and with its ready-made symbolic apparatus of eschatological judgment
and the separating of those who will enjoy an eternity of contemplation
from those who do not. The rich symbolic eschatology apparatus, largely
Orphic, on which Plato draws in the *Gorgias* and *Republic*,[57] continued to
have a half-life in carriers of Platonism such as Iamblichus and Porphyry.
Augustine, however, never calls on them, restricting himself entirely to
Scripture and moving freely in a non-Marcionite manner between the
New and Old Testament. The fully elaborated eschatology of *The City
of God* is the fruit of biblical exegesis, albeit one that depends on previous exegetical labors and the commonsense of the Christian tradition.
Given Heidegger's methodological decisions, already apparent six to
seven years before the publication of *Being and Time*, Augustine's kind of
holistic interpretation of the biblical text with attention to his numerous
claims concerning God and God's relation to the world that is, was, and is
to come has no warrant and its results can only be disavowed.

Now, it would be stretching the truth to say that Heidegger's early
Catholic interlocutors foregrounded his excision of classical eschatology
or attempted to describe its mechanisms. Yet this is not to say that they
had no sense of it. For example, the very logic of Balthasar's antagonism in
Apokalypse to emergent forms of eschatological thought, whether idealistic, vitalistic, or exaggeratedly finitist, makes sense if and only if Balthasar
is committed to the Augustinian view of the eternal destiny of human
being made to enjoy superabundant life in God. Such a commitment
becomes fully explicit only much later, especially in Theo-Drama, vols. 4
and 5, which speaks to all four eschata, and insists on the importance of
resurrection, while expressing some reservations about Augustine's views
on hell.[58] In his mature work, as earlier in *Apokalypse*, it is clear that German Idealism is the proximate target, since its influence is more obvious

57. I am thinking of the way Plato cycles more nearly "mythic" material, likely of
an Orphic origin into his texts. I am thinking especially of the function of the gods of
judgment, Aecus, Minos, and Rhadamanthus in the Gorgias and Er in the *Republic*.

58. Balthasar's most concentrated treatment of the eschata is to be found in *Theo-
Drama*, vol. 5.

and the response necessarily more urgent given its practical translation in Marxism. This is the view shared by Henri de Lubac who rails against the Marxist immanentization of history in the 1940s and who takes up the issue again late in his career. To the extent to which Augustine's eschatology finds itself as one side of a binary, then, the dominant binary in the cases of both Balthasar and de Lubac is Augustine-Hegel. In addition, to the extent that time and history are rendered under the aspect of salvation history, the binary is between two very different forms of Trinitarian thought with very different understandings of the intra-divine Trinity and its relation to salvation history. At the same time, it should not be denied that Balthasar—if not necessarily de Lubac—can be thought to critically link Augustine and Heidegger. One obvious place is at the end of *Wahrheit*, where having both appropriated and emended Heidegger's model of truth as *aletheia*, Balthasar ends up inveighing against the absoluteness of temporality and its agonistic structure of endless search.[59] Against this he affirms the ecstasy of each self is towards eternity and God as absolute truth and goodness. There is enjoyment as well as search, fruition as well as longing.

If a prize, however, had to be given to the most eminent supporter of the binary between Augustine and Heidegger, it would have to be Przywara, on whose *Analogia Entis* Balthasar's 1947 text on truth significantly depends. Of course, in *Analogia Entis* Przywara argues that formally speaking the "creaturely metaphysics" he has elaborated prepares for a full-scaled theological elevation which supposes revelation. This, undoubtedly, would involve the elaboration of a full-scaled Trinitarian theology and a Christology that does not reject the person of Christ even as it does justice to his soteriological significance. To this one can add that the dynamism of the finite subject, who as "essence- in-and-beyond-existence"—to use Przywara's accurate but awkward designation—enters an entirely different dimension when joined with God in and through death. What allows us to fill out *Analogia Entis* in a theological manner and to feel assured that the theological content is in significant part Augustinian is Przywara's huge anthology of Augustine in which if there is coverage of all the philosophical and theological contributions made by Augustine,[60] there is a particular emphasis on passages that underscore

59. Balthasar, *Theo-Logic*, vol. 1, 203–5.
60. Przywara brought out the anthology of Augustine's writings roughly at the same time he published *Analogia Entis*. Sooner than most of Przywara's work, and probably because of the availability of translations of Augustine, it came out in English

our desire for God who as infinite *esse* is the origin as well as term of all human desire. Moreover, the theologian Augustine does not forbid discussion of the heaven in which the fulfillment of our desire consists. This fulfillment is in the vision of the triune God who gives rest, but also perpetually induces ecstasy.[61] Przywara seems to suggest that the beatific vision of the West and *epekstasis* of the Greek East are not contraries and that Augustine is able to construct a Western equivalent to "eternal becoming" which pays full respect to the eternal nature of the milieu in which the ecstatic enjoyment of God is enacted.

In truth neither Przywara nor Stein provide fully-developed eschatologies of the sort that Balthasar does somewhat later. Undoubtedly, part of the reason is their greater proximity to Heidegger's foreclosing the possibility of a Christian death, but also his shutting down of traditional eschatology, which ironically is an implication of his eschatological exacerbation of the prescribed orientation of *Dasein*. They are contemporaries in a way that Balthasar is not, and Heidegger has more the form of an overwhelming crisis for thought than he will later. As we have seen already, this does not mean that Balthasar despises dealing with Heidegger's thanatology, even beyond *Apokalypse*, vol. 3 (1939) and *Wahrheit* (1947).[62] Nonetheless, he has the luxury of branching out into the construction of an eschatology, deeply grounded in the patristic tradition (East and West), in Aquinas and Bonaventure, not to exclude Dante. The Augustine brushed aside in Heidegger's pre-*Being and Time* reflections on the Bishop of Hippo, and repressed in the context of *Being and Time* (which makes great use of his notion of *cura* only to correct it in an authentically philosophical direction) makes a triumphant return in Balthasar's eschatological and Trinitarian investigations in the trilogy and in *Theo-Drama* in particular. In the return of Augustine, Heidegger's thanatology is not only exposed as an abstraction from a complex human reality of great ambiguity, but also as an idol in which the very vulner-

---

just before WWII as *An Augustinian Synthesis*.

61. In *Analogia Entis*, 181, Przywara makes much of a passage from Ps 130:11 commented on by Augustine and highlighted by him in his anthology: "so that he who is to be found may be sought, he is hidden." See also *Analogia Entis*, 176–77, 183, 231–32, 235.

62. See Balthasar's principled rejection of anxiety rather than joy being the primordial human disposition, see *Der Christ und die Angst*; also Balthasar, *Gottesfrage*. For an English translation of the latter book, see *God Question*. The hidden God rather than the apocalypse of death is the ultimate horizon for finite, temporal, and fallible human being.

ability of the self is exalted to the level of the divine that gets displaced. For our three major Catholic thinkers, and arguably for Rahner also, Heidegger is a passionate voice recalling death from the oblivion it has suffered in modernity. His is an act of remembrance which Christian theology can ignore only at its peril. A great rememberer, it turns out that Heidegger is also a great forgetter, since the death he makes central to the definition of human being ultimately evacuates it. If these 20th-century Catholic theologians remain faithful to a Christian thanatology they do not consider refuted by Heidegger, they also suggest a Christian—and more specifically Catholic—thanatology after him, one purged of certainty, but not of faith and hope, and the love that is their *raison d'être* and their point of integration. They find intimations in the matrix of human life that death may be merely an interruption rather than a violent cessation, a pretext of a rebounding into more exuberant life that shows no signs of entropy.

Of course, this refurbished thanatology serves as the foreground for a fully elaborated eschatology, which has a variable Augustinian outline. Thus, one is speaking—and necessarily so—of an Augustine after Heidegger, an Augustine who refused to die on Heidegger's say-so in the early 1920s, and whose voice is repressed in *Being and Time*. This is an Augustine present in the three Catholic thinkers who have gone to their difficult and hopeful death, one intimated in Stein, heaved to by Przywara, and critically developed by Balthasar. This is the Western master of eschatology who essentially defines the eschatological project of Benedict XVI for whom the apocalypse of death has not arrived. Benedict notably does not perseverate about death, or try particularly hard to dislodge it from the axial position it enjoys in Heidegger. Benedict is aware of his great 20th-century Catholic predecessors for whom the proper response to the oblivion of death is hopeful mindfulness rather than obsession. They remind him that he does not need to make the case, but also help cement the conviction that traditional eschatology has not yet been outbid. This is especially true of Augustine. His eschatological thought has not been outbid by the immanentism of Hegel or Mark. Nor has it been outbid by the immanentism of Heidegger. When it comes to rendering the full horizon of the eschaton, which is precisely what will never become concept, who is a greater guide than he, who is a greater witness to the hope that we have in Christ who witnesses in turn to the Father's loving embrace for ever and ever.

BIBLIOGRAPHY

Aries, Philippe. *Attitudes to Death: From the Middle Ages to the Present.* Translated by Patricia Ranum. Baltimore: Johns Hopkins, 1975.

―――. *The Hour of Our Death: The Classic History of Western Attitudes to Death over the Last One Thousand Years.* Translated by Helen Weaver. New York: Vintage, 1983.

Balthasar, Hans Urs von. *Apokalypse der deutschen Seele: Studie zu einer Lehre von letzen Haltungen*, vol. 3: *Zur Vergöttlichung des Todes.* Einsiedeln, Switzerland: Johannes Verlag, 1993.

―――. *Der Christ und die Angst.* Einsiedeln, Switzerland: Johannes Verlag, 1951.

―――. *The Glory of the Lord: A Theological Aesthetics*, vol. 5: *The Realm of Metaphysics in the Modern Age.* Translated by Oliver Davies et al. Edited by Brian McNeil and John Riches. San Francisco: Ignatius, 1991.

―――. *The God Question and Modern Man.* Translated by Hilda Graef. New York: Seabury, 1958.

―――. *Die Gottesfrage des heutigen Menschen.* Einsiedeln, Switzerland: Johannes Verlag, 1958.

―――. *Theo-Drama: Theological Dramatic Theory*, vol. 5: *The Last Act.* Translated by Graham Harrison. San Francisco: Ignatius, 1998.

―――. *Theo-Logic: Theological Logical Theory*, vol. 1: *Truth of the World.* Translated by Adrian J. Walker. San Francisco: Ignatius, 2000.

―――. *Theo-Logic: Theological Logical Theory*, vol. 2: *The Truth of God.* Translated by Adrian J. Walker. San Francisco: Ignatius, 2004.

―――. *Theo-Logic: Theological Logical Theory*, vol. 3: *The Spirit of Truth.* Translated by Graham Harrison. San Francisco: Ignatius, 2005.

Caputo, John D. *The Mystical Element of Heidegger's Thought.* New York: Fordham University Press, 1986.

Derrida, Jacques. *The Gift of Death.* Translated by David Wills. Chicago: University of Chicago Press, 1995.

Gadamer, Hans-Georg. "The Marburg Theology." In *Heidegger's Ways*, translated by John W. Stanley, 29–44. Albany, NY: SUNY, 1994.

Guardini, Romano. *Rilke's Duino Elegies: An Interpretation.* London: Darwen Finlayson, 1961.

Heidegger, Martin. *Being and Time.* Translated by John McQuarrie and Edward Robinson. Oxford: Blackwell, 1967.

―――. *Contributions to Philosophy (From Enowning).* Translated by Parvis Emad and Kenneth Maly. Bloomington: Indiana University Press, 1990.

―――. "Letter on 'Humanism.'" Translated by Frank A. Capuzi. In *Martin Heidegger: Pathmarks*, edited by William McNell, 239–78. Cambridge: Cambridge University Press, 1998.

―――. "The Ontotheological Constitution of Metaphysics." In Martin Heidegger, *Essays in Metaphysics: Identity and Difference*, translated by Kurt. F. Leideker, 33–67. New York: Philosophical Library, 1960.

―――. "Phenomenology and Theology." In *The Piety of Thinking: Essays by Martin Heidegger*, edited by J. Hart and J. C. Maraldo, 5–21. Bloomington: Indiana University Press, 1969.

————. *The Phenomenology of Religious Life*. Translated by Matthias Fritsch and Jennifer Anna Gosetti-Ferencei. Bloomington: Indiana University Press, 2004.

————. "What Are Poets For." In *Poetry, Language, Thought*. Translated by Albert Hofstadter, 89–142. New York: Harper & Row, 1971.

Hemming, Laurence Paul. *Heidegger's Atheism: The Refusal of a Theological Voice*. Notre Dame: University of Notre Dame Press, 2002.

Kant, Immanuel. *Religion within the Boundaries of Mere Reason*. Translated by George di Giovanni. In *Religion and Rational Theology*, edited by Allen W. Wood and George di Giovanni, 41–215. The Cambridge Edition of the Works of Immanuel Kant 6. New York: Cambridge University Press, 1996.

Kisiel, Theodore. *The Genesis of Heidegger's Being and Time*. Berkeley: University of California Press, 1993.

Lesurdo, Dominico. *Heidegger and the Ideology of War: Community, Death, and the West*. Translated by Marella and Jon Morris. New York: Humanity, 2001.

MacQuarrie, John. *An Existential Theology: A Comparison of Heidegger and Bultmann*. London: SCM, 1955.

Murdoch, Iris. *Bruno's Dream*. London: Penguin, 1969.

Nietzsche, Friedrich. *Nietzsche*, vol. 3: *The Will to Power as Knowledge and Metaphysics*. Translated by Joan Stambaugh et al. Edited with notes by David Farrell Krell. New York: Harper & Row, 1987.

O'Leary, Joseph. *Questioning Back: The Overcoming of Metaphysics in the Christian Tradition*. Minneapolis: Winston, 1986.

O'Regan, Cyril. *The Anatomy of Misremembering: Balthasar's Response to Philosophical Modernity*, vol. 1: *Hegel*. New York: Crossroad, 2014.

————. "Answering Back: Augustine's Critique of Heidegger." In *Human Destinies: Philosophical Essays in Honor of Gerald Hanratty*, edited by Fran O'Rourke, 134–84. Notre Dame: University of Notre Dame Press, 2013.

————. "Kant: Boundaries, Blind-Spots, and Supplements." In *Christianity and Secular Reason: Classical Themes and Modern Developments*, edited by Jeffrey Bloechl, 87–126. Notre Dame: University of Notre Dame Press, 2012.

Przywara, Erich. *Analogia Entis: Metaphysics: Original Structure and Universal Rhythm*. Translated by John R. Betz and David Bentley Hart. Grand Rapids: Eerdmans, 2014.

————. *Analogia Entis: Metaphysik, Ur-Struktur und All-Rythmus*. Einsiedeln, Switzerland: Johannes Verlag, 1962.

————. *An Augustinian Synthesis*. Translated by C. C. Martindale. Eugene, Oregon: Wipf & Stock, 2014.

Rahner, Karl. "The Concept of Existential Philosophy in Heidegger." Translated by A. Tallon. *Philosophy Today* 13:2 (1969) 126–37.

Richardson, William J. *Heidegger: Through Phenomenology to Thought*. Dordrecht: Martinus Nijhoff, 1963.

Ricoeur, Paul. *Time and Narrative*, vol. 1. Translated by Kathleen McLoughlin and David Pellauer. Chicago: Chicago University Press, 1984.

Schürmann, Reiner. *Meister Eckhart, Mystic and Philosopher: Translations with Commentary*. Bloomington: Indiana University Press, 1981.

Sheehan, Thomas. *Karl Rahner: The Philosophical Foundations*. Athens: Ohio University Press, 1987.

Siewerth, Gustav. *Das Schicksal der Metaphysik von Thomas von Aquin zu Heidegger.* Einsiedeln: Johannes Verlag, 1959.

Stein, Edith. *Endliches und Ewiges Sein: Versuch eines Aufstiegs zum Sinn des Seins.* Freiburg: Herder, 1949.

———. *Finite and Eternal Being: An Attempt at an Ascent to the Meaning of Being.* Translated by Kurt F. Reinhardt. Washington, DC: ICS, 2002.

———. *On the Problem of Empathy* (rev. 3rd edition). Translated by Walraut Stein. Washington, DC: ICS, 1989.

———. *Science of the Cross.* Translated by Josephine Koeppeli. Edited by D. L. Gelber and R. Leuven. Washington, DC: ICS, 2003.

———. *Welt und Person.* Louvain: Éditions Nauwelaerts, 1962.

Van Buren, John. *The Young Heidegger: Rumor of the Hidden King.* Bloomington: Indiana University Press, 1994.

Welte, Bernard. *Gesammelte Schriften II/2: Denken in Begegnung mit den Denkern II: Hegel, Nietzsche, Heidegger.* Freiburg im Breisgau: Herder, 2007.

Wolfe, Judith. *Heidegger's Eschatology: Theological Horizons in Martin Heidegger's Early Work.* Oxford: Oxford University Press, 2013.

Zimmerman, Michael E. *Heidegger's Confrontation with Modernity: Technology, Politics, Art.* Bloomington: Indiana University Press, 1990.

Chapter 10

"I go and know not whither"

Death, Eternity, and the Immortality of the Soul in Karl Barth

Marc Cortez

MODERN THEOLOGIES OF DEATH typically begin by affirming that death is one of the fundamental anthropological problems. When the movie finishes, and even the credits have been replaced by the black screen beyond which we cannot see, will our story continue or will we be nothing more than a memory? This according to Verne Fletcher is "the mystery of death," whether this "will be, or will not be, the prelude to nothingness."[1]

For many Christians, though, it is not entirely clear why death should constitute such a fundamental problem: not for the redeemed, at least. Although the existential realities of death might involve pain and anxiety, there is no real question about the *whither* of death. After all, death is a consequence of sin introduced at the fall, and, consequently, it is something that has been entirely overcome through Christ's redemptive work. Additionally, even though we are still broken people and continue to experience the lingering reality of death, our continued existence is secured by the fact that we have immortal souls. Together these two affirmations entail the conviction that death should not pose any particular

---

1. Fletcher, "Some Reflections," 16.

challenges for the Christian. Death might still be painful and difficult, but the real "problem" of death has already been answered.

In modern theology, though, each of these affirmations—death as a consequence of sin and the continued existence of the soul—have come under increased scrutiny. Indeed, many influential theologians have explicitly rejected both, arguing instead that death itself is part of God's created order *and* that humans do not continue to exist after death in virtue of the fact that they have immortal souls.[2] If these theologians are correct, then traditional answers fail, and the problem of death looms for the Christian as well.

In this paper, we will use the theology of Karl Barth to explore some of the theological motivations behind such arguments. Other modern theologians have developed their own ways of dealing with death that differ from Barth in important ways. Nonetheless, the broad influence of Barth's approach makes it a good candidate for close study. Additionally, Barth is one of the few modern theologians who has made death a central category of his theology. Although he developed his views most extensively in the last third of his volume on theological anthropology, "Man in His Time,"[3] that discussion draws extensively on his earlier discussion of divine temporality (II/1). He subsequently develops his position further in his discussions of divine providence (III/3), theological ethics (III/4), and the theology reconciliation (IV).[4] With Barth, then, we have the opportunity to consider a theology of death in which our view of death is importantly related to a broad range of theological issues.

Our study will unfold in three parts. First, we will see why Barth thinks it is necessary to make a distinction between death in itself, which is a creational good, and death as we currently experience it, which is a consequence of sin. In the process, we will see that Barth thinks any adequate view of death must begin with the fact that Jesus himself died, and why he contends that this requires us to affirm that mortality and finitude are inherent to human nature. In the second section, we will consider several arguments Barth offers for why it is to our benefit that we are temporally limited in this way, each of which involves a rejection

2. E.g., Tillich, Pannenberg, Jüngel, and Harshorne.

3. Barth, *Church Dogmatics* III/2, 437–640.

4. It is also important to recognize that although he develops his most extensive arguments in the *Church Dogmatics*, he also addresses the topic at some length in his Romans commentary, his lectures on 1 Corinthians and Romans 5, and the *Göttingen Dogmatics*.

of the idea that we live eternally in virtue of having immortal souls.[5] Finally, we will explore some of the implications and potential difficulties involved in Barth's argument, suggesting ways in which some of the key insights of Barth's approach might be retained even if we choose not to follow him at every turn.

Even Jesus Died: Viewing Human Death Christologically

Death as the Sign of Judgment

The first step to understanding Barth's view of death is to recognize the distinction he draws between death and judgment. Although he recognizes that the two are inseparably related in the Bible, he still thinks that we can and should discern the difference between them.

Barth begins by arguing that the Bible almost universally views death in entirely negative terms.[6] Although the Old Testament authors only make the connection between sin, death, and judgment explicit in the early chapters of Genesis, Barth maintains that they consistently viewed death as an unnatural consequence of sin. Whatever we might say about the person after death, they no longer truly live. Thus, the dead are described as mere shadows, unable to worship God or continue as members of his covenant community. The New Testament picture of death is materially identical to that of the Old Testament, with the exception that the connection between death and judgment becomes even clearer.[7] It is "not a part of man's nature as God created it."[8] By the time he is done considering all the biblical data, then, Barth can only conclude that any

---

5. Barth's objections to dualist ontologies are not limited to his views on death. Indeed, he dedicates another large portion of III/2 to explaining the inseparable body/soul relationship in a way that rejects traditional accounts of the soul (III/2, 325–436). I have dealt with those arguments at some length elsewhere, though, and will be focusing this discussion specifically on how he deals with the soul in the context of his theology of death (Cortez, *Embodied Souls*).

6. III/2, 598. Unlike many biblical scholars, Barth does not try to find a more positive account of death in the Old Testament descriptions of "good" deaths—heroic deaths, dying after a long and faithful life, etc.

7. III/2, 599. Thus, "We learn nothing materially new when we formally enter New Testament ground." (III/2, 613).

8. III/2, 600.

idea of death being "a friendly or at least a conceivably neutral fate" is alien to the biblical material.[9]

At first glance, such concessions might seem to eliminate any possibility of finding a positive and creational aspect to death. Yet Barth argues that it is important to realize that this entire picture is based on death "as it actually encounters us."[10] The vast majority of the biblical data, and all of our personal experience, involve death in this sinful and fallen world. Thus, no matter how unanimous they might be in proclaiming death to be negative and evil, they are necessarily limited in their ability to reveal whether death is inherently associated with sin and guilt or only contingently so.

The difficulty is that between our creation and our eventual death, "there stands the fact of the abysmal and irreparable guilt."[11] With this in view, it stands to reason that the biblical authors would cast death in largely negative terms. After death, we stand before God himself, and we do so as those who have broken covenant and have lived faithlessly.[12] If this were not the case, it might be possible to face death with some level of confidence, even defiance. However, "it is not the enemy but God who is to be feared."[13]

According to Barth, then, we need to distinguish death from sin, guilt, and judgment. "Death is not in itself the judgment. It is not in itself and as such the sign of God's judgment. It is so only *de facto*. Hence it is not to be feared in itself or necessarily, but only *de facto*."[14] This is the lens through which Barth reads all of the biblical passages portraying death as a consequence of sin that needed to be conquered in Christ. The threat of death that became an actual curse as a consequence of sin was the threat that death would be experienced as judgment.[15] This is the "sting of death" defeated by Jesus on the cross (1 Cor 15:55). Although we continue to experience biological death, we need no longer fear the accompanying judgment because Jesus has already faced that judgment

9. III/2, 601. See also IV/1, 307; II/2, 588–93; IV/1, 253; IV/4, 16.
10. III/2, 596.
11. Ibid., 695.
12. Ibid., 607.
13. Ibid., 608.
14. Ibid.,, 632.
15. Ibid., 633; see also IV/1, 234.

for us. Understood in the sense of death-as-judgment, our death already lies behind us.

The picture Barth develops is much like a guilty child standing before the door leading to her father's study. Even if she is convinced that her father is good and gracious, she still fears what lies beyond the door. She knows that she deserves judgment and punishment. Maybe she even fears complete rejection, the loss of her father's love. Should we be surprised if this child transferred some, maybe even all, of her trepidation about the coming judgment to the door itself? If we had the chance to interview her before entering the room, she might well talk about how much she feared that door, how much she wanted to avoid opening the door, even touching it. The door could easily become an object of terror in its own right.

In itself, though, the door is no more than that, a point of transition from one place to another. Indeed, we could easily imagine another scenario in which the same child comes home from school excited to tell her father about all the exciting things that happened during the day. Racing down the hallway eager for the father's embrace, she approaches that same door. Would that not change how she views the door and the language she uses to describe it?

According to Barth, we are limited by the fact that almost all the information we have about death comes from the first scenario. We are always already those who stand before the door in guilt, fearing the coming judgment. So we experience the door as a great evil. Yet none of this establishes the fact that this is the only way to view death. "It is clear beyond all doubt that there are certain connexions between blessing and life, cursing and death. But this is no proof that death is intrinsically a curse, nor life a blessing."[16] Might it not be the case that the second scenario is still possible, one in which death is merely the point of transition from one place to another?

In itself, then, death is "man's step from existence into non-existence."[17] Barth thus associates death even with the passing of Enoch and Elijah.[18] In their case, however, we see that the transition does not have to be associated with judgment.[19] Death is not judgment itself, but it

16. III/2, 588.

17. Ibid., 632.

18. Ibid., 635–637.

19. Although Barth does not raise this in the context of his various discussions of death, he also contends that the transformation of living believers at the *parousia*

has become so closely associated with judgment that it is now its clearest sign. "Death, as it actually encounters us men, is the sign of God's judgment on us. We cannot say less than this, but of course we must not try to say more either."[20]

However, by making this distinction, Barth has not yet reached his goal. Thus far, he has merely established the conceptual possibility that despite the Bible's consistently negative portrayals of death there might still be a more positive, creational view of death lurking in the background. We have not yet seen any real reason for thinking that this conceptual distinction is valid in reality. Might it not be the case that the biblical authors consistently view death as a negative consequence of sin because that is precisely what it is? To answer this question, we must turn to Barth's christological argument.

The Mortality of the Messiah

There are many ways in which Barth could have tried to establish the reality of this conceptual distinction. Some have argued that it is inherent to any living process that it eventually comes to an end. Others contend that the finite nature of creation requires the temporal limitation of living creatures, otherwise they would eventually overpopulate the world. And we could probably postulate still further arguments. For Barth, though, these will always remain secondary arguments at best. They may help delimit the concept "mortal," but none is adequate for establishing that human persons are in fact mortal in this way.

Throughout his theological anthropology, Barth contends that a proper understanding of the human person must always begin with the humanity we see revealed in Jesus Christ. We must recognize the ways in which Jesus differs from other humans, not least as a consequence of his deity, but he remains the only one in whom true humanity is both revealed and grounded.[21] Important for our purposes, though, is the fact that Jesus lived a fully sinless life, thus revealing as much as possible the nature and shape of sinless humanity. It should come as no surprise, then, that Barth similarly orients his discussion around a christological analy-

---

constitutes another kind of transition without passing through death-as-judgment (IV/3.2, 924–925).

20. III/2, 596.

21. For more on this, see Cortez, "Madness," 15–26.

218

sis of death. "His death, resurrection and coming again are the basis of absolutely everything that is to be said about man and his future, end and goal in God."[22] This is what provides the real ground for his contention that we must discern a creational basis for death in addition to its function as the sign of judgment.

From this christological starting point, Barth draws two important conclusions. First, Jesus' death shows us that death is in some way necessary for being human. The "simplest and most obvious consideration" that arises when we consider this question in light of Jesus is, "Like all men, the man Jesus has His lifetime: the time bounded at one end by His birth and at the other by His death; a fixed span with a particular duration within the duration of created time as a whole."[23] No theology of death should neglect the fact that even Jesus died.[24]

Many would respond that Jesus' death was itself a consequence of sin. By taking all of our sins upon himself, Jesus rendered himself liable to death and judgment. Thus, even here the Bible affirms the inseparability of the two. I will have more to say in a moment about what the cross reveals about the relationship between death and judgment. Here it suffices to point out that, for Barth, we simply cannot neglect the anthropological significance of his death. If he is going to serve as the revelatory center of our theological anthropology, offering our only real glimpse of sinless humanity, we must account for the fact that even Jesus' life ended in death. For Barth, the only reasonable conclusion is that Jesus "had to be able to die."[25] Contrary to any anthropology that depends on some inherently immortal soul, and any attempt to view Jesus' death merely as a consequence of sin, Barth contends that Jesus "had to have this finitude in order that He might take this end upon Himself."[26] In other words, even if the way that Jesus *experienced* death was closely connected to sin and judgment, as indeed it was, the *mere fact* that his sinless humanity was capable of dying means that we need to understand mortality as part of God's creational vision for human persons. Thus, "if it seems to be for Him an anthropological necessity, the determination of His true and

22. III/2, 624.

23. Ibid., 440.

24. Thus, "there is no human greatness and grandeur which is not exceeded, overshadowed and fundamentally called in question by death: not even that of the promised and manifested Messiah and Son of Man" (III/2, 601).

25. III/2, 630.

26. Ibid.

natural being as man, how can we maintain that all this has nothing to do with the nature of man as created good by God?"[27]

This is the primary basis on which Barth argues that death-as-transition is necessary to human nature. In Jesus we see that to be human is to be finite and mortal, and "mortality means subjection to death, and death means the radical negation of life and therefore of human existence."[28] Thus, all human persons have an "allotted span," which "begins at a certain point, lasts for a certain period and finally comes to an end."[29]

Some might object that Jesus himself clearly feared his own death (Matt 26:36–46).Thus, Jesus apparently did not view death as a "neutral" door through which one might experience either judgment or bliss. Instead, Jesus appeared to view death as intrinsically evil, something he would far prefer to avoid and to which he only submits after a long night of anxious wrestling before the Father. His fears were confirmed on the cross, where his Cry of Dereliction manifested the agony of divine judgment (Matt 27:46). How then can we view Jesus' death as pointing to any concept of death that is intrinsic to human nature? Clearly this demonstrates the opposite: death is part of God's judgment on sin.

Barth, however, agrees with nearly all of this proposed counterargument.[30] Indeed, Barth stresses the agony of Jesus' death on the cross, viewing the Cry of Dereliction as a declaration that Jesus, the one human who was "wholly and unreservedly for God," took our judgment upon himself and experienced hell, which Barth defines as "an annihilatingly painful existence in opposition" to the Father.[31] This is "the eternal death which Jesus suffered for us," the cup he chose to drink.[32] Rather than downplaying the painful reality of Jesus' death, Barth views it as the only true experience of death-as-judgment.

Nonetheless, he contends once again that although we must say this, we may not say more than this. The fact that Jesus experienced death-as-judgment does not necessitate the conclusion that death is *only* a negative reality. Instead, Barth argues that the *voluntary* nature of Christ's death requires a different conclusion. The key here is Barth's contention that

27. III/2, 630.

28. Ibid., 625.

29. Ibid., 554.

30. See esp. IV/1, 306–307.

31. III/2, 603.

32. II/1, 420.

even if we affirm that Jesus' death was an anthropological necessity, this does not mean he had to die the *particular* death he did. Instead, Jesus freely willed to take our sin upon himself and experience death-as-judgment. If this is the case, however, then we must draw a distinction between death-in-itself, which was a necessary part of Jesus' human existence, and death-as-judgment, which he freely took to himself as a redemptive work.[33]

This is what makes it possible for Jesus' people to experience death differently. If death and judgment were identical, then we would all still be experiencing God's judgment in the event of death, this despite the fact that "death" has been defeated through the cross and resurrection. Instead, Barth contends that although we still face death-as-transition, and we will continue to experience considerable trepidation in this event as we go to face God in our broken and sinful condition, we should nonetheless view death-as-judgment as something over which Jesus has already triumphed. Thus, "A strict identity of dying and judgment in death is possible only if we ignore the fact that God has acted for us at Calvary."[34]

On this basis, Barth goes back and addresses the New Testament material again, finding at least some hints of this distinction. For example, he contends that since Hebrews talks about a judgment that comes *after* death (Heb 9:27), these cannot be identical events.[35] He draws the same conclusion from the reference to a "second death" in Revelation.[36] And he points out a number of occasions in which the NT authors refer to death without any indication that it should be viewed negatively (e.g., 1 Thess 5:10; 1 Cor 3:22; Rom 8:38; 14:7f; Phil 1:20). In this context, he contends that the common euphemism of "falling asleep" to refer to death is the way the New Testament describes the experience of death for those who have been freed from death-as-judgment.[37]

33. III/2, 628.
34. III/2, 629.
35. III/2, 637.
36. III/2, 634, 637.
37. III/2, 639. He goes on to reject the idea that "sleep" means they still exist. The term refers to *falling* asleep (something we witness) not *being* asleep.

The Positive Benefit of Creaturely Limitation

If Barth had stopped with his distinction between death-as-judgment and death-as-transition, viewing the latter as a creational good inherent to being the kinds of creatures God made humans to be, his argument would not necessarily have any implications for the immortality of the soul. It is entirely possible to agree with Barth on the nature of death and conclude that the soul is that which establishes the continuity of the human person through the transition of death. On such a view, Adam and Eve would have been created mortal, not merely contingently so. Even without sin, they would have experienced the transition of death, though without the fear of judgment. For them too, the transition would have culminated in their resurrection and entrance into eternal life, a transition in which their soul is what ensures their continued existence in eternity.

However, Barth does not stop here. The greater part of his argument concerning death has to do with a number of positive benefits that he associates with being finite and mortal beings. These arguments do not serve as the basis for his contention that we are necessarily mortal, a role that he reserves for his christological argument. Nonetheless, he does view them as strengthening the account, providing reflections on why a good and gracious God might have constituted human nature in this way. Each of the benefits he associates with human morality challenge long-standing views about the "immortality" of the human person, regardless of whether this is understood in terms of the immortality of the soul.

History, Uniqueness, and Covenant

One of Barth's most fundamental reasons for arguing that limitation is good for human persons is that he thinks it is only by having a finite history that we have a meaningful identity. According to Barth, human persons constitute themselves as the persons they are in and through their actions in time. This is Barth's famous actualism at work.[38] Persons are not metaphysical "substances" in which their identity is grounded in some stable, underlying essence. Instead, Barth contends that I establish my identity in and through the history of my personal actions and relations. "And in so far as I am caught up in this movement from my

38. See esp. Hunsinger, *How to Read Karl Barth*.

beginning to my end, my life becomes my history—we might almost say my drama—in which I am neither the author nor the producer, but the principal actor . . . I myself am in this movement."[39] Indeed, "We might almost say that he is himself his time in the sequence of his life-acts."[40]

The significance for understanding death, though, is Barth's contention that unless such a history has an end it cannot really constitute a person's identity. "A history without an end would not be a history."[41] Although Barth does not unpack all the details of his argument, the thought seems to be that if we are constituted by the particular acts that comprise our histories, and if these histories are never complete, then there is a very real sense in which I do not have an identity. *Who* I am would continue to unfold as through the never-ending sequence of actions in time. No matter how much time transpired, I would never have a determinable identity. "In an infinite and unending time he would obviously be an indefinite being dissolving both behind and before. He would have no centre, and therefore would not be himself. To be himself he must be constituted by his existence in time, by the appointed limits of birth and death."[42] Without both a beginning and an ending, nothing would be "genuinely defined."[43]

In the same way, Barth connects temporality with the uniqueness of the human subject. If our temporal histories are that which provide our identities, they are also that which makes human persons "irreplaceable, indispensable, and non-interchangeable."[44] The time of our human history may not be much, but it is ours and it comprises "our place in the cosmos and in history."[45] Without complete histories, our unique identities would be lost in the never-ending succession of past, present, and future.

Indeed, Barth argues that unlimited time would cause problems even for the identity of God himself. If we mistakenly envision God as either timelessly eternal or existing in some infinite temporality, we would

39. III/3, 232.

40. III/2, 521.

41. III/3, 233.

42. III/4, 572–573.

43. III/2, 565. As Verne Fletcher affirms, "one would be incapable of determining the shape of one's life, of deciding what shall be one's definitive commitments and loyalties" ("Some Reflections," 9).

44. III/3, 231.

45. III/4, 579.

render God's own identity indeterminable.[46] Instead, Barth contends that we should think of God as having his own eternal temporality.[47] God has a determinable identity because he himself is the sum total of all that he is and does throughout his own eternal history. This does not mean, however, that his identity somehow develops over time, which would be the consequence of viewing him as existing in an infinite series of temporal moments. Instead, the past, present, and future that constitute the divine identity occur in an eternal simultaneity. In this way, Barth contends that God too is "single and unique" as a consequence of his personal history.[48]

The key for our purposes, though, is the argument that the history that constitutes personal identity needs to have both a beginning and an end. "[T]aken together the two events do constitute the outline of the disposing or limitation of the life of all of us."[49] Unlike God, who is *eternally* temporal, we are *finitely* temporal. For our histories to be complete, the temporal succession of past, present, and future must some day come to an end. As the temporal limit that brings our personal histories to conclusion, death is necessary for us to have determinate identities.

Some might wonder at this point whether it is really all that necessary for us to have determinate identities in this sense. What would be so wrong about suggesting that our identities remain forever undetermined? Certain postmodern conceptions of the self might be quite happy to affirm that our identities remain eternally in flux. According to Barth, however, this alternative would itself render us unable to participate as God's covenant co-partner in his plans for creation. For Barth, this is the essence of what it means to be human, and it requires that the human person be a unique subject, which in turn requires temporal finitude.[50] The concern appears to be that without the distinct identity constituted by my particular history, there would be no unique *I* to whom God could relate as Counterpart. This historical uniqueness is what marks me out as a particular, an individual self with a particular role to play in God's covenantal purposes.

46. III/2, 565.

47. see. esp. II/1, 608–77.

48. III/4, 572. Indeed, "The eternal singleness of God Himself is reflected in the small creaturely once-for-allness of this life of his which has a single beginning and a single end" (232).

49. III/3, 229.

50. III/2, 565.

Definite People, Definite Atonement

Another argument Barth offers for the benefit of temporal limitation is that without finitude there could be no real salvation. In a state of unending life in which our personal histories had no conclusion, there would be no way to secure our salvation. "What would become of us if in an endless life we had the constant opportunity to achieve a provisional ordering of our relationship with God and our fellows?"[51] For Barth, this could only mean the eternal possibility of breaking fellowship and again falling back toward the nothingness that currently plagues us. "Long life and an ample measure of time can only mean more opportunities. And an infinite measure of human life can only mean an infinite number of opportunities."[52] Instead of unending bliss, this would leave us in the position being "compelled to aspire continually" and "condemned to perpetual wanting and asking and therefore dissatisfaction."[53] For Barth, this is a better picture of Hell than of Heaven.

Barth takes the argument a step further and suggests that the atonement itself can only be effective if we are in fact finite beings. "We have to be finite, to be able to die, for the ἐφάπαξ of the redemption accomplished in Christ to take effect for us."[54] He does not unpack this argument in any detail, but the concern again seems to relate to the difficulties of envisioning the human life as an unbounded set. Barth uses the same "once-for-all" language to describe the idea of being a temporally bounded person. Birth and death are the "two events which give to human life its character of once-for-allness."[55] And God himself is "once-for-all" in his eternal temporality.[56] Barth seems to think, then, that there is a connection between the once-for-allness of the atonement and the once-for-all nature of temporal beings. For the atonement to be a real event that impacts real beings, both must have the kind of identity that comes from their historical, and therefore temporally limited, determination.

A second possibility, though, is that Barth is concerned that infinitely unending human life would require a similarly infinite and unending atonement. The problem here would not be with the quantity of

51. III/2, 631.

52. Ibid., 561.

53. Ibid., 562.

54. Ibid., 631.

55. III/3, 231.

56. III/4, 571–72.

sin such unending lives would produce, as though Barth were concerned about the possibility that our sins might eventually surpass the amount of atonement made available through the cross. Christ's work on the cross cannot be measured in such quantitative terms. Instead, Barth's concern more likely deals again with the fact that such an unlimited set (i.e., the unbounded set of all unendingly future sins) has no real identity. He is thus raising the question of whether Christ's death on the cross could have the kind of once-for-all application in which *all* sins are already in view and addressed on the cross. Rather than a redemptive event that was already *applied*, we would need one that was unendingly *appliable*.

Rather than revising the meaning of the cross in this way, Barth thinks it preferable just to accept the fact that God built temporal limitations into the fabric of creation. "To belong to Him we must be finite and not infinite. Finitude, then, is not intrinsically negative and evil. There is no reason why it should not be an anthropological necessity, a determination of true and natural man, that we shall one day have to die, and therefore merely have been."[57]

My Time, My Place, My Contribution

According to Barth, a third major benefit is that temporal finitude grants full significance to our personal histories. If we lived unending lives, we would no longer be able to view any particular time, even an extended period of time, with any real urgency.[58] After all, if our years are unlimited, how can we possibly think that a decision I make in *this* moment, or even a series of decisions I make over the course of a few decades, has any real significance? Would not such years and their corresponding actions be mere a mere drop in the infinite ocean of my unending life?

Barth raises this concern most acutely in his volume on the ethics of creation (III/4). There Barth argues that the uniqueness that comes from the human person's particular history is what gives significance to the person's actions in creation. This uniqueness means first that these actions are mine and mine alone. "The time in which we live is our place. It may be a modest place, but it is ours. As such, it is our place in the cosmos and in history."[59] The uniqueness of my particular history is such that I

57. III/2, 631.
58. Ibid., 633.
59. III/4, 579.

make a contribution only *I* can make. Second, though, this uniqueness involves the idea that these events cannot be repeated. "'Unique' means this one time exclusively. It means once and not twice; once and never again."[60] Between the two, then, the fact that my history is limited to just *these* years, the ones bounded by my birth and death, means that *these* years are my unique and unrepeatable contribution to what God is doing in creation. These years and these alone are my distinct work as God's covenant co-partner.

It comes as no surprise, then, that Barth thinks this places particular urgency on how we use the time that we have, especially in light of the fact that we cannot know when it will come to an end. "For now, in his present time, he has his unique opportunity, and since he does not know how long it will last he must seize and use it."[61] Since every moment is a unique and precious part of my unrepeatable history, everything I do should be "tested by the question whether it is a seizing or neglecting of the unique opportunity presented to him in his time."[62]

For Barth, this urgency is entirely lost when we emphasize instead infinitely unending life. Without temporal finitude, my actions may still have *significance*—after all, they remain actions of obedience or disobedience before my Creator—but they have no *urgency*. With an infinite number of years ahead, does it really matter if I do something in the next few minutes? It can wait.[63]

Finite Creatures Before a Gracious God

The final benefit of temporal finitude we will consider is Barth's argument that such a view helps us understand our true dependence on God's grace for every moment of existence. An obvious question that comes to mind given Barth's claim that the history of human persons must come to and end at some point is what this means for the human person *after* death. Although a discussion of Barth's views on eternity and the resurrection would take us too far afield at this point, we need to deal with this at least briefly to understand how Barth relates his view of death to God's grace.

60. Ibid., 571.

61. Ibid., 580. Thus, "The urgency of the divine command carries with it a warning to seize our limited time as a unique opportunity" (III/4, 580).

62. Ibid., 580.

63. For a similar conclusion, see Fletcher, "Some Reflections," 9.

As we have seen, Barth is clear throughout that death is the end of the personal history of a human being. Whatever we might want or need to say about me after I die, we must say that my history has concluded. The time between my birth and death is the *only* time I have, which is why I must live it with urgency. Barth thus rejects any attempt to affirm a post-mortem continuity of the human person through appeal to an immortal soul.[64] For Barth, appeals to the immortal soul are almost always attempts to reassure ourselves in the face of death.[65] Even Jesus lived a finite, human life. Although Barth spends a fair bit of time discussing Jesus' resurrection, the "Easter time" between the resurrection and the ascension, and the nature of his own eternal life,[66] he rejects the conclusion that we should view any of this as suggesting that Jesus "was given further time beyond the unique time of his given life on earth back then."[67] The human life of Jesus is likewise drawn up into and preserved in God's eternal love.[68]

Because we legitimately desire the gift of life to continue, we appeal to some indestructible entity that can ground our continued existence even through our own deaths.[69] Instead, Barth contends that the human person should simply recognize his finite mortality and understand that the only thing he can do in death is "throw himself upon God's free grace."[70]

The fact that God remains the gracious God who is always "for us" in Christ means that my death will not involve the complete negation of

64. This is, of course, at least partly because he has already rejected the idea of a separable soul in his discussion of the body/soul relationship.

65. "Apart from God, the human will try to avoid this knowledge, perhaps by ascribing 'to himself, or at least to his soul, an infinitude, a so-called immortally'. Or he might say that 'in any case he is not yet dead', or he may console himself with the thought that the species will live if not the individual. All of this is 'a typical expression of fear', a sign that those who conceive of themselves as godless cannot 'face themselves', and have too weak an ego to accept the thought of their own mortality (III/4, 591)." See also III/4, 593.

66. Se esp. III/2, 437–511.

67. III/2, 477; cf. I/2, 53.

68. For more on Barth's view of the *parousia*, see Bolt, "Exploring Karl Barth's Eschatology," 225–26.

69. Even though temporal finitude is inherent to creatureliness, Barth contends that longing for more time is still a legitimate human desire because we recognize that our vocation as human persons is more than we can accomplish in any finite period (III/2, 555).

70. III/2, 569.

my existence. "One day we shall cease to be, but even then He will be for us. Hence our future non-existence cannot be our complete negation."[71] But this does not mean that we can presume upon God and demand that his grace requires him to sustain our existence in particular ways.[72] Any existence that we have in death cannot be the mere continuation of our personal histories, otherwise we would undermine everything Barth has established with his other arguments. Instead, human persons continue to exist as objects of God's love.[73] "What shall we be? Come what may, we shall be what we shall be under and with God; what we can and may and must be on the basis of His eternal future, i.e., those who are loved by Him to whom He will give time to live."[74] Thus, the human person has no "beyond" of his or her own. Instead, "God is his beyond."[75]

All of this entails the rejection of an immortal soul as the ground of the human person's continuing and unending life after death. For Barth, such arguments appear to be attempts to ground the certainty of our continued existence in ourselves rather than depending on the grace of God. He is well aware that it is entirely possible to view the soul, not as intrinsically immortal, but as eternally sustained by the life-giving grace of God. But he ultimately finds even these more nuanced accounts of immortality unconvincing. Even though these affirm the necessity of grace, they do so in ways that "would not be natural or obvious."[76] On such an account, it would be far too easy to forget that this unending life is a gift and begin to think of it as a possession that belongs intrinsically to human nature. "He would be blinded by the illusion that he can rely on many other things as well as God, and especially on himself."[77]

On the contrary, the human person should recognize mortality as "a powerful invitation and direction to throw himself upon God's free

71. III/2, 611.

72. Ibid., 610.

73. Ibid., 611.

74. Ibid., 545.

75. Ibid., 632. Schurr points out that Barth routinely use language that suggest continued personal existence, so we must take that into account. Yet he maintains nonetheless that "Barth does not seem to have provided the categories within which the identity of subjective continuity beyond death could be affirmed, but he nevertheless insists on it, and with his present emphasis on durable eternity could allow for it" (Schurr, "Brunner and Barth," 102).

76. III/2, 569.

77. Ibid.

grace."[78] In death, we see that God alone is "the source of life" and the event in which we will remain eternally.[79] Indeed, according to Barth, this is the real meaning of the excluding Adam and Eve from the Tree of Life. This was not an act of wrath, and certainly not of envy, but of grace. In this act, God prevented Adam an Eve from living forever, which would have been a curse that would have fundamentally undermined their ability to rely on God in his grace.[80] If we understand death rightly as it is revealed in Jesus Christ, then, we can see that death is the event that pushes us to face the inevitable limitation of our own resources and to throw ourselves into the eternal arms of our gracious God.

Some Critical Reflections

Barth thus offers a robust theology of death in which there is much to appreciate.[81] Anyone seeking to maintain traditional views on the human person's continued history in an unendingly eternal existence should reflect deeply on the questions Barth raises about the implications this has for the significance of our current existence. Such views should reflect further on how to affirm the eternality of the human person without undermining the urgency and importance of our pre-mortem histories. And they should offer more robust ways of explaining why it is that these few pre-mortem years play such a significant role in shaping our identities on into eternity. Although the concern today lies more with a tendency to neglect eternity, we should not fail to consider the ways in which an overemphasis on eternity could undermine human history and agency in important ways.

I also find much to appreciate in Barth's robustly christological analysis of human death. Unlike many theologians who begin their theologies of death with discussions of Genesis 2–3 or the relevant scientific data, Barth rightly contends that a Christian view of death should revolve around the shocking reality that the Messiah himself died. Yet as much

78. Ibid.
79. III/2, 353.
80. Ibid., 635.
81. In keeping with the purposes of this paper, I am not going to respond to Barth's position merely by rehearsing arguments for the existence of a substantial soul. As interesting as such discussions might be, we need to reserve them for another time. Instead, I will focus specifically on the particular aspects of Barth's arguments regarding death and the necessary finitude of the human person.

as there is to appreciate in this starting point, some important questions need to be asked here as well. To begin, it is not clear to me that Barth's conclusions are the only, or even the most likely, outcome of such a starting point.[82] We do not have time here to address Barth's lengthy discussions of Jesus' resurrection and the conclusions we should draw from his own appearances between the resurrection and the ascension, which Barth refers to as "Easter time," but it does seem to me that these warrant at least a revision of his clear rejection of any post-mortem history for the human person. Indeed, Barth himself contends that "Jesus has a further history beginning on the third day after His death and therefore after the time of His first history had clearly come to an end."[83] However, Barth rejects the conclusion that we should take this as warrant for affirming the post-mortem history of the human person since this subsequent time is "simply the time of the revelation of the mystery of the preceding time of the life and death of the man Jesus."[84] At this point, it is difficult to avoid the impression that rather than beginning with Jesus' death and resurrection as the starting point for understanding humanity, a certain conception of temporal finitude is driving the christological analysis here. If we had not already determined that humans could have no history after death, would we really draw the conclusion that this was anything other than a continued history of the incarnate Christ?[85]

Similar questions arise when we consider Jesus' state between his death and resurrection. If human persons have no continued existence after death, must we affirm a cessation of the incarnation during Holy Saturday? This is one of the difficult questions faced by any physicalist account of the human person. If Christ's human time comes to and end at death, so must the incarnation. Granted, on this interpretation, the incarnation would resume with the resurrection, but such a temporal gap in the incarnation would run counter to long-standing convictions about the permanence of Christ's incarnate state. And it would also generate some interesting questions about whether we should talk instead

82. See esp. Berkouwer, *Triumph*, 329–41.

83. III/2, 441.

84. Ibid., 455.

85. We should keep in mind that Bath cannot respond here with an appeal to Christ's divinity since he affirms that this is the incarnate Christ in his humanity. Indeed, Barth repeatedly emphasized the *bodily* resurrection of Jesus specifically to ensure his continued humanity. For more on this, see esp. Hitchcock, *Karl Barth*.

about *two* incarnations rather than merely the continuation of the same incarnation.

Barth himself would not likely have found such objections convincing. He would probably respond by appealing to the idea that human persons are sustained in God's love after their death. Thus, even on Holy Saturday, the incarnation "continues" in much the same way that all human persons continue to exist in eternity. To do this, however, he must contend that the resurrection does not effect any real change in Jesus' ontological condition. At death, Jesus had already entered the post-mortem state of inclusion in God's time. As important as the resurrection might be in Barth's theology, it would seem to constitute a revelation of the truth of Jesus' historical existence rather than transformation of his human condition. Once again, then, we must ask if this is really the only, or even the most likely, conclusion to draw from the christological data itself. If we had not already drawn conclusions about the necessary finitude of the human person, would we really read the resurrection narratives in this way? To me, that seems unlikely.

I raise these christological concerns first because of the foundational role they play in Barth's theology of death. If we were to draw different conclusions on the basis of this christological starting point, much of the warrant for Barth's view of death, including his most important arguments for the necessity of creaturely finitude, would be significantly weakened. Nonetheless, we should still raise some questions about other aspects of Barth's argument.

The aspect of Barth's argument that has received the most attention and criticism has to do with the nature of creaturely existence in eternity. Is it really adequate to say that we continue to exist in eternity only insofar as we continue to be loved by God and that we have no continued history of our own? To many, this sounds like a denial that the human as a personal subject actually continues. Instead, we only "live" in God's memory. Even a sympathetic interpreter like Nathan Hitchcock, who defends Barth against those who criticize him for undermining creaturely agency, ultimately concludes that his view of the resurrected state cannot sustain the affirmation that the human person continues to have any meaningful existence.[86]

Another issue worth considering is Barth's argument that temporal finitude is necessary to ground uniqueness and identity. This seems to

86. Hitchcock, *Karl Barth*.

neglect the possibility that an infinite set can still have a discrete identity. Consider, for example, the set of all even numbers. Although such an upwardly unbounded set is infinite in the same sense as many conceptions of creaturely life in eternity, it is not clear why we would need to say that such an upwardly unbounded set has no identity. Surely we can differentiate this set from the set of all odd numbers, despite the fact that both are unlimited. If that is the case, then we might have reason to question whether it is truly the case that a similarly unlimited historical existence might still have a unique, personal identity.

This latter point becomes even more pressing if we think about human personhood and identity as being somewhat more settled than Barth allows. Many of Barth's critiques about unlimited time have to do with the idea that in such a state we could have no certainty that we would continue to be the kinds of people we are now. Eternity would give us boundless opportunity to change course and reverse decisions made earlier in life, thus making it impossible to have any determinate identity. There is an extent to which this might not be such a bad thing. Allowing human identity to be more malleable in eternity might help address concerns about resurrected life being overly "static." But we can affirm the continued development of the human person in eternity without allowing the kind of radical reversal that Barth fears. Surely at least some creaturely decisions and actions are the kind that shape a person to such an extent that we would view them as permanent features of that person's identity. For example, I made a decision twenty years ago to get married, a decision that has surely shaped everything that follows. However we understand the post-mortem status of my marriage, it is hard to conceive of any future condition in which my identity will not always be marked by the reality of having-been-married for the last twenty years. That is irreversibly part of who I am as a unique subject. If that is true for marriage, it seems difficult to deny that it might also be true for Christian conversion. Barth's worries about personal identity in an unending future do not seem to account adequately for these kinds of identity-forming events.

From the opposite direction, we should ask whether Barth's way of establishing identity does not run into problems of its own. Barth establishes our identity within the limits of our current histories and then grounds the continued existence of those personal histories in God's eternal love. That may be reassuring for those who have lived lives relatively free of tragedy, but what about the rest? As Verne Fletcher asks, "Will

God 'cherish throughout endless ages' the 'actual being' of the desperate, the abjectly poor, the famine-stricken, the agonizing, the tortured?"[87] Similarly, how do we deal with concerns about justice when human history itself comes to an end with death? Although Barth may have a way of answering such questions, they go unaddressed in this theology of death.

Finally, Barth's concerns about the "immortality" of the soul undermining our dependence on grace at least needs to be developed with greater rigor. As we have seen, Barth is well aware that one can affirm the soul's continued existence without appealing to some kind of inherent immortality, but he thinks that all such approaches leave the human person on an unavoidable trajectory toward self-reliance. While those affirming the soul should hear this as an important warning, especially in light of popular conceptions of the soul that continue to view it as inherently immortal, the tradition has consistently emphasized the creaturely nature of the human person and consequently humanity's dependence on God's sustaining grace for any continued existence. At the very least, Barth owes us a more sustained articulation of why such an approach cannot meaningfully affirm a sufficiently grace-based ontology despite such historical consistency.

To conclude, then, Barth offers a robust theology of death that is an important challenge to many traditional perspectives on this important topic, not least of which is his insistence on the importance of developing Christian views of death in which Christ himself stands at the center. Nonetheless, I think we can identify a whole range of issues on which Barth's view itself needs to be challenged or clarified.

BIBLIOGRAPHY

Barth, Karl. *Church Dogmatics*. Edited by G. W. Bromiley and T. F. Torrance. 4 vols. Edinburgh: T & T Clark, 1936–75.

Berkouwer, G. C. *The Triumph of Grace in the Theology of Karl Barth*. London: Paternoster, 1956.

Bolt, John. "Exploring Karl Barth's Eschatology: A Salutary Exercise for Evangelicals." In *Karl Barth and Evangelical Theology*, edited by Sung Wook Chung, 221–35. Grand Rapids: Baker Academic, 2006.

Cortez, Marc. *Embodied Souls, Besouled Bodies: An Exercise in Christological Anthropology and Its Significance for the Mind/Body Debate*. London: T & T Clark, 2008.

87. Fletcher, "Some Reflections," 26.

———. "The Madness in Our Method: Christology as the Necessary Starting Point for Theological Anthropology." In *The Ashgate Research Companion to Theological Anthropology*, edited by Joshua Farris and Charles Taliaferro, 15–26. Aldershot, UK: Ashgate, 2015.

Fletcher, Verne H. "Some Reflections on Death." Theological Review 31:1 (2010) 4–59.

Hitchcock, Nathan. *Karl Barth and the Resurrection of the Flesh: The Loss of the Body in Participatory Eschatology*. Eugene, OR: Wipf & Stock, 2013.

Hunsinger, George. *How to Read Karl Barth: The Shape of His Theology*. Oxford: Oxford University Press, 1991.

Schurr, George M. "Brunner and Barth on Life after Death." *Journal of Religious Thought* 24:2 (1967) 95–110.

Chapter 11

A Good Christian Death

Brent Waters

THIS IS AN EXPLORATORY exercise. I am exploring, in an abbreviated manner, some initial ideas on what could be ascribed as a good death for a Christian. I begin with a simple but direct question: What is a good death? Answering this question is conditioned by a variety of factors such as time, social location, particular circumstances, and personal convictions and beliefs. For instance, my thinking about death has changed a great deal from when I was a young seminarian to now being referred to as a "seasoned" professor. An elderly woman with hordes of adoring children and grandchildren might prefer to linger awhile in their company, while an old man without family or friends might hope for a quick death while asleep. Some ancient Athenian philosophers awaited death with eager anticipation, for at last the soul would be freed from its temporal and physical bondage—Socrates tells a joke and drinks the hemlock. Whereas the twentieth-century philosopher, Hannah Arendt, offers a more sobering appraisal of death as "the only reliable law of life," that consigns "everything human to ruin and destruction."[1]

Moreover, death is particular and personal. Although death is a universally shared human fate, it is not encountered or experienced in a universal manner. We do not grieve the demise of people in general, but mourn the loss of friends and loved-ones. Someone *I* have known and loved is now dead. When we contemplate our own impending deaths, we do not confront an abstraction, but an approaching, concrete reality that

1. Arendt, *Human Condition*, 246.

is deeply personal, fraught with an uneasy mixture of anxiety and hope. The death I shall inevitably face will be *my* death.

What is a good Christian death? The tradition does not speak with a singular voice, for again various teachings, emphases, and changing circumstances come into play. Although the martyrs died in exemplary ways, martyrdom is not *the* normative objective. The martyrs did not seek death, but rather died faithfully in the face of persecution. St Augustine explicates with great clarity the Pauline teaching that nothing this side of eternity can compare with what awaits us on the other side, so that death should not be feared. Yet this defender of mediocre Christians[2] is not surprised when the dying long for an "extension of life in this pitiable state, and the deferment of their death."[3] Jeremy Taylor counsels, "He that would die well must, all the days of his life, lay up against the day of death," adding that without this preparation, we cannot face death with grace, faith, and charity.[4] There is also the petition from the Great Litany that reads, "and from dying suddenly and unprepared, Good Lord, deliver us."

Although the tradition does not speak about a good death with a singular voice, may some promising themes be gleaned from the preceding excerpts? From the examples of the martyrs we learn that a good Christian death is a faithful one. The martyrs remained true to their faith to the very end. Augustine reminds us that our desires are often disordered in respect to death. Even the promise of eternal life does not negate the preciousness of the life in hand. Taylor teaches us that a good death is the outcome of lifelong preparation. Death is the fitting end of a life lived well. The Great Litany warns that a quick and easy death is an unwanted occurrence from which we should plead to be spared. A time to consent to one's inevitable demise, however brief, is needed before life comes to an end.

These are all useful themes, but their immediate utility is not apparent; they require some framing. How might we go about constructing such a frame? For the purpose of this exercise, I want to pose, as my starting point, another question derived from the two commandments to love God and neighbor: what does it mean to die in love and fellowship with God and neighbor? We must be clear about who is asking this

2. See Markus, *End of Ancient Christianity*, ch. 4.
3. Augustine, *City of God*, XI/27, p. 461.
4. Taylor, *Rule and Exercises*, Kindle location 832.

question in order to better understand the eventual answer. This does not mean conducting a detailed exegesis of the biblical source, but rather who is asking this question for the purpose of this exercise. The short answer is: I am—a late modern Christian who enjoys relative affluence and easy access to medical care, and who has reached an age that is no longer on the sunny slope of the mortality divide. Although these factors are not determinative, they both inform and obscure how I think about a good Christian death. In what follows I often use the first person singular pronoun. This is not, hopefully, self-indulgence, but to acknowledge that death is always particular and always personal. Explicating what a good Christian death entails is not aided if I refuse to contemplate how I might aspire to die in love and fellowship with God and my most immediate neighbors.

Christians are commanded to love God and neighbor. Although the two commands are discrete, they are also interwoven, presupposing and reinforcing each other. I cannot love God and hate my neighbor, or vice-versa. Although these two loves are related they nonetheless require a proper ordering. It is God alone who should be loved with our entire being, and all lesser loves, despite their immediacy and importance, must be arranged accordingly. If I love my wife, daughter, career, or country more than I love God, my life becomes bent and disordered. At its most basic, the love of God is the acknowledgment that God is the creator of heaven and earth, and therefore the source and giver of life. At its most basic, the love of neighbor is the acknowledgment that my neighbors are fellow creatures, each one created in the image and likeness of God, and they too, like me, are recipients of the gift and loan of life.[5]

It is important to remember that one's life is simultaneously a gift and a loan. Our lives are not something we create and are thereby entitled to do with as we wish and possess it for as long as we might like. My life is given and loaned to me and must eventually be surrendered back to the giver. As recipients, then, our lives are not our own.[6] I am a custodian of a loaned gift entrusted to my care. As creatures we do not choose the circumstances in which we receive life. I did not choose my parents, nor did they choose me, and I often do not select the neighbors with whom I share my life with theirs. As creatures, we are interdependent. Unlike God, I am not self-sufficient and depend upon the assistance of others

5. See Kilner, *Life on the Line.*
6. See Barth, *Church Dogmatics*, III/4, and Meilaender, *Limits of Love*, ch. 7.

to survive and to flourish. As creatures, we perform the custodianship of our lives in a fallen world, weakening or imperiling the very interdependency we require in being custodians of our lives. In ordering my lesser loves—bonds of imperfection—I often sin against God and neighbor, because all too frequently I mistake love for the will to power.

Most importantly, for the purpose of this exercise, as creatures human beings are embodied and therefore finite and mortal. Particular bodies constrain what we might desire and will and are able to do. I lacked the physical attributes to fulfill my fondest boyhood dream of becoming a major league pitcher. Bodies deteriorate and eventually fail. I have reached that point where playing baseball is a memory and not an active pastime, and I know that eventually my life will come to an end. Creatures live in the time allotted to them, and eventually it runs out.[7] I do not have sufficient time to do everything I might want to do, for the "what has been" of my life expands as the "not yet" recedes. Remembrance slowly takes precedence over anticipation. The fact that finitude and death are natural offers little solace in confronting this awkward dance between past and future, because as Karl Barth concedes, the prospect of an impending and certain death remains a "monstrous" reality that, try as we might, cannot be ignored or evaded.[8] Consequently, it is not surprising that medicine wages a desperate but futile campaign against finitude and mortality, or at the very least tries to ease their grisly grip.

Is there anything that Christians might or should say in the face of this "monstrous" reality? Two things, perhaps. First, allotted time is what makes creaturely life possible, for it is the "form of human existence."[9] "If man had no time, if his existence were timeless, he would have no life."[10] Creation and its creatures cannot be eternal; otherwise it would be another God. Life in and constrained by time is the only way that creatures can live. Second, although death will have its say, it does not have the final word. In the resurrection of Jesus from the dead, a second history is inaugurated. Easter is an event that takes place in time, but also anticipates its fulfillment in eternity. The resurrection, as well the ascension, is a proleptic sign of the *parousia*. "The being of Jesus in time is not merely a being in the present or the past. It is also . . . a being in the

7. See Barth, *Church Dogmatics*, III/2, 47.

8. See ibid., 516–17.

9. Ibid., 520.

10. Ibid., 437.

future, a coming being."[11] And in that coming the time of creatures, my time, is taken up into God's eternity. The necessity of allotted time and its fulfillment in Jesus' resurrection, ascension, and *parousia* does not negate the monstrous reality of death, but it does (or should) ease its sting.

It is in baptism that we catch a glimpse of this admittedly uneasy resolution of creaturely finitude and mortality with the eternity of the creator. Again as Barth reminds: "Who are Christians? Those who by baptism into Jesus' death have been buried with Him (Rom 6:4); who can no longer live unto themselves, but only unto Him who died and rose again for them (2 Cor 5:15)."[12] It should be added, that baptism is also an initiation into the church as the body of Christ on earth. And it is here where Christians learn how to live no longer unto themselves, and to do so as finite and mortal creatures in fellowship with other finite and mortal creatures.

A few suggestive contours of what might constitute a good Christian death can now be roughly sketched. To die in love and fellowship with God and neighbor requires the proper ordering of these loves. The love of God, as the origin and destination of life, delineates and delimits all other important but nonetheless lesser loves. Disordering occurs when the penultimate is confused with the ultimate; when, for example, I love life more than God.

To die in love and fellowship with God and neighbor requires the faithful reception of life as gift and loan. To be baptized is to also affirm that our lives are not our own but are to be lived for God and neighbor. Consequently, we find our freedom in the very constraints imposed upon us as temporal creatures. In dying as a Christian, I should ideally not become self-absorbed but remain mindful of God and my neighbors. It is in living in fellowship with neighbors that I also live in fellowship with God. Hell is not other people, but their absence.

To die in love and fellowship with God and neighbor requires the faithful stewardship of the gift and loan of life entrusted to our care. As stewards, we are accountable to God and neighbor, but accountable as finite and mortal creatures. Consequently, to be a faithful steward or custodian, I must also consent to the finitude and mortality endemic to my creaturely status. Consent, however, is not affirmation, for death is an enemy, but there are both good and bad ways to fight; neither premature

11. Ibid., 485.
12. Ibid., 470.

surrender nor hopeless struggling to the bitter end constitute good stewardship. A good steward endeavors to bring one's life to its fitting and timely end.

To die in love and fellowship with God and neighbor requires lifelong preparation, for, following Taylor, our deaths ultimately reflect our lives. Somewhat like a story, a life has an opening and concluding chapter, and a good ending depends upon the quality of the chapters preceding it. In preparing for death I become a better custodian of the gift and loan of life entrusted to my care; I learn, hopefully, to surrender it back faithfully to its source as my allotted time runs out. And in such surrender I can also be embraced by the hope of resurrection into the eternal life of God, but not as some idle fantasy of cheating death. I first consent to my finitude and mortality in order to be raised gracefully into God's eternity.

In order to say a bit more about what the qualities mentioned above might entail, some contrast is needed. Contemporary medical practice offers such a background. Nothing about these preceding qualities should be construed as diminishing the importance of embodiment, for it is as embodied beings that we are created and loved by God, a status attested to by the incarnation.[13] To the contrary, there is nothing at all wrong with wanting to live long and healthily, or to relieve unremitting pain and suffering so long as these desires enable rather than distort a love of God and neighbor. Medical care in general, and particularly at the end of life, can both assist and thwart the stewardship of our lives. In what follows I identify, briefly, some cultural forces shaping medical practice that tend to militate against Christians from pursuing a good death, one that is in love and fellowship with God and neighbor. Specifically, I am pondering how should we assess the growing and simultaneous dedication of late modern medicine to both extend longevity and assist the dying to achieve a death at a time and means of their choosing? What are some of the cultural forces driving this twofold commitment?

In part, there is the late modern project of mastering nature and human nature.[14] Nature is perceived as, at best, indifferent and, at worse, inimical to human flourishing. Technologies are used to assert greater control over natural vicissitudes more in line with human desires and values, providing greater material comfort and presumably more fulfilling lives. Medical technologies in particular play an increasingly central role

13. See Waters, *This Mortal Flesh*.
14. See Grant, *Technology and Justice*.

in asserting this mastery. Advances in diagnostic, preventive, therapeutic, and enhancement techniques have promoted longer, more productive, and happier lives. Medicine has not only become a powerful tool in both preserving and improving physical capabilities, but also enhancing the wellbeing of mind and soul. Medicine, to at least some extent, is reshaping human nature by enabling relatively good health over an extended period of time into a widespread expectation rather than a rare occurrence. If humans flourish by asserting greater control over nature and human nature, then cannot the same be said for controlling the natural process of dying and death?

The prominent role the will plays in shaping the identities and actions of late moderns is another cultural force. Closely associated with the attempt to master nature and human nature, the will, however defined or understood, serves as the central source for late moderns in constructing their desires, actions undertaken in satisfying them, and thereby their identities. The will is both the source and expression of one's evolving identity. Both nature and human nature are effectively reduced to artifacts of the will. Since the will plays such a crucial role, then eliminating any unnecessary constraints enables human flourishing. Ideally, constraints against the will should be freely chosen rather than unwillingly imposed. In response, various political policies and social customs are devised that simultaneously seek to eliminate unwanted constraints and enlarge the range of choices that one can make in forming and asserting one's will. These schemes, however, largely fail to address two significant constraints, namely, finitude and mortality. Since humans are embodied they are also finite and mortal beings, and a body, particularly an aging one, exerts many unwanted limitations against the will.

Late moderns turn to medicine to ameliorate their finite and mortal limitations. To some extent, this recourse has not been in vain. Medical advances have not only extended longevity, but they have also helped maintain physical and mental vitality as people grow older. Although medicine has helped to relieve the constraints of finitude and pushed back those of mortality, they have not been overcome, so the will remains fettered. Eventually, everyone dies despite the best medical efforts at hand. Yet again late moderns turn to medicine to help them forge one last, defiant gesture: if mortal constraints cannot be conquered, at least medical care can help patients choose the time and means of their death. If the lives of late moderns are artifacts of the will, then so too should be their deaths.

Another cultural force reflects a reaction to the success of medicine at prolonging life. Many late moderns will live for long periods of time, but many will also die slowly and in pieces, a fate that most find highly undesirable and best avoided. Ironically, the same medical care that enables patients to live longer also keep them alive too long. The same medical care that enriches the lives of its beneficiaries fails them in the end. As a remedy, patients again turn to medicine to help protect themselves from unwanted treatments that merely serve to delay death rather than prolong life in any meaningful sense. When a patient (or surrogate in cases of incompetency) reaches a point where it is determined that the quality of one's life has diminished so extensively that it is no longer worth living, then medical care should assist the patient in achieving a death that is deemed to be more desirable.

Increasingly, medicine is acquiescing to this demand for assistance in achieving a desirable death. My concern here is not to assess whether this acquiescence is good or bad, for both healthcare providers and patients, but to highlight a tension it creates or exacerbates in the practice of medicine. Traditionally, medicine has largely, though not entirely, been regarded as the champion of preserving life rather than taking it. This did not always dictate a drawn-out and ultimately futile campaign against a mortal enemy, but there was a reticence to aid this foe in having its eventual way. Care and comfort should be provided to the dying, but the eventual death would be an act of necessity rather than choice. This is, in part, why modern medicine's frequent inability to differentiate the difference between curing and caring (and when the former should give way to the latter) helped exacerbate a fear of death that appeared unduly prolonged and overly burdensome.[15]

Finally, there is transhumanism. Transhumanists believe that nature or evolution has bequeathed to humans a poor host or prosthetic of the will. The inherent fragility and lack of endurance over time restricts rather than enables what individuals might will to do. This weakness is most apparent in the fact that people die, a reality that transhumanists often characterize as a terrible waste, tragedy, or injustice. Their proffered solution is to use technology to construct a superior host or prosthetic of the will, one that enhances personal capabilities and performance while enduring for a greatly expanded period of time, perhaps forever. They envision a golden, posthuman future in which if death occurs it is a matter

---

15. See Ramsey, *Patient as Person*, ch. 3.

of choice or a rare, unfortunate accident. Over time, humans will merge with their technology, evolving into superior, posthuman beings that can enjoy the benefits of nearly endless time.

It is tempting to dismiss the transhumanists as daydreamers indulging wild fantasies, for much of the technological development they envision may very likely prove infeasible. The temptation, however, should be resisted. Even if the anticipated technological innovations never come to fruition, transhumanist discourse is nonetheless influencing expectations of overcoming, or at least pushing back, finite limitations among the broader public. These expectations in turn place a demand upon medical care to both extend longevity and enhance performance, while also insisting that it assist patients in constructing a desirable end when the limits of mastering finitude are eventually reached, at least for the time being. To a large extent, transhumanist discourse is hyperbolic description and commentary on how humans already perceive themselves;[16] As Katherine Hayles contends: "People become posthuman because they think they are posthuman."[17]

Taken together these cultural forces pose challenges for pursuing a good death that can be said to be Christian, especially in respect to the expectations that we bring to extending and ending life, and how medical practice responds accordingly. In the first instance, Christians are not called to a life of comprehensive mastery over nature and human nature. Having said this, however, an important qualification needs to be made. In rightfully affirming the goodness of creation and the creatures inhabiting it, Christians should avoid romanticizing nature. Late moderns are largely correct in assuming that nature is often indifferent or inimical to human flourishing. Plagues, earthquakes, and hurricanes are all natural, but rarely, if ever, lifted up as cherished events. "The history of human culture is in part the history of the development of human defenses against the threat of nature."[18] There is no reason to deny that asserting some mastery over nature has greatly benefitted humankind, and any thought of returning to a more primitive age as being somehow an improvement is little more than reckless nostalgia. Arendt is correct in her insistence that although humans are born into nature, they must

16. See Waters, *Christian Moral Theology*.

17. Hayles, *How We Became Posthuman*, 6.

18. Gustafson, *Ethics*, 105.

construct a world fit for their habitation.[19] Adam and Eve, after all, were gardeners tending a garden and not survivors wandering the wilderness of Eden.

Such mastery, however, is not and should not be absolute. The world that humans construct remains part of God's creation. Reticence in asserting mastery over nature is both prudent and faithful. Prudent because of unintended environmental, social, and political consequences, and faithful because human life is properly oriented toward the proleptic or eschatological end of the *parousia*. Creation finds its fulfillment in Christ and not in human mastery.

This reticence is even more crucial in respect to mastering human nature. If life is a gift and loan rather than self-possession, then caution is required in exercising its faithful stewardship. A loan as well as a true gift always has implicit strings attached regarding its use. If an artist, for example, entrusts me with a sculpture she has created it comes with the expectation that I should display and enjoy it rather than using it for a doorstop or hiding it in the basement. Consequently, caution should be taken to prevent extending longevity and controlling the means of death as mere or pointless acts of mastery for their own sake. Rather medical care throughout and at the end of life should be guided, in part, by discerning how particular treatments either facilitate or discourage one's stewardship of the gift and loan of life; either enabling or diminishing love and fellowship with God and neighbor within one's allotted time.

Such mastery is especially troubling, even potentially perilous, when it is asserted exclusively to serve the will of those seeking mastery, serving no other purpose than that of the self. As Augustine acknowledged, such attempts at self-mastery undertaken by people plagued by disordered desires is to fall more deeply into the abyss of sin. Or as Nietzsche recognized, self-mastery quickly degenerates into the nihilistic will to power. The will, then, becomes the centerpiece of human identity, and the more unfettered the better. Late moderns in effect perceive their lives as artifacts of their will, and bringing one's life to an end is *the* final act of will.

This means that one can never consent to the inherent finitude and mortality of being a creature, because they are the last constraints against the will that must be warred against. But in failing to consent to finitude and mortality, the will becomes bent and out of alignment, for humans will themselves to become something other than the creatures they were

19. See Arendt, *Human Condition*.

created to be. Particularly for the Christian, a good life does not entail self-mastery for the sake of asserting the will, but aligning one's will, through grace, with God's will. Is not the same alignment true in regard to death, so that in both living and dying should not our prayer be: not my will but thy will? Does this mean that God wills us to die? No, but God does will us to be creatures, entailing the inherent finitude and mortality endemic to such a status. To aspire to be infinite and immortal is to aspire to be inhuman, and thereby depriving humans of the very richness of life that these limitations make possible; that joy is inexplicable without suffering. In the novel, *Shadowlands,* Joy, who is dying, tells her husband, C. S. Lewis, "that the pain, then, is part of the happiness, now." She goes on to add: "That's the deal."[20] Consenting to finitude and mortality is, in short, the prerequisite for a life of preparing for a good and faithful death; honoring the terms of the deal.

The allure of assisted dying is most explicable as a fearful reaction to the success of medicine to prolong life, sometimes for too long. When the goal is to delay death as long as possible, the patient often dies little by little, confined to a hospital attached to an array of machines and monitoring devices, and visited occasionally by family, a few friends, and various medical professionals. As Paul Ramsey insists: "If the sting of death is sin, the sting of dying is solitude." "Desertion is more choking than death, and more feared. The chief problem of dying is not to die alone."[21] For many, if not most, this prospect is undesirable, even dreadful, and best evaded if possible. Given this fear, to opt for assisted dying is understandable.

Understandable, but it is not a good alternative, at least for a Christian. To choose the time and means of one's own death is to surrender the gift and loan of life on our terms and not God's. A good Christian death, at least ideally,[22] is a matter of timing within the time we are allotted.[23] Neither abandoning the gift too early nor clutching it too avidly is an act of faithful stewardship. A good Christian death is neither hastened too quickly nor delayed interminably.

A good Christian death, however, is not Stoic. Here a pastoral note needs to be highlighted. A good death is not necessarily heroic or serene.

20. Fleischer, *Shadowlands,* 239. Based on the screenplay and stage play by William Nicholson.

21. Ramsey, *Patient as Person,* 134.

22. I am aware that I am ignoring accidental or sudden deaths.

23. See Waters, *Dying and Death.*

The end of life is often accompanied by great pain and suffering. This reality should not be ignored or easily dismissed. Pain is said to build character, but it can also destroy the soul. As Taylor observed: "For there is the voice of man, and there is the voice of the disease, and God hears both; and the louder the disease speaks, there is the greater need of mercy and pity, and therefore God will the sooner hear it."[24] In this respect, good palliative care or hospice is a fitting response to hearing the voice of the disease. But this is not enough in pursuing a good *Christian* death. Following Ramsey again, what "does loyalty…to the dying require of us?[25] It certainly requires medical care, but it also requires maintaining the bonds of imperfection in which we live together in our allotted times. We assist others in dying faithfully by keeping company, and being attentive, for the time being, to their needs and not fixating on our impending loss and grief.[26]

Transhumanist rhetoric raises to a feverish pitch the Promethean underpinnings of the late modern project of mastery and will to power— a bit like encountering Nietzsche on steroids. For them, finitude and mortality are not merely unfortunate or distasteful features of being temporal creatures, but unmitigated evils that must be conquered. The disease of aging must not only be treated, but cured. To make death always a matter of choice and never a necessity is the ultimate artifact and triumph of the will. To come to terms with, much less consent to finitude and mortality, is to commit treason against life itself.

Such audacious verbosity must give Christians some pause, for they recognize it as the language of a counterfeit salvific religion. Humans must be saved from their finitude and mortality, from their creaturely status. Yet to achieve this goal they must completely reconstruct humans into something better than human, the posthuman; to be born again into willful artifice. This is little more than reversing the incarnation, for salvation does not come from the Word made flesh, but in flesh made data. And what is the promised heaven on earth: immortality as endless time.[27] This is a death wish, for in stripping humans of their allotted time, transhumanists also preclude any prospect of life within time that requires a beginning and end. In this respect the transhumanists are

---

24. Taylor, *Rule and Exercises*, Kindle location 1249.

25. Ramsey, *Patient as Person*, 131.

26. See Murdoch, *Sovereignty*.

27. See Grant, *Time as History*.

correct that in order to achieve endless time, humans must stop being human. This is a hellish destiny, quite different than the Christian hope of death, resurrection, and eternal fellowship with the triune God. The point here is not whether or not the transhumanists can actually achieve their goal, but the extent to which their religious rhetoric begins to form the expectations and imagination of late moderns who are no doubt susceptible to their proffered promise of ultimate mastery. The challenge for Christians is to offer a counter narrative of properly ordered rather than disordered desires, a task they have often undertaken and need to undertake once again.[28]

At this point it would be customary for someone like me, trained as a moral theologian, to suggest ways that other Christians might resist the cultural forces that militate against them in pursuing a good death. Instead, I am going to turn my attention inward, to concentrate on a specific question: if I someday I face the prospect of a long, painful death, of dying slowly and in pieces, would I accept an offer of assisted dying, a quick and easy exit? I wish I could say, without hesitation, certainly not! But I know better. I think it would prove to be a real, attractive temptation. On those occasions when I have faced an illness requiring a brief stay in the hospital, I have discovered that I am not a very good patient, particularly when it comes to pain—I greedily imbibe any medication offered. I grow restless when extended convalescence is required, tending to withdraw into myself in a petulant, bitter, and fearful manner. I would also like to spare my family the spectacle of watching me die slowly, the time spent in a futile, gut-wrenching vigil, and the financial burden incurred. I would like to spare them this emotional suffering and material hardship. Moreover, I simply do not like the feeling of being out of control. I am, after all, deeply embedded in a late modern culture committed to mastery, the centrality of the will, and a pervasive fear of death. In my most unguarded moments I see my mortality as nothing more than a monstrous reality.

Yet as a Christian I know I should resist the offer. But how? I think I should begin by remembering my baptism. I have already died and been raised in Christ. It is not so much the end of my first birth that should command my attention, but the destiny of my second birth. This is not to deny the reality of my impending, physical death; the death of my body. It is merely to place it in its proper context of the temporal bracketed by

28. See Waters, *From Human to Posthuman*.

the eternal. Augustine is right, we are pilgrims, and all pilgrimages come to an end.

Next, rather than withdrawing into and isolating myself from others, I would try to remember that I have never lived as an autonomous individual, but always in bonds of fellowship. From the beginning my life has been shared with family, friends, colleagues, and strangers, many of whom have changed over time, but the human bonds of imperfection have always been there. Is there really any compelling reason to break them while dying? Hopefully, the Eucharist would also pervade my thoughts and imagination. This shared meal at the Lord's Table is emblematic of the Christian life. In dying in Christ we are already resurrection in Christ and share a foretaste of this new life in the church. In the breaking bread and sharing the cup we learn about the love, grace, and fellowship that binds us together in this earthly pilgrimage. We also catch a glimmer of our eternal destiny in Christ, for this simple, sacramental meal also anticipates a heavenly, unending banquet when all that is not well is made well. Even in the darkest recess of my suffering, I hope the Eucharist will remind me that I am never really and shall not be alone. And so, more mundanely, I also hope I would muster the courtesy to accept even the most awkward attempts of expressing care or love as moments of grace, reminding me that I was not created to be alone. Ramsey is right; it is dying alone that I fear more than death.

Although at the end of life it is more blessed to receive than to give, I would try to remember that I still have responsibilities to others. Ramsey is again right to insist that we have duties to the dying, but what are the duties that the dying have to the living? The decision of when to die is not exclusively mine alone to make, particularly if I aspire to be in love and fellowship with my neighbors, particularly those to whom I am most intimately related. What say do my loved-ones rightfully have regarding my treatment? To what extent am I obliged to try to honor their expectations, particularly since they may be as fearful for what lies ahead? My death is admittedly my own, but not exclusively; it shall effect others for good or ill. Dying effectively exposes the deceit of so-called autonomy. If the living should not abandon the dying, then should not the dying also resist abandoning the living, at least to the point where their own voices have not been silenced by the voice of illness?

I think I would also try to resist the offer of assisted dying in order to not to jeopardize the souls of my healthcare providers. Medicine is properly a practice dedicated to preserving life. This does not require a long and ultimately fruitless struggle to delay death for every minute and second possible. Yet Scripture teaches that death is an enemy, and fraternizing or conspiring with an adversary is never a good idea. But there are honorable defeats. I think I would want those caring for me to ease the physical pain as much as possible, to help me maintain the bonds or fellowship with those I love, to treat me not so much as a dying patient but a fellow human being who is dying. Reciprocally, Taylor's words are also instructive when he urges the dying person not to be "ungentle and uneasy to the ministers and nurses that attend us, but to take their diligence and kind offices as sweetly as we can."[29] In this respect, I hope my request of medicine would not be to help me die, but to help me consent to my mortality and their finitude.

Finally, I would try to be attentive and receptive to God, particularly a God who may seem to be absent in my suffering—at least that was Jesus' experience on the cross. I would try to remember that in exercising the ending of my stewardship of the gift and loan of life that was entrusted into my care, I am now being called to entrust it back to its source. It is the final act of faith that my life is not simply a short, accidental emergence out of the abyss of nothingness only to be pulled back down into nothing. In surrendering myself to God, the source and end of life, I would try, despite my failing strength, my fear, to remember that my life is, has been, and shall be, in the words of Michel Quoist, "a long throb of love towards Love eternal."[30]

BIBLIOGRAPHY

Augustine, *City of God*. Translated by Henry Bettenson. New York: Penguin, 1972.

Arendt, Hannah. *The Human Condition*. Chicago: University of Chicago Press, 1998.

Barth, Karl. *Church Dogmatics*. Edited by G. W. Bromiley and T. F. Torrance. 4 vols. Edinburgh: T & T Clark, 1936–75.

Fleischer, Leonore. *Shadowlands*. New York: Signet, 1993.

Grant, George. *Technology and Justice*. Notre Dame: Notre Dame University Press, 1986.

———. *Time as History*. Toronto: University of Toronto Press, 1995.

Gustafson, James. *Ethics from a Theocentric Perspective*, vol. 1. Chicago: University of Chicago Press, 1981.

Hayles, N. Katherine. *How We Became Posthuman: Virtual Bodies in Cybernetics, Literature, and Informatics*. Chicago: University of Chicago Press, 1999.

29. Taylor, *Rule and Exercises*, Kindle location 1288–1304.
30. Quoist, *Prayers*, 16.

Kilner, John. *Life on the Line: Ethics, Aging, Ending Patients' Lives, and Allocating Vital Resources.* Grand Rapids: Eerdmans, 1992.

Markus, R. A. *The End of Ancient Christianity.* Cambridge: Cambridge University Press, 1990.

Meilaender, Gilbert. *The Limits of Love: Some Theological Explorations.* University Park, PA: Pennsylvania State University Press, 1987.

Murdoch, Iris. *The Sovereignty of Good.* London: Routledge, 2001.

Quoist, Michel. *Prayers.* Franklin, WI: Sheed and Ward, 1999.

Ramsey, Paul. *The Patient as Person: Explorations in Medical Ethics.* New Haven: Yale University Press, 1970.

Taylor, Jeremy. *The Rule and Exercises of Holy Dying.* Amazon Digital Services, 2010. Kindle edition.

Waters, Brent. *Christian Moral Theology in the Emerging Technoculture: From Posthuman Back to Human.* Farnham, UK: Ashgate, 2014.

———. *Dying and Death: A Resource for Christian Reflection.* Cleveland, OH: United Church, 1996.

———. *From Human to Posthuman: Christian Theology and Technology in a Postmodern World.* Aldershot, UK: Ashgate, 2006.

———. *This Mortal Flesh: Incarnation and Bioethics.* Grand Rapids: Brazos, 2009.

Chapter 12

Resting in the Peace of Jesus
Christian Living toward Dying

GILBERT MEILAENDER

"A THEOLOGY WHOSE CENTRAL message is the biography of a crucified Jew cannot avoid speaking about death, whether it be his death or
ours."[1] There is probably no single best way to do this, but I will take my
direction from Karl Barth's repeated attempts to think about our humanity from three different—though complementary rather than compet-
ing—angles of vision.

In the massive and never completed volumes of his *Church Dogmatics* Barth envisions ethics as offering an account of human action that
corresponds to the threefold form of God's action in creation, reconciliation, and redemption.[2] Because we are God's creatures, there must be
some account that accepts, honors, and celebrates the limits of our finitude and the time we are allotted. Because we are sinners whom God has
in Jesus acted to reconcile, our life moves toward death and is disordered
in countless ways that come under God's judgment. And because we are
heirs of the future God has promised, because he knows us by name, we
are promised that one day we will come to share in the life eternal that

1. Pelikan, *Shape of Death*, 5.
2. Barth himself provides a succinct description of his approach in three places:
(1) 549–50 of volume II/2 of the *Church Dogmatics*; (2) 24–26 of volume III/4; and
(3) 6–11 of *The Christian Life*, a fragment of the unfinished discussion of the ethics of
reconciliation in volume IV.

Father, Son, and Spirit live. I want to borrow not the substance but the structure of Barth's account, using it as an approach for thinking about the spirituality of Christian dying.

Without attempting in any way to do justice to the richness of Barth's lavishly developed structure, I simply suggest that Christian moral reflection on almost any important topic—in this instance, the death toward which we live—cannot ignore any of the three angles of vision that Barth distinguishes. These three angles do not simply follow one another in lockstep sequence, nor does any one ever replace another. But even if, as Barth himself noted, it is difficult to combine the three, it is still important, as he put it, to recall that our task is "to accompany this history of God and man from creation to reconciliation and redemption, indicating the mystery of the encounter at each point on the path according to its own distinctive character."[3]

If we do not begin from within the contours of this Christian story, we may still come to understand some truth about human nature, but we are not likely to see the truth about human destiny. For if our vision is restricted to created life but does not include reconciled and redeemed life, we will have little to say about the life God promises in the new creation. At best we will think in terms of something rather like an indefinitely extended continuation of this life, and sooner or later it will become clear that we cannot make sense of such a notion.

Thus, for example, the philosopher Samuel Scheffler suggests that, understandable as it may be that we might "wish that our lives could go on forever," that wish is "confused." Rather than enhancing the pleasure we take in life, living forever would, Scheffler thinks, actually undermine the kind of value life has. For that value depends on the limitations of natural, finite life. "A life without temporal boundaries would no more be a life than a circle without a circumference would be a circle. So whatever the eternal existence of a being might be like, it would not be just like our lives only more so."[4] Scheffler can make little sense of imagining creatures who are like us but who do not experience the kinds of bodily limits that characterize our experience. Such creatures would never have to act or make decisions "against the background of the limits imposed by the ultimate scarce resource, time. But every human decision is made against

---

3. Barth, *Church Dogmatics*, III/4, 26.
4. Scheffler, *Death and the Afterlife*, 100.

that background, and so in imagining immortality we are imagining an existence in which there are, effectively, no human decisions."[5]

Scheffler is a distinguished philosopher, and we have little reason to disagree with him on his own terms. But we need not confine ourselves to those terms. Because we love, trust, and hope in Jesus—who was not simply resuscitated on the third day but (rather) raised to a life that is genuinely new and not just more of the same—our understanding of death can and must be shaped by the three angles of vision Barth delineates. Hence, I will seek here, as he put it, "to accompany this history of God and man from creation to reconciliation and redemption."

Created Life

I know of a peaceful eventide;
And when I am faint and weary,
At times with the journey sorely tried,
Thro' hours that are long and dreary,
Then often I yearn to lay me down
And sink into blissful slumber.[6]

Our days and years are lived out east of Eden, and it is for our good that the cherubim with flaming sword stand guard, lest any of us should seek a way to the tree of life. This earthly life could never satisfy the deepest desire of the human heart, and, hence, it is good that the course of life should move through decline to death. That is the deepest truth about human life, but we can begin nearer to the ground.

Created life is a gift, but also a burden. We are living organisms, bodies animated by soul. That is, we are not just "things," not inanimate objects. This is especially clear in the German language, which makes a distinction not present in many other languages—the distinction between *Leib* and *Körper*.[7] Lacking soul, our bodies are purely material things, corpses. To be living organisms is, therefore, a great gift, but it is a

---

5. Scheffler, *Death and the Afterlife*, 99.

6. This is one of the stanzas from Magnus Landstad's hymn, "I know of a sleep in Jesus' Name." Langstad (1802–1880) was a Norwegian pastor who authored many hymns. His *Hymnary* was widely used in Norwegian churches. Here and in the two other stanzas from this hymn cited later I use the translation of the hymn from *The Lutheran Hymnal* of 1941.

7. Barth, *Church Dogmatics*, III/2, 377.

gift that comes to us also as a task. We call that task metabolism. Through constant exchange of substances with our environment we sustain our existence as living beings. This means, however, that we constantly hover "between being and non-being."[8] We cannot just persist indefinitely, the way a rock is "simply and fixedly what it is, identical with itself over time, and with no need to maintain that identity by anything it does."[9]

For us, by contrast, continuing to live is always a task, sometimes a burdensome task, and we have life "strictly on loan."[10] Because we are finite organisms, the course of human life, unless ended prematurely by illness or accident, has a natural trajectory of growth and development through decline to death. Sooner or later the fires of metabolism burn themselves out, and *Leib* becomes *Körper*. And thus, as the poet John Hall Wheelock writes, "The dead are the only ones who never die."[11]

Our time is never unlimited; it is always, as Barth puts it, an "allotted time."[12] That does not make it any less a gift. It simply means that our time is not God's timeless eternity, and it invites us constantly to remember that we are not Creator but creatures. It seems right, therefore, that Odysseus, offered the choice between an immortal life with the nymph Calypso and a return home to his wife Penelope, should choose the latter. He chooses, that is, to be a man, not a god, accepting a life that is strictly on loan and that moves inevitably toward death. For that is the nature of our allotted time, a time in which decline must come and, sooner or later, we grow "faint and weary."

To acknowledge that it is a burden to maintain our life over time does not mean that this life lacks goodness or sweetness. Quite the contrary. This is a world that invites our love. "Shall not a man sing as the night comes on?" Wheelock asks. Although we know that sooner or later the fires of metabolism burn themselves out in our bodies, "[t]he fury and joy of every sound and sight" along the way cannot and should not be denied.[13] It is right that we should love these sounds and sights, right that we should enjoy the beauty of life, right even that we should say, as

8. Jonas, "Burden and Blessing," 35.

9. Ibid.

10. Ibid., 36.

11. Wheelock, "Song On Reaching Seventy," 20–21.

12. Barth, *Church Dogmatics*, III/2, 553–572.

13. Wheelock, "Song On Reaching Seventy."

the poet does, "More time—oh, but a little more."[14] Desire for longer life and grief at the death of those we love are not wrong for Christians. Our funerals are not—or should not be—simply celebrations of life and rejoicing that the deceased loved one is now "in a better place." They should be occasions for sadness, even if we acknowledge that the one we loved has arrived at a "peaceful eventide" and a "blissful slumber."

About finite human life we must always, therefore, say both that its sweetness elicits our love and that, in the end, it will fail us. Describing St. Augustine in his classic study of the *City of God*, J. N. Figgis captured this two-sidedness in its most pronounced form.

> In Augustine there were struggling two men, like Esau and Jacob in the womb of Rebecca. There was Augustine of Thagaste, of Madaura, of Carthage, of Rome, of Milan, the brilliant boy, the splendid and expansive youthful leader, "skilled in all the wisdom of the Egyptians," possessed of the antique culture, rhetorical, dialectic, Roman—the man of the world, the developed humanist with enough tincture of Platonism to gild the humanism; and there is the Augustine of the "Confessions," of the "Sermons," of the "De Civitate," the monk, the ascetic, the otherworldly preacher, the biblical expositor, the mortified priest. These two beings struggle for ever within him, the natural man filled with the sense of beauty and the joy of living, expansive, passionate, artful—and the supernatural Christian fleeing from the world, shunning it, burning what he adored, and adoring what he burnt, celibate and (at times) almost anti-social.[15]

Surely it is understandable that we should desire more of this life and that only with difficulty can we learn to accept that our bodies must wither and decline.

But the deepest truth remains that of the angel with the flaming brand at Eden: More of this life could never fully satisfy our love's longing; for what we want is not simply quantitatively more of this life, but a beauty that is qualitatively different. "In other words," Josef Pieper writes, "the allaying of the thirst cannot consist simply in the mere continued existence of the thirster."[16] We know ourselves as people who are always on the way, always wanting a fulfillment not yet given. Barth is right,

---

14. Ibid.

15. Figgis, *Political Aspects*, 114.

16. Pieper, *Happiness and Contemplation*, 36.

therefore, to say that an unlimited span of this life would actually be bad for us, condemning us to "perpetual wanting."[17]

Thus, both aspects of our creatureliness—the limits of our finite condition, and the inner freedom to soar beyond those limits in longing for a good not yet fully possessed—suggest that, however lovely this life may be, death cannot simply be bad for us. On the one hand, the limits of our finitude help to shape and form lives that are distinctively human. To be finite organisms, animated bodies, is to live a life that has not just duration but also a characteristic shape—from infancy, through maturity, to decline and death. The moments of such a life are not identical; they take their specific character from their place in the whole. That is what a distinctively human—and limited—life is like. And on the other hand, the metabolic exchanges by which we work to sustain ourselves as animated bodies also bear witness that a human being cannot be reduced to the matter of those exchanges; for they indicate, Hans Jonas observes, that a human being has "a sort of freedom with respect to its own substance, an independence from that same matter of which it nonetheless wholly consists."[18] This life has its own special beauty, but it does not finally quench the thirst it evokes in us. As a character in Wallace Stegner's *The Spectator Bird* says, "A reasonably endowed, reasonably well-intentioned man can walk through the world's great kitchen from end to end and arrive at the back door hungry."[19]

Eventually, therefore, we need to come "faint and weary" to "eventide," yearning to "sink into blissful slumber." That is the truth of our created life.

Reconciled Life

O Jesus, draw near my dying bed
And take me into Thy keeping
And say when my spirit hence is fled,
"This child is not dead, but sleeping."
And leave me not, Savior, till I rise
To praise Thee in life eternal.

17. Barth, *Church Dogmatics*, III/2, 562.
18. Jonas, "Burden and Blessing," 35.
19. Stegner, *Spectator Bird*, 69.

Thus far, limiting our perspective to created life, we have noted two reasons for thinking that death is not necessarily bad for human beings. Because we are created as living bodies, death is built into the shape of a meaningful human life. And because we are created with a thirst for God, more of this same life could never answer to the love that moves us. How is it, then, that St. Paul characterizes death not as a good to be desired but as the wages of sin and the last enemy?[20] Evidently death is not only the natural end of human life but also something other and more than its natural end.

To a limited extent we can make sense of this on the basis of ordinary human experience. If created life is filled with beauty and sweetness, then its loss is reason for sadness. If we seem to be characterized by a thirst never satisfied in this life, death might seem to announce that our created life is vain and futile. But sadness and futility do not quite add up to judgment or punishment, and the fact that death comes to every living organism cannot fully reconcile us to it. For *my* death is not merely a participation in what is universal, what is common to all human beings. My death is also unique. That is the point of Ivan Ilyich's often quoted reflections on the standard syllogism: "All men are mortal, Caius is a man, therefore Caius is mortal." This, Ilyich reflects, "had always seemed to him correct as applied to Caius, but by no means to himself. That man Caius represented man in the abstract, and so the reasoning was perfectly sound; but he was not Caius, not an abstract man." On the contrary, he had been a little boy with a particular mother and father, particular toys, particular school experiences, particular loves. "Caius really was mortal, and it was only right that he should die, but for him, . . . Ivan Ilyich, with all his thoughts and feelings, it was something else again. And it simply was not possible that he should have to die. That would be too terrible."[21]

However true it may be, therefore, to note that our finite life must inevitably move toward its end, death "as it actually encounters us" has the character of judgment, for it encounters us "as sinful and guilty men."[22] We may say that one who dies has "passed" or "passed away," but those comfortingly passive formulations fail to articulate the real truth. For one who dies has been summoned—summoned for judgment. Jaroslav Pelikan noted that Cyprian—Bishop of Carthage in the mid-third

---

20. Rom 6:23; 1 Cor 15:26.
21. Tolstoy, *Death of Ivan Ilyich*, 79–80.
22. Barth, *Church Dogmatics*, III/2, 597.

century AD—seems to have been the first Latin writer to use the word *ar-cessitio* ("summons") to refer to death. That summons is no gentle "pass-ing" from this life, perhaps to a better place. "To Cyprian the idea of the summons connotes the authority of the Supreme Judge to order a man into his presence and to demand an account from him of all that he has been and done." To simply "pass away" in death may be sad, but it does not really call us into question. If, however, death is a summons, then it confronts us with "the irresistible call of the Summoner"—to personal encounter with One who rightly judges us.[23] If ever we had thought we were in charge of our own lives, we now will see how vain such notions were.

As Ivan Ilyich understood, the summons is in no way abstract; it is directed to each of us individually, and it judges our loves as misdirected. So the Letter to the Hebrews notes, "it is appointed for men to die once, and after that comes judgment" (Heb 9:27). How is it that, in the face of such judgment upon our misdirected loves, we might nonetheless find the faith to say "come, sweet death" to such a summons?

That happens only as we pray, "O Jesus, draw near my dying bed, And take me into thy keeping." For, as the Letter to the Hebrews also notes, if we must die once and face judgment, so also "Christ, having been offered once to bear the sins of many, will appear a second time, not to deal with sin but to save those who are eagerly waiting for him" (Heb 9:28). When we rest in the peace of Jesus, faith trusts what is not necessarily evident to sight. For, as Barth notes, only in the case of Jesus is submission to death as *judgment* (and not simply as biological necessity) freely chosen. As the "first-born among many brethren," he took upon himself the judgment of all, "to put away sin by the sacrifice of himself."[24] He is, therefore, "the judge judged in our place."[25]

Here faith discerns the answer to Ilyich's bewilderment at the par-ticularity of his death, a death that he cannot and should not experience as generic. If each of us dies as a unique individual, each of us is also uniquely one for whom Jesus is the judge judged in our place. Meditating upon his own brush with death, Richard Neuhaus once recalled Potter's Field on Hart Island in New York City. There thousands of unclaimed dead, once particular lives now reduced to nameless corpses, have for

23. Pelikan, *Shape of Death*, 69.
24. Rom 8:29; Heb 9:26; Barth, *Church Dogmatics*, III/2, 628.
25. Barth, *Church Dogmatics*, IV/1, 211–283.

almost two centuries been buried in numbered boxes. But in the middle of Potter's Field a large stone stands, inscribed with the words, "He Knows Them by Name."[26] Each may be but a number in Potter's Field, but before God none is merely a generic human being.

This truth, that God knows each of us by name, has particular significance in the case of those who die—as we say from the perspective of our finitude—"prematurely." They do not enjoy a full life with its characteristic shape from infancy, through maturity, to decline and death. And if the meaning and worth of life were judged only from the perspective of the shape of a full life, and not also by remembering that in every moment of life we are equidistant from God, premature death of one whom we love might well lead us to despair. But the days or weeks of a child who dies soon after (or even before) birth are not only days of a life tragically cut short, though of course they are that from the perspective of a normal life span. They are also the days or weeks of a God-aimed spirit, whose every moment is lived before One for whom a thousand years are but as yesterday when it is past, and they do not count less or have any less worth because they never progress to maturity or old age (Ps 90:4). Jesus will draw near such a child's dying bed as surely as he will the deaths of those who live out their allotted threescore years and ten—or, if by reason of strength, still more.

In the end, then, the One who summons each of us at death is One with the power and authority to say, "'This child is not dead, but sleeping.'" To be sure, it is, as the Letter to the Hebrews says, "a fearful thing to fall into the hands of the living God"(Heb 10:31). But when that living God is the judge judged in our place, we "fall into *His* hands and not the hands of another."[27]

Redeemed Life

I know of a morning bright and fair
When tidings of joy shall wake us,
When songs from on high shall fill the air
And God to His glory take us,
When Jesus shall bid us rise from sleep,
How joyous that hour of waking!

26. Neuhaus, *As I Lay Dying*, 60.
27. Barth, *Church Dogmatics*, III/2, 609.

Misdirected as our loves often are, faith trusts that they can be redeemed—and so, we live in hope for life beyond death. We should not too quickly suppose, however, that there is nothing at all analogous to death in the promised life to come, nor should we suppose that entry into God's own eternal life must entirely await the end of this life.

May we not say, subject of course to the proviso that for now we speak from faith not sight, that in the life of the Triune God there is something akin to dying—a kind of "continual self-abandonment"?[28] From eternity the Father gives all that he is and has to the Son, who offers that begotten life back to the Father in perfect obedience, through the bond of love that is their Spirit. Each of the three persons is marked by self-abandonment, "each losing itself in common enterprise pursued without jealousy or conflict," entirely at one in continuous self-giving.[29] When the Son offers himself on the cross in human history, he does here among us what he does from eternity in the glory of his Father. Hence, C. S. Lewis, picturing the eternal life of the Triune God as a dance in which each continually abdicates his place and gives way to the other, writes: "All pains and pleasures we have known on earth are early initiations in the movements of that dance," though Lewis adds (no doubt calling St. Paul to mind), "but the dance itself is strictly incomparable with the sufferings of this present time."[30]

It is also true that the promised life of the new creation touches us even now, as we still live toward death. "If any one is in Christ, he is [present tense!] a new creation," St. Paul writes, enunciating in his own idiom the Johannine teaching that to know Jesus, whom the Father has sent, is life eternal (2 Cor 5:17; John 17:3). To be baptized into Christ is to begin a pilgrimage toward the full realization of a redeemed life in which we already share. Thus, in his *Small Catechism* Luther describes baptism as signifying "that the old Adam in us with all sins and evil desires is to be drowned and die through daily contrition and repentance, and on the other hand that daily a new person is to come forth and rise up to live before God in righteousness and purity forever."[31] This means that the death toward which we live is the last gasp of a life the Holy Spirit has been putting to death in us since our baptism, and the redeemed life we

28. Lewis, *Problem of Pain*, 139.
29. Placher, *Narratives*, 71.
30. Lewis, *Problem of Pain*, 141.
31. Kolb and Wengert, *Book of Concord*, 360. Translation slightly revised.

will share in the new creation is the full realization of "the first fruits of the Spirit" (Rom 8:23), already present in our life here and now.

Of course, acutely aware as we are that "our outer nature is wasting away" day by day and that we have not yet put on the promised "eternal weight of glory," we can only live in hope (2 Cor 5:16–17). Which means, inevitably, that we must ask, for what exactly do we hope? And this is by no means an easy question to answer. We hope to rest in the peace of Jesus, to be taken into the imperishable, eternal life of God. That promised eternal life is not simply an immortal, bodiless life; for, after all, as Pelikan notes, the existence of the fallen angels should remind us that in itself "there is nothing desirable about living forever."[32]

Nor is the promised life easily thought of simply in terms of a continued existence of the soul apart from the body. To be sure, there is something quite natural about that way of thinking. Contrasting an inner and outer self captures something true of our lived experience. As truly as I know that the component parts of my body are constantly being replaced throughout life, I also have a sense that in, with, and under this constant change I—what we are pleased to call my "self"—somehow persist. Nevertheless, if a human person is the *union* of soul and body, if that is what a genuinely human life means, then to think of death as the dissolution of the body while the soul lives on untouched cannot be comforting. For it would mean that death was essentially "the *threat* of a bodiless life," and it would make almost inexplicable Christian hope for the resurrection of the dead.[33]

Unsurprisingly, therefore, Christians have sometimes struggled to explain how it is that the souls of believers can be happy after death, how prior to the general resurrection they can fully flourish if separated from the body. St. Thomas addresses the question directly, though I at least am not sure what to make of his response. As he does so often, Thomas seeks to divide and clarify the question. On the one hand, the souls of the saints in heaven see God, a vision that does not depend on bodily senses but that provides everything a created soul could desire. In this sense perfect happiness does not require the presence of the body. But on the other hand, although the desire of the separated soul is fully satisfied and at rest, possessing the good it desires, from another angle we can say that "it does not possess that good in every way [i.e., bodily] that it would wish

32. Pelikan, *Shape of Death*, 23.
33. Barth, *Church Dogmatics*, III/2, 352. Italics added.

to possess it. Consequently, after the body has been resumed, Happiness increases not in intensity, but in extent."[34]

I confess to not finding this especially helpful, but Richard Neuhaus, attempting mightily to make good use of it, offered an imaginative way to understand St. Thomas's point. Even though the separated soul is entirely at rest and fully satisfied in the beatific vision, still, Neuhaus suggests, it "desires the body to share the joy. It is just a little like a very happy traveler sending a postcard to a friend, 'Wish you were here.'"[35] Whether we find this helpful will depend, I suppose, on whether we think it helpful to picture the relation of soul and body in the human person as somehow analogous to the relation of happy traveler and friend left behind. It may be better simply to admit that, living for now as those who are always on the way but do not yet rest in the peace of Jesus, we can only say that the risen Lord has taken the departed saints into his keeping and will one day bid them rise from sleep.

Hence, rather than beginning with an anthropology (of soul and body, inner and outer, material and spiritual) that may eventually leave as many questions unanswered as answered, perhaps we should begin from the heart of Christian faith. Those who have died in Christ may be, as St. Paul writes, "away from the body," but they are "at home with the Lord" (2 Cor 5:9). No longer beset by "fighting without and fear within" (2 Cor 7:5), they are at peace. And because the Lord with whom they are at home is the resurrected Christ, the Living One, they too must somehow live in him. Quite rightly, therefore, even now week after week in the Eucharist we offer our praise (in the words of the 1928 *Book of Common Prayer*) "with Angels and Archangels, and with all the company of heaven." Or, to put it in the language of the Letter to the Hebrews, we "have come to Mount Zion and to the city of the living God, the heavenly Jerusalem, and to innumerable angels in festal gathering, and to the assembly of the first-born who are enrolled in heaven, and to a judge who is God of all, and to the spirit of just men made perfect, and to Jesus" (Heb 12:22–24).

For now, then, as we live toward our dying, we wait in hope for the great day of resurrection still to come. If we die before that day comes, we will rest in the peace of Jesus, trusting that on "a morning bright and fair" he will "bid us rise from sleep" to share with all who have hoped in him that joyous "hour of waking."

---

34. ST I-II, q. 4, a. 5, ad 5.
35. Neuhaus, *As I Lay Dying*, 91.

BIBLIOGRAPHY

Barth, Karl. *Church Dogmatics*. Edited by G. W. Bromiley and T. F. Torrance. 4 vols. Edinburgh: T & T Clark, 1936–75.

Figgis, J. N. *The Political Aspects of St. Augustine's "City of God."* London: Longmans, Green, 1921.

Jonas, Hans. "The Burden and Blessing of Mortality." *Hastings Center Report* 22:1 (1992) 34–40.

Kolb, Robert, and Timothy J. Wengert, eds. *The Book of Concord: The Confessions of the Evangelical Lutheran Church*. Minneapolis: Fortress, 2000.

Lewis, C. S. *The Problem of Pain*. London: Fontana, 1957.

Lutheran Church–Missouri Synod. *The Lutheran Hymnal*. St. Louis: Concordia, 1941.

Neuhaus, Richard John. *As I Lay Dying: Meditations upon Returning*. New York: Basic, 2002.

Pelikan, Jaroslav. *The Shape of Death: Life, Death, and Immortality in the Early Fathers*. New York: Abingdon, 1961.

Pieper, Josef. *Happiness and Contemplation*. South Bend, IN: St. Augustine's, 1998.

Placher, William C. *Narratives of a Vulnerable God*. Louisville: Westminster John Knox, 1994.

Scheffler, Samuel. *Death and the Afterlife*. Oxford: Oxford University Press, 2013.

Stegner, Wallace. *The Spectator Bird*. Garden City, NY: Doubleday, 1976.

Tolstoy, Leo. *The Death of Ivan Ilyich*. New York: Bantam, 1981.

Wheelock, John Hall. "Song On Reaching Seventy." In *Songs of Experience: An Anthology of Literature on Growing Old*, edited by Margaret Fowler and Priscilla McCutcheon, 20–21. New York: Ballantine, 1991.

NAME/SUBJECT INDEX

Adam, 4, 61n60, 101, 105–6, 111,
    114, 118, 138, 141, 143,
    149–50, 221, 229, 244
Ambrose, 2, 51–52, 55n43, 58n49,
    62, 72, 106–7
annihilation, 2–3, 8–11, 14, 22,
    23n49, 27–34, 36, 38–39,
    177, 187
Anselm, 6, 125–27, 129
apotheosis, 47–48, 67, 185
Aqedah, 153
Aristotle, 191
Ars moriendi tradition, 2
Athanasius, 16, 58n49, 129
atheism, 199
atonement, 8, 224–25
Augustine, 2–6, 8, 58–65, 72–73, 97,
    105–114, 125–26, 128–29,
    148n50, 181, 183, 188,
    194n36, 202–3, 205–8, 236,
    244, 248, 255
    on suffering, 97, 105–114

Balthasar, Hans Urs von, 3, 8, 179,
    189–93, 196–98, 205–7
baptism, 6, 127, 135, 144–45,
    146n42, 148n50, 149, 156–
    57, 239, 247, 260
Barth, Karl, 2, 8–9, 70, 212–33,
    238–39, 251–59, 261
Basil the Great, 51, 54, 72, 74–75, 86
beatific vision, 78, 207, 261–62
Benedict of Nursia, 112
    Rule of, 112
Berrigan, Daniel, 23n48

Bonaventure, 203, 207
Bonhoeffer, Dietrich, 1
Bulgakov, Sergius, ix, 2–3, 7, 160–78
    condemntation of, 169
Bultmann, Rudolf, 185

Camus, Albert, 191
Cavadini, John, 4–5, 55, 58n49
celibacy, 49, 51, 255
Cicero, 3, 44–48, 57, 62n61, 63
    on grief, 44–48
Christ. *See* Jesus Christ.
communion of the saints, 169
concupiscence, 6, 136–37, 141–45,
    156n78, 157, 184
Confession, sacrament of, 169
cremation, 119
Cullmann, Oscar, 4, 70, 88, 90
Cyprian of Carthage, 257–28

Daniélou, Jean, 73
death,
    as divine punishment, 5, 7,
        107–8
    "good" Christian death, 9,
        58n49, 235–49
    as natural, 58n49, 257
    relation to sexuality, 48–50, 52
    as separation of soul and body,
        87, 107, 118, 185n17, 203
    as sleep, 10, 220
Derrida, Jacques, 180n3, 187n24,
    193
devil. *See* Satan
Didymus the Blind, 51

265

SCRIPTURE INDEX

Job (*continued*)

16:13–14	32
17:2	32
17:11	32
17:13–16	32
18:21	11
19:6–8	32
19:7–9	38
19:9–10	32
19:10	38
19:25–27	36–37, 39
21:26	33
21:34	26
22:5	26
22:21	26
22:29	26
23:11–13	33
23:16–17	33
24:24	33
27:2	33
27:8	33
27:10	33
29:4	33
30:19	26
30:22	33
30:23	33
32:1	26
32:2	26
33:17	26
33:27–28	26
34:12	26
24:21	26
36:26	27
37:14	27
37:23	27
38:4	34
38:7	35
38:17	35
38:36–37	35
39:26	35
41:11	35
42:2–3	35
42:3	27
42:5–6	27
42:7	27
42:11	36
42:12	36

42:17	12, 36

Psalms

90	149
90:4	259
116:15	95
119:71	147n44
123:7 (LXX)	83
143:2	148n50

Ecclesiastes 58n49

Song of Songs

8:6	168

Isaiah

14:9 (LXX)	122
35:10	85
52:2–3	94
52:4–5	94
52:9	94
52:12	94

Ezekiel

37	81

Daniel

3:23–27	168

Matthew

6:12	148n50
19:14	84
26:36–46	219
27:46	219

Luke

20:34–36	49n28

John

1:4	125
12:24	129
14	67

17:3	260

Romans

5:6–10	65n70
5:10	80
6:4	239
6:5	130
8:22–23	171
8:23	261
8:38	220
12:2	147n44
14:7	220

1 Corinthians

3:22	220
15	79–80, 88
15:20	89
15:28	89
15:42–50	152
15:51	77
15:51–53	164
15:52	81
15:53	viii
15:55	123, 215

2 Corinthians

4:10–12	170
4:16	143
5:9	262
5:15	239
5:16–17	261
5:17	89, 260
7:5	262
7:8–11	60
12:9	100

Galatians

2:20	146

Philippians

1:20	220
1:23	167
2:7	67
3:13	92

Colossians

1:15–17	129
3:1–3	127

1 Thessalonians

4:3	147n44
5:10	220

Hebrews

6:19–20	83
9:27	220, 258
9:28	258
10:1	83
10:31	259
12:1	1
12:22–24	262

1 John

1:8	148n50